Mastering
Negotiable Instruments
(UCC Articles 3 and 4) and
Other Payment Systems

Carolina Academic Press Mastering Series

RUSSELL WEAVER, SERIES EDITOR

Mastering Bankruptcy
George W. Kuney

Mastering Civil Procedure
David Charles Hricik

Mastering Criminal Law
Ellen S. Podgor, Peter J. Henning, Neil P. Cohen

Mastering Evidence
Ronald W. Eades

Mastering Intellectual Property
George W. Kuney

Mastering Legal Analysis and Communication
David T. Ritchie

**Mastering Negotiable Instruments (UCC Articles 3 and 4)
and Other Payment Systems**
Michael D. Floyd

Mastering Products Liability
Ronald W. Eades

Mastering Statutory Interpretation
Linda D. Jellum

Mastering Negotiable Instruments (UCC Articles 3 and 4) and Other Payment Systems

Michael D. Floyd
Samford University, Cumberland School of Law

Carolina Academic Press
Durham, North Carolina

Library of Congress Cataloging in Publication Data

Floyd, Michael D.
  Mastering negotiable instruments (UCC Articles 3 and 4) and other payment systems / by Michael D. Floyd.
     p. cm. -- (Carolina Academic Press mastering series)
  Includes bibliographical references and index.
  ISBN 978-1-59460-366-2 (alk. paper)
  1. Negotiable instruments--United States. 2. Payment--United States. I. Title. II. Series.

  KF957.F56 2008
  346.73'096--dc22

                                            2008025889

Carolina Academic Press
700 Kent Street
Durham, NC 27701
Telephone (919) 489-7486
Fax (919) 493-5668
www.cap-press.com

Printed in the United States of America

For my students, who teach me so much

Contents

Part Three
Other Payment Systems

Series Editor's Foreword

The Carolina Academic Press Mastering Series is designed to provide you with a tool that will enable you to easily and efficiently "master" the substance and content of law school courses. Throughout the series, the focus is on quality writing that makes legal concepts understandable. As a result, the series is designed to be easy to read and is not unduly cluttered with footnotes or cites to secondary sources.

In order to facilitate student mastery of topics, the Mastering Series includes a number of pedagogical features designed to improve learning and retention. At the beginning of each chapter, you will find a "Roadmap" that tells you about the chapter and provides you with a sense of the material that you will cover. A "Checkpoint" at the end of each chapter encourages you to stop and review the key concepts, reiterating what you have learned. Throughout the book, key terms are explained and emphasized. Finally, a "Master Checklist" at the end of each book reinforces what you have learned and helps you identify any areas that need review or further study.

We hope that you will enjoy studying with, and learning from, the Mastering Series.

Russell L. Weaver
Professor of Law & Distinguished University Scholar
University of Louisville, Louis D. Brandeis School of Law

Acknowledgments

I am grateful to the Cumberland School of Law and Samford University for enabling me to teach and explore the topic of this book and other subjects that interest me. I particularly appreciate Dean John Carroll, Associate Dean Corky Strickland, Vice Dean Jim Lewis, and Director of Faculty Development Brannon Denning for the many ways that they support my efforts. My years toiling in the commercial law vineyard have been educational and enjoyable thanks in large part to Samford colleagues Howard Walthall and Paul Kuruk, former Samford colleagues Larry Ahern, Steve Ware, and Tim Zinnecker, University of Alabama colleagues Bill Henning and Gene Marsh, University of Tennessee colleagues George Kuney, Bob Lloyd, and Tom Plank, and many others. I have gained much knowledge and many good friends from participating in the Alabama Law Institute's law reform efforts; in that work I learned much that is relevant to this book from Douglas Arendall, Hamp Boles, Richard Carmody, David Carroll, Rob Couch, Penny Davis, Ed Dean, Bill Hairston, III, Palmer Hamilton, Wallace Malone III, Bob McCurley, Ron Sims, Hon. James Sledge, Joe Stewart, Stephen Trimmier, Sam Upchurch, and Larry Vinson. I am fortunate to have had outstanding student research assistants: most recently Anna Smith, Carolyn Lam, and Heather Sharp. Special thanks are due to Janice Brantley, my Assistant who handles innumerable details, arrangements, and problems with consistent skill, dedication, grace, and good humor. Thanks also to Russ Weaver and the editors at Carolina Academic Press, who have been exceptionally accommodating in this project.

I acknowledge my indebtedness to authors whose books I regularly turn to for insight and guidance: James J. White & Robert S. Summers, Uniform Commercial Code (5th ed. 2000); Fred H. Miller & Alvin C. Harrell, The Law of Modern Payment Systems (2003 & Supp. 2006); Frederick M. Hart and William F. Willier, Negotiable Instruments Under the Uniform Commercial Code (2007). Similarly, I have great admiration and appreciation for the authors of books I have used to teach this material: Ronald J. Mann, Payment Systems and Other Financial Transactions: Cases, Materials, and Problems (3rd ed 2006) (and previous editions); Robert L. Jordan, & William D. Warren, Commercial Law (3rd ed. 1992); and David C. Epstein, James A. Martin, William H. Henning, & Steve H. Nickles, Basic Uniform Commercial Code: Teaching Materials (3rd ed. 1988).

Of course, if anything in this book is wrong, misguided, trivial, or boring, that responsibility is entirely my own.

Last, but most important, I note my gratitude, love, affection, and appreciation for Annette and our children — John, Sarah, Ellen, and Russell — who bring tremendous joy and meaning to my world.

> Michael D. Floyd
> Samford University,
> Cumberland School of Law
> Birmingham, Alabama
> June 2008

Mastering Negotiable Instruments (UCC Articles 3 and 4) and Other Payment Systems

Chapter 1

Introduction

Roadmap

- Commercial law
- Commercial transactions
- Payment systems
- Payment transactions
- Transaction phase
- Litigation phase

Every day, countless people engage in numerous and varied commercial transactions that are fundamental to their lives. Unlike some other areas of law, only rarely does a commercial law transaction or case generate widespread popular interest.

Some commercial transactions involve large amounts of money and are memorable in the life of an individual, a family, or a business: common examples include major purchases, debt prepayments, and receiving or paying a judicial award. Such large transactions usually have a dramatic effect on the lives of the individuals involved, though they rarely appear in newspapers or on broadcast news. Even these major transactions appear routine in the functioning of our economy and society as a whole.

Commercial law also encompasses myriad smaller transactions, infinitely more numerous and varied than the major marker-event transactions of our lives. Most of these transactions are almost invisible until we start thinking about them. Buying toothpaste and frozen pizza at the grocery store with a debit card, paying for a dinner out with a credit card, and mailing a check to the finance company for a car payment are all commercial transactions that many of us engage in at least monthly, and often more frequently. In the overwhelming majority of cases, these transactions go exactly as the parties expect: the seller or lender gets its money, the buyer or borrower gets (or gets to keep)

3

the property or service that was provided, and no one gives a thought to the law that governs the transactions or to the systems that track and facilitate them.

The fact that most people rarely think about commercial law doesn't make it unimportant or simple, though. In fact, the seamlessness of most commercial transactions is a tribute to the success of the governing law and systems. Looking below the surface of these transactions reveals a rich and complex body of law and related institutions. These are essential to our ability to undertake these transactions and are available to resolve the occasional dispute. A portion of this body of law and the related systems are the subject of this book.

Payment systems comprise one area of commercial law and transactions. Other areas often addressed in law school commercial law courses include sales of goods (UCC Article 2) and secured transactions (UCC Article 9). The law of bankruptcy is closely associated with commercial law, because the planning and systems for transactions must take account of what can go wrong with the parties' financial situations.

Payment systems and the individual payment transactions that the systems facilitate often intersect with other areas of commercial law. If the buyer of goods must pay for them in full when they are delivered, often the buyer will issue a check (a particular type of negotiable instrument) to the seller. Alternatively, if the buyer and the seller agree that payment for the goods may be made in installments, often the seller will require the buyer to sign a promissory note (another type of negotiable instrument) documenting the payment terms. If the seller is not entirely confident about the buyer's promise to pay, the seller may require that the note be secured with collateral, following the rules in UCC Article 9.

Chapter 2 of this book provides an overview of the various bodies of law, regulation, and private ordering that govern commercial transactions. Part One (Chapters 3 through 11) explores the law of negotiable instruments. This law once governed the overwhelming majority of payment systems. Other types of payment systems have emerged in recent years, with a corresponding development of new law. However, negotiable instruments remain important both as pervasive payment systems in their own right, and as the prototypical payment system from which the newer types evolved.

Part Two of this book (Chapters 12 through 16) explores the law of check collection. A check is a particular type of negotiable instrument, and checks remain an important mechanism for making payments. Part Three (Chapters 17 through 19) explores the law of credit cards, debit cards, and wire transfers (called "funds transfers" in the UCC), which developed in the 20th Century to address perceived limitations of the older systems.

As you work through legal issues, it's important to recognize that a lawyer may advise a client as to either of two very different stages of a transaction:

(1) the *transaction-planning* phase, in which lawyers and their clients analyze how to comply with the law as to events that haven't yet occurred, or (2) the *litigation* phase, in which the events have occurred and the analysis focuses on the legal significance of those events. Lessons learned in litigation are potentially useful for transaction planning, and vice versa. However, the analysis of a particular problem will be very different depending on whether you're in the transaction-planning phase or the litigation phase. If you're in the transaction-planning phase, the safe course is to assume that all the rules are effective and make sure you comply with each and every one of them. In that phase, you focus on how to do a future transaction exactly right, and still have that opportunity. By contrast, in the litigation phase the transaction is already done (perhaps badly, by someone else), and you're figuring out how to clean up the mess. Your focus is on exploring all possible interpretations of the applicable law, as applied to facts you cannot change, in the hope of finding one that gives your client a favorable result.

Checkpoints

- Commercial transactions pervade our lives and dealings.
- The vast majority of commercial transactions go smoothly.
- The law governs resolution of the relatively few problems that occur.
- The law shapes the systems necessary to process and record transactions and governs disputes when things go wrong.
- Payment systems and payment transactions are types of commercial transactions and often intersect with other areas of commercial law.
- It's important to recognize whether you're at the transaction-planning phase or the litigation phase, because the analysis and strategies differ significantly.

Chapter 2

The Law Governing Payment Systems: Uniform Law, Other State Law, Federal Law, Private Ordering Arrangements, and International Law

---

Roadmap

- Uniform Commercial Code
- Federal statutes and regulations governing payment transactions
  - Expedited Funds Availability Act, and Federal Reserve Regulations J and CC
  - Truth in Lending Act, and Federal Reserve Regulation Z
  - Subchapter VI of the Consumer Credit Protection Act governing electronic fund transfers, and Federal Reserve Regulation E
  - Electronic Signatures in Global and National Commerce Act (E-Sign)
  - Equal Credit Opportunity Act
  - Fair Credit Reporting Act
- State laws beyond the Uniform Commercial Code
  - State statutes prohibiting fraudulent and deceptive practices
  - Uniform Electronic Transactions Act
- Judicial decisions
- Private ordering arrangements
- United Nations Convention on International Bills of Exchange and International Promissory Notes

---

Payment transactions are governed by a complex (but finite and under-standable!) interaction of state statutes, federal statutes, federal administrative regulations, state and federal judicial decisions, and private ordering arrangements. The state statutes are primarily states' enactments of the Uniform Commercial Code. Federal statutes include the Expedited Funds Availability Act, the Consumer Credit Protection Act, and the Check Clearing for the 21st Century Act. The federal statutes often authorize accompanying administrative regulations that flesh out the requirements of the statutes. Private ordering arrangements include clearinghouse rules, the *Uniform Customs and Practices for Documentary Credits* and *International Standby Practices* governing letter-of-credit transactions, and various other types of private contracts. This book focuses on United States law. However, in addition to the United States' laws governing domestic transactions, increasing globalization creates more and more need for understanding laws and systems beyond the borders of the United States.

A. The Uniform Commercial Code (UCC) and Other State Law

The primary state statutes are found in the Uniform Commercial Code (the UCC), the most successful of many attempts to make state legislation uniform across the United States. The UCC was promulgated by the American Law Institute (the ALI) and the National Conference of Commissioners of Uniform State Laws (NCCUSL). Both the ALI and NCCUSL continue to oversee the UCC and have proposed periodic amendments over the years since it was originally approved in 1952. The UCC is issued by the ALI and NCCUSL as the "Official Text," but it does not become binding law in a state until state legislatures adopt it.

The UCC is divided into "Articles." Articles 3 and 4 are the portions with primary importance for the law of payment systems, though the general definitions and other provisions in Article 1 apply to Articles 3 and 4 (and to all other Articles of the UCC). Article 3 governs "Negotiable Instruments," and contains the majority of the law on that subject; Article 4 governs "Bank Deposits and Collections." The current Official Text of Articles 3 and 4 reflects a major revision in 1990 and a less extensive revision in 2002. All of the states in the U.S. except New York and South Carolina have adopted the 1990 revisions. 2 Frederick M. Hart & William F. Willier, Negotiable Instruments Under the Uniform Commercial Code § 1C.01 fn 2. (2006). As of June 1, 2007, six states have adopted the 2002 revisions. *Id.* § 1D.01 fn 2.

Other state laws beyond the UCC also affect commercial transactions. Many states have non-uniform statutes governing unfair or deceptive trade practices, passing bad checks, fraud, practices in particular types of businesses, etc.

B. Federal Statutes and Regulations

Historically the UCC was the primary source of commercial law, but Congress has increasingly enacted federal statutes applying to various types of commercial transactions and practices. Perhaps the most pervasive is the Expedited Funds Availability Act (EFAA), codified at 12 U.S.C.A. §§ 4001–4010, and discussed in Chapters 13 and 14 of this book. This statute (and its related regulations, commonly referred to as "Reg. CC") require banks to make deposited funds available to depositors more quickly than was required by UCC Article 4. Because requiring accelerated availability of funds would increase risks on the banking system if the collection of the related checks were not also accelerated, the EFAA and Reg. CC establish additional deadlines that require banks to return dishonored checks to the drawee more promptly than is required by Article 4 in most cases.

Congress directed the Board of Governors of the Federal Reserve System to prescribe regulations to help implement the EFAA. The Federal Reserve Board subsequently issued the regulations codified at 12 CFR Part 229. These regulations are commonly referred to as "Regulation CC," reflecting a widely-used convention for referring to Federal Reserve Board regulations. The lettering system reflects the fact that A is the first letter of the alphabet, so the regulations in 12 CFR Part 201 are "Regulation A." Z is the 26th letter, so the regulations in 12 CFR Part 226 are "Regulation Z." Starting over with double letters for Part 227 ("AA") results in Part 229 being "Regulation CC." Cognoscenti often refer to these regulations as "Reg. Z," "Reg. CC," etc.

Part B of Regulation CC provides greater detail than the EFAA itself on the availability rules for various types of deposits. Part C of Regulation CC fleshes out the rules to speed up the check collection system, to reduce the risk that a bank will make funds available to its depositor and only later find out that the check was no good. Subpart A of Regulation J, 12 CFR Part 210, provides rules for the collection of checks through the Federal Reserve Banks, which play an enormous role in the check collection system.

Another significant federal entry into payment systems law is the Truth-In-Lending Act (TILA). This statute is Subchapter I of the Consumer Credit Protection Act, and is codified at 15 U.S.C.A. §§ 1601–1666j. TILA establishes disclosure requirements for consumer credit transactions and imposes some substantive requirements for credit terms, particularly in credit card transactions. The Federal Reserve Board's Regulation Z, 12 CFR Part 226, provides regulations related to TILA.

Other significant federal legislation includes Subchapter VI of the Consumer Credit Protection Act, governing debit card transactions and other consumer electronic fund transfers. This statute is codified at 15 U.S.C.A. §§ 1693–1693r; the related Federal Reserve Board regulations appear in Regulation E, 12 CFR Part 205. Other federal statutes affecting payment transactions, sometimes mentioned in payment systems courses but usually left for more extensive coverage in consumer protection law courses, include

(1) the Fair Credit Reporting Act, (FCRA, Subchapter III of the Consumer Credit Reporting Act, codified at 15 U.S.C.A. §§ 1681–1681x);
(2) the Equal Credit Opportunity Act (ECOA, Subchapter IV of the Consumer Credit Protection Act), codified at 15 U.S.C.A. §§ 1691–1691f, and the related Federal Reserve Board Regulation B, 12 CFR Part 202; and
(3) the Fair Debt Collection Practices Act (FDCPA), Subchapter V of the Consumer Credit Protection Act, codified at 15 U.S.C.A. §§ 1692–1692p.

UCC section 3-102(c), and Official Comments 3 and 4 to section 3-102, address the relationship between UCC Article 3 and federal law. Official Comment 5 to section 3-102 discusses the relationship between Article 3 and the United Nations Convention on International Bills of Exchange and International Promissory Notes, discussed in Section E of this Chapter.

Another body of law with a complex relationship to payment systems and transactions is found in the federal and state statutes governing electronic transactions. The UCC developed in an era when paper documents were the norm. Modern technology now allows many transactions to proceed electronically without any actual piece of paper being produced. The federal Electronic Signatures in Global and National Commerce Act (E-Sign), and the closely related Uniform Electronic Transactions Act (UETA) are in force (as of May 2007) in the District of Columbia and all the states in the U.S. except Georgia, Illinois, and New York. *See* 7A Uniform Laws Annotated at Supp. 96 (Supp. 2007). These statutes validate electronic substitutes for paper documents in many legal contexts. However, both of these statutes explicitly defer to the rules of UCC Articles 3 and 4, which require negotiable instruments to be "written," as discussed more fully in Chapter 3 of this book. Consequently, negotiable instruments still may not be in electronic form, despite the enactment of E-Sign and UETA. However, even in the world of negotiable instruments, the trend is toward electronic documents and electronic processing; a significant recent example of a specific statute accommodating that trend is the Check Clearing in the 21st

Century Act of 2003 (Check 21), a federal statute that validates electronic substitutes for paper checks in the check processing system in specified circumstances. The Check 21 Act is discussed in Chapter 14 of this book.

One other federal regulation deserving brief mention is Reg. J, 12 CFR Part 210. This regulation governs check collection by the Federal Reserve Banks and funds transfers through the Fedwire system. This regulation usually gets only passing attention in the typical law school Payment Systems course. However, a commercial lawyer should be at least aware of its existence, and should consult it for rules applicable to dealings with the Federal Reserve Banks.

C. Judicial Decisions

The law governing commercial transactions includes judicial decisions interpreting the statutes and regulations, though judicial decisions in commercial law are usually less important for the development of the law than in some other legal fields. Federal and state courts in the U.S. (and in other countries) occasionally decide a major commercial law case, but such cases rarely have widespread impact on the nature of commercial law transactions overall, nor do they often get headlines outside the business section of the newspaper. Rather, even the "landmark" cases tend to be interpretive decisions clarifying previously uncertain technical issues. Far more often, commercial law judicial decisions apply settled law to resolve a dispute between parties as to a particular transaction. Of course, those cases are very important to the parties before the court, but rarely does the resolution of particular litigation generate anything more than passing interest in the wider legal or business community, let alone on MTV or in *People* magazine (though the folks who appear on MTV and in *People*, and their fans, are frequent participants in commercial transactions).

D. Private Ordering Arrangements

Most (though not all) provisions of the UCC provide "default rules." That is, the UCC states a rule, and that rule applies if the parties don't agree on a different rule to govern their particular transaction. (Incidentally, the word "default" is also used in a very different way to mean failure to pay as agreed. Usually it is clear from the context which meaning of the word applies, but this is a potential source of confusion that you should be alert to.) One example of private ordering arrangements that supersede the default rules of the

UCC is clearing-house rules. Banks are often members of clearing-houses, which facilitate the processing of the checks drawn on the various member banks of the clearing-house. UCC Article 4 often refers to the rules of such clearing-houses as supplementing or superseding the rules in the UCC itself. *See, e.g.*, UCC § 4-203(b)(3), 4-301(d)(1), 4-303(a)(3).

Another major example of a private ordering arrangement is in the highly specialized law governing letters of credit, which is discussed further below in Section E of Chapter 10. Letters of credit are governed by UCC Article 5, but it has long been standard practice in drafting letters of credit for the parties to agree that the transaction will be governed by the *Uniform Customs and Practice for Documentary Credits* or the *International Standby Practices*. Each of these two books contains a set of rules that looks like a statute, but it has not been enacted by Congress or a state legislature. Instead, these are rules developed and published by the International Chamber of Commerce. They govern a particular transaction when the parties incorporate them by reference and agree to be bound by them.

E. International Law

This book focuses on the United States' rules for payment transactions. Increasingly, though, business crosses national borders, and payment transactions must follow.

The United Nations Commission on International Trade Law (UNCITRAL) undertook a major effort in the latter part of the 20th century to create a consistent international set of rules for some (though not all) negotiable instrument transactions. The outcome of that project was the United Nations Convention on International Bills of Exchange and International Promissory Notes (the UN Convention). The United States signed the UN Convention in 1990, but has not ratified it. *See* Fred H. Miller & Alvin C. Harrell, The Law of Modern Payment Systems ¶ 1.03[3][C] at 22 (2003); 2B Frederick M. Hart & William F. Willer, Negotiable Instruments Under the Uniform Commercial Code § 18.01 (2006). If the U.S. ratifies the UN Convention, it will preempt the UCC for instruments governed by the UN Convention. *See* UCC § 3-102 Official Comment 5. However, the UN Convention specifies that it only applies to bills and notes that indicate that they are cross-border transactions and reflect the parties' intent that the UN Convention apply. *See id.*

The UCC Article 3 Official Comments highlight a numbers of similarities and differences between the UN Convention rules and the corresponding UCC rules. *See* UCC §§ 3-102 Official Comment 5, 3-104 Official Comment 5, 3-

118 Official Comment 7, 3-203 Official Comment 6, 3-205 Official Comment 4, 3-302 Official Comment 8, 3-305 Official Comment 8, 3-306 Official Comment, 3-412 Official Comment 4, 3-413 Official Comment, 3-414 Official Comment 7, and 3-415 Official Comments 6 and 9. Further discussion of the Convention appears in Fred H. Miller & Alvin C. Harrell, The Law of Modern Payment Systems ¶ 1.03[3][C] at 22–23 (2003), and 2B Frederick M. Hart & William F. Willer, Negotiable Instruments Under the Uniform Commercial Code Chapter 18 (2007).

F. Mastering the Statutes

As you work through the remainder of this book, you will gain the best mastery of the material if you keep a copy of the statutes alongside and refer to the actual statutory language as you read the explanations in this book. The goal of this book is to help you understand the meaning and application of the words in the statute. Ultimately, though, there is no substitute for being able to read and understand the statutory language itself.

G. A Note on Citations

Citations in this book are intended to facilitate ease of reference and readability of the text. To advance those primary goals, citation forms sometimes intentionally sacrifice slavish compliance with the details and nuances of the *BlueBook*. Unless otherwise noted, the citations to the Uniform Commercial Code are to the 2007 Official Text.

Checkpoints

- Articles 3 and 4 of the Uniform Commercial Code (UCC) historically have been the primary source of the law governing payment transactions and systems.

- Federal law increasingly affects payment transactions and systems.

  - The Expedited Funds Availability Act, together with the related Federal Reserve Regulations J and CC, set standards for when banks must make deposited funds available to the depositor, and impose corresponding requirements to speed up the check collection process.

  - The Truth in Lending Act (Subchapter I of the Consumer Credit Protection Act), and Federal Reserve Regulation Z specify rules governing credit card transactions, as well as other types of consumer credit transactions.

  - Subchapter VI of the Consumer Credit Protection Act and Federal Reserve Regulation E specify rules governing debit cards and other consumer electronic fund transfers.

- State laws beyond the UCC also affect payment transactions in particular ways.

  - Bad check statutes.

  - More general statutes prohibiting fraudulent and deceptive practices.

- Judicial decisions in payment transaction cases are primarily directed to interpreting the statutes and applying them to the facts of particular disputes.

- Private ordering arrangements also play an important role in shaping payment transactions.

- Increasing globalization of transactions leads to the increasing importance of international law.

- Full understanding of the laws expressed in this book requires you to read and understand the statutory language itself, not just the explanations.

Part One

Negotiable Instruments (UCC Article 3)

Chapter 3

Drafts and Notes

Roadmap

- Negotiable instrument
- Instrument
- Note
- Draft
- Check
- Cash
- Promise
- Order
- Issue
- Payee
- Maker
- Drawer
- Payor bank

Many more types of payment systems existed at the end of the 20th century than at the beginning, and that trend continues. Credit cards, debit cards, wire transfers, and various other methods for facilitating transactions were inconceivable in 1900 but commonplace in 2000. The law struggles to keep pace with commercial and technological change, and the evolution of payment systems law will almost certainly continue for the foreseeable future.

A. Drafts and Notes as Types of Payment Systems

Prior to the electronic revolution, most payment transactions used cash, a "draft," or a "note." (A "check" is a particular type of draft.) Cash transactions are numerous, but they are a shrinking part of the payment landscape and a minor factor—perhaps invisible—in most law school courses on payment systems. The law of notes and drafts remains important and is still a significant part of law school payment systems courses.

Notes and drafts are referred to collectively as "negotiable instruments," or simply "instruments," reflecting the definitions in section 3-104 of the Uniform Commercial Code (UCC). The law governing negotiable instruments was once the core of law school courses on payment systems; such courses were usually named "Negotiable Instruments" or (earlier) "Commercial Paper."

Negotiable instruments law remains important despite the proliferation of newer payment systems. The law governing these long-used payment systems is still worth studying for at least two reasons.

First, negotiable instruments still play a major role in everyday commercial transactions. Therefore, the law governing notes and drafts still applies to many modern commercial transactions. Payment systems courses in law school (and many bar exams) still focus on negotiable instruments law. Lawyers who represent financial institutions (banks, finance companies, savings institutions, credit unions, insurance companies, brokerage firms, etc.) routinely deal with negotiable instrument transactions and disputes. Most other lawyers have less frequent dealings with disputes on the law governing notes and drafts. However, any lawyer whose client is concerned about being paid, making a payment, or borrowing money is affected by this body of law. Lawyers also regularly have such concerns for themselves.

Second, the newer types of payment systems (credit cards, debit cards, wire transfers, etc.) evolved from notes and drafts. The people who wrote the law governing these newer payment systems were familiar with the law governing notes and drafts. In the new systems, they sought to preserve the good things from negotiable instruments law and alleviate problems with negotiable instruments. Consequently, the legal framework governing modern payment systems continues to build on the systems for notes and drafts.

As we will see shortly, a note requires only two parties, and a draft has a minimum of three parties (though sometimes one bank or another person will play two of the three roles required for a draft). These, however, are the minimums. Other parties may get involved in the original obligation, the process of collection, or as purchasers of the instrument. These include co-makers, indorsers, accommodation parties and other sureties. The roles of these other parties are discussed in Chapters 8 and 10 below.

Notes and drafts are the most common types of negotiable instruments, but UCC Article 3 also applies to other specialized types of instruments, discussed in Chapter 4 below. *See also* UCC § 3-104. As if that weren't already enough to make this body of law complex, UCC Article 4 also provides different terminology that applies to negotiable instruments and a few other things. UCC Article 9 also has a partially-overlapping set of definitions.

Despite the general trend toward allowing electronic substitutes for paper documents in many areas of commercial law, negotiable instruments governed by UCC Article 3 must all be in writing. This rule is clear, though seeing it requires you to work through a couple of UCC sections. The term "negotiable instrument" is defined in section 3-104(a) as a "promise or order." The definitions of both "promise" in section 3-103(a)(12) and "order" in section 3-103(a)(8) provide that they must be "written."

These requirements for written documents remain in force despite the enactment, at the end of the 20th century, of federal and state legislation generally allowing electronic substitutes for written documents. *See* Electronic Signatures in Global and National Commerce Act § 103(a)(3) (2000), 15 U.S.C.A § 7003(a)(3) (2007); Uniform Electronic Transactions Act § 3(b)(2), 7A U.L.A. 235 (2002).

Congress enacted a more limited statute in the early 21st century to permit electronic substitutes for the traditional movement of checks in the check-collection process. *See* Check Clearing for the 21st Century Act (Check 21 Act), 12 U.S.C.A. §§ 5001–5018 (2004). The Check 21 Act is discussed below in Chapter 14.

B. Note Terminology and Functions

The essential difference between a note and a draft is reflected in UCC section 3-104(e): a note is a "promise" to pay, and a draft is an "order" to pay. UCC section 3-103(a)(12) and (a)(10) defines those terms. UCC section 3-104(e) says that "[a]n instrument is a 'note' if it is a promise...." Section 3-103(a)(12) defines "promise" as "a written undertaking to pay money signed by the person undertaking to pay."

The most prevalent use of notes is to document an obligation to repay borrowed money. If you have ever obtained a loan from a financial institution — and if you haven't yet, you will someday — you undoubtedly signed a promissory note as part of the transaction, reciting the terms of your promise to repay the money you borrowed.

For various reasons we will explore below, some documents that evidence a promise to pay money may not qualify as negotiable instruments governed by the UCC—even though the parties may call them "notes." Conversely, sometimes notes governed by UCC Article 3 are used in transactions that don't fit the usual money-lending pattern. Nevertheless, thinking of a note as an obligation to repay borrowed money is a useful place to start.

The typical note is "issued" (a term defined in UCC section 3-105) in exchange for a loan of money and is the legal document that evidences the promise to repay. Thus, a note only requires a minimum of two essential parties: the borrower (called the "maker" in UCC parlance, section 3-103(a)(7)) and the lender (called the "payee").

UCC section 3-103(a)(7) defines the term "maker" as "a person who signs or is identified in a note as a person undertaking to pay." The term "payee" is not defined in the UCC, though it is widely used and usually easily understood to mean the person who is to receive payment. In most cases it's easy to determine who the payee is by looking at the instrument. Section 3-110 provides a somewhat convoluted mechanism for making this determination in some unusual cases, and the rule in that provision works for the simple cases, too. More on that in Chapter 16 below.

In a typical note transaction, the *maker* borrows money and signs a note to confirm the terms of repayment; the note serves as evidence that the maker will repay the debt to the *payee*. A note can be helpful in the payee's collection efforts if the maker fails to pay as agreed; once a note is dishonored, the payee has the choice of suing on the note or the underlying obligation, as discussed further in Chapter 11. A negotiable note also comes to embody the obligation to pay: "An instrument is a reified right to payment. The right is represented by the instrument itself." UCC § 3-203 Official Comment 1 (third paragraph).

Another common use of a note is in a purchase of goods on credit. If you buy a car from a car dealer on credit, and no financial institution is involved to provide financing, you would sign a note payable to the car dealer in exchange for the car. Conceptually this transaction could be divided into two parts—the purchase and sale of the car, and the loan of the money for the purchase price, which makes this use of the note identical to the prior example. The law has sometimes treated credit purchases of goods differently than loans to obtain the money to buy goods, but economically they are equivalent transactions.

C. Draft Terminology and Functions

UCC section 3-104(e) says that "[a]n instrument is ... a 'draft' if it is an order." Section 3-103(a)(8) defines "order" as "a written instruction to pay money signed by the person giving the instruction." Because drafts are the primary basis for the check collection system, transactions involving drafts are governed not only by UCC Article 3, but also by UCC Article 4 and the various federal laws and regulations governing check collection. See Part Two of this book below.

A "check" is a particular type of draft. UCC section 3-104(f) defines the term "check" as "(i) a draft, other than a documentary draft, payable on demand and drawn on a bank or (ii) a cashier's check or teller's check." In a typical draft transaction, the drawer needs to pay money to the payee, so the drawer draws a draft instructing the drawee to give some of the drawer's money to the payee. In most such transactions, the drawee is a bank and the draft is a check. Part Two of this book considers the elaborate mechanism by which banks collect checks.

Unlike a note, which may have as few as two parties, the typical draft is a three-party instrument. It is an instruction (an "order") by one party (the "drawer," UCC section 3-103(a)(5)) addressed to a second party (the "drawee," UCC § 3-103(a)(4), or "payor bank," UCC § 4-105(3)), instructing that second party to make payment to the third party, the "payee."

As discussed above for notes, the term "payee" is not defined in the UCC, though it is widely used and usually easily understood to mean the person who is to receive payment. In most cases it's easy to determine who the payee is by looking at the instrument. Section 3-110 provides a somewhat convoluted mechanism for making this determination in some unusual cases; the rule in section 3-110 works for the simple cases, too. More on that in Chapter 16 below.

UCC section 3-103(a)(5) defines the term "drawer" as "a person who signs or is identified in a draft as a person ordering payment." More commonly, you would say that you "wrote a check" if you signed as drawer.

UCC section 3-103(a)(4) defines "drawee" as "a person ordered in a draft to make payment." When you write a check, the drawee is your bank where you deposited the money to pay the check; the name and other identifying information about that bank are pre-printed on your checks. For drafts that are not checks, the drawee may or may not be a bank, and the name of the drawee may or may not be pre-printed on the draft.

The drawee is referred to as the "payor bank" in UCC Article 4; that definition appears in section 4-105(3). Section 4-105 also defines other roles that a bank may play with respect to a particular draft.

In most cases, the drawee is not directly liable on a draft because the drawee has not signed the draft. If only the drawer has signed a check, only the drawer is liable on that check. Unless your bank signs a check that you write (which almost never happens), your bank is not directly liable on that check. *See infra* Chapter 8. The bank's responsibility is limited to paying your funds to the payee *if* you have funds available in your account. Moreover, even if your bank wrongfully refuses to pay your check when it should have paid it, your bank owes liability for wrongful dishonor *only to you* as drawer of the check; the bank has no direct liability to the payee of the check. *See infra* Chapters 8 and 14. For these reasons, sometimes a payee will not be willing to rely on just liability of the drawer to insure payment. In such cases, the payee might insist on a specialized types of check — a cashier's check, teller's check, or certified check — which provide the payee with a claim against a bank, which is usually a more valuable claim than one against the average drawer of a check. These and other specialized types of negotiable instruments are discussed below in Chapter 4.

Checkpoints

- Notes and drafts were the primary payment systems historically and are the primary focus of UCC Articles 3 and 4.

- A check is a particular type of draft.

- Other types of payment systems developed in the late 20th century; the law governing those newer payment systems reflects experience notes and drafts under the UCC.

- A note is a promise to pay and requires at least two parties, a payee and a maker.

- A draft is an order to pay and requires at least three parties, a payee, a drawer, and a drawee (or payor bank).

- UCC Article 3 requires notes and drafts to be "written," though recent federal legislation facilitates processing checks in electronic form.

- The drawee or payor bank is not liable directly to the payee on most drafts, though certain specialized types of checks can provide such liability.

Chapter 4

Specialized Negotiable Instruments

Roadmap

- Cashier's check
- Teller's check
- Certified check
- Traveler's check
- Certificate of deposit
- Article 9 Instrument
- The peculiar and difficult terms "accept" and "acceptance"
  - Certified checks
  - Bankers' acceptances

As we saw in the previous Chapter, notes and drafts are the typical negotiable instruments you are likely to run across on a regular basis, and checks are the typical form of drafts. However, you may also run across a few types of specialized negotiable instruments from time to time. This Chapter explains those specialized types of instruments.

A. Cashier's Checks

As we will see in Chapter 8 of this book below, liability on a negotiable instrument arises from signing the instrument. Someone who has not signed an instrument (either by their own hand or via an agent) is not liable on the instrument itself. Consequently, the bank on which your checks are drawn is not liable to the payee on your checks; that bank's name is printed on the check, but that does not constitute a signature. *See* UCC §§ 3-401 and 1-201(b)(37).

Your bank's incentive to pay your checks is largely based on the bank's potential liability for wrongful dishonor, discussed in Chapter 14 below.

Sometimes it is useful to have a bank directly obligated on a check, to give the payee greater assurance of being paid. If you sell someone your car, you want to be assured of getting your money before you let the buyer drive off in the car. The buyer's personal check may not be sufficient assurance because it will only be paid if there is money in the buyer's account at his or her bank. A cashier's check is one convenient method for assuring payment, by adding a bank's signature—and therefore, that bank's liability—on the check itself.

A "cashier's check" is defined as "a draft with respect to which the drawer and drawee are the same bank or branches of the same bank." UCC § 3-104(g). In effect, the bank is ordering itself to pay the indicated amount to the payee. Because the bank, itself, has signed the check, the bank is liable to the payee for payment. The general liability rule for drawers of drafts in UCC section 3-414(b) would reach that result; that rule is discussed below in Chapter 8. However, liability on cashier's checks is governed by the same liability rule as for notes. UCC §§ 3-412, 3-414(a). Essentially, a cashier's check issued by a bank is equivalent to a promissory note issued by that bank.

B. Teller's Checks

Teller's checks serve a similar function to cashier's checks. Both have a bank's signature, so the payee of a teller's check, like the payee of a cashier's check, can demand payment from a bank. The essential difference between a teller's check and a cashier's check is that a teller's check is signed by one bank, but drawn on a different bank. Consequently, the bank signing the check is liable as drawer. *See* UCC § 3-414. By contrast, a cashier's check is signed by the same bank on which it is drawn.

A "teller's check" is defined as "a draft drawn by a bank (i) on another bank, or (ii) payable at or through a bank." UCC § 3-104(h). Teller's checks are often used by savings banks, credit unions, and other financial institutions that are included in the definition of "bank," UCC § 1-201(b)(4), but prefer to maintain a checking at another (usually larger) bank.

C. Certified Checks

A certified check is a check that has been "accepted" by a bank. UCC § 3-409(d). As discussed more fully below in section G of this chapter, the terms "accept," "accepted," acceptance," etc. have a narrow, technical, and counterintuitive meaning in UCC Article 3.

When someone draws a check on a bank and that bank "certifies" or "accepts" it, the bank agrees to be liable to the payee *on the check*. Checks show the name of the bank on which they are drawn (the "drawee"), but that printed name of the bank is not a signature, so the bank is not liable to the payee on the check. The payee can only demand payment as a matter of right from someone who has signed the check; in the usual case, the drawee never signs the check.

The drawee is potentially liable for wrongful dishonor if it fails to pay a check that was properly payable; however, that liability is owed to the *drawer*, *not* to the payee. These rules are discussed further below in Chapters 8 and 14. Of course, most checks are paid when the payee (or a bank acting on behalf of the payee) presents the check to the drawee, through the mechanism discussed below in Chapter 12. However, those payments occur because of the drawee's obligations to the drawer, not because the drawee owes any legal obligation directly to the payee.

Certified checks are rare in modern banking practice. A few decades ago, banks more commonly certified their depositors' checks. If you were making a large purchase, you might write your personal check to the seller and get your bank to certify that check. Your bank would set aside funds from your account to pay the check, and the seller would have your bank's assurance that the check would be paid. Today this service is provided almost entirely by cashier's checks and teller's checks.

The reason for this shift has more to do with accounting than law: cashier's checks and teller's checks are easier to keep track of than individual account holders' checks that an officer of the bank may have certified. Each cashier's check and teller's check is created on a separate pre-printed check form, and those forms can be printed with consecutive numbers. This makes it easy for an auditor to make sure the employee responsible for these checks is not issuing them without keeping appropriate records. Certified checks, by contrast, are created by stamping and/or writing on the depositor's check form. If a bank officer forgets (accidentally or intentionally) to record certified checks, the bank may not find out about its liability on those checks until they are presented for payment. By that time, the misbehaving bank officer may have disappeared.

D. Traveler's Checks

A traveler's check may in form be either a note or a draft. As their name suggests, they are designed to allow travelers to carry funds in a form that is relatively easy to convert to cash far from home, but (unlike cash) is replace-able if lost or stolen. When you buy traveler's checks, you enter your "speci-men signature" on each check. *See* UCC § 3-104(i)(iv). Then, when you want to cash a traveler's check, you fill in the name of the payee and sign the check a second time. This second signature is called a "countersignature." *See id.* Comparing the countersignature to the specimen signature gives the payee some assurance that the person cashing the traveler's check is the same per-son who originally bought it.

Traveler's checks are still available and in use, though their popularity has decreased as travelers have gained access to money by other, more convenient means. Cash is now readily available from networked automated teller ma-chines (ATMs) in much of the world. Alternatively, a number of different credit cards are readily accepted across national borders.

Traveler's checks are subject to some special rules. Understanding the first rule requires us to note that the requirement of a countersignature could make a traveler's check "conditional" and therefore not a negotiable instrument. *See infra* Chapter 5. However, a special carve-out from the definition of "conditional" allows traveler's checks to be negotiable instruments covered by Article 3. *See* UCC § 3-106(c).

The second special rule provides that the absence of a required countersig-nature is a potential defense to payment of a traveler's check, but even a trav-eler's check lacking the required countersignature may be negotiated from one holder to another. *See id.* The mechanics and rules of holders, negotiation, etc. are discussed below in Chapter 5.

E. Certificates of Deposit

A deposit of money in a bank account creates a debtor-creditor relation-ship between the bank and the depositor. The bank is the debtor, obligated to repay the money in the account on the terms agreed upon when the deposit was made. (Notice that this is the mirror image of borrowing from a bank, where the bank becomes the *creditor*.)

Deposits in bank accounts may be documented in a variety of ways. Among the more formal ways a bank can acknowledge a deposit is by issuing a nego-tiable "certificate of deposit." *See* UCC § 3-104(j).

If a certificate of deposit (commonly called a "CD") meets all the require-ments for being a negotiable instrument discussed in Chapter 5 below, the CD is covered by the rules in UCC Article 3. Such a CD is treated as a note of the bank that took the deposit. *See* UCC § 3-104(j). This means that the depositor can transfer ownership of the deposit to someone else simply by transferring or negotiating the CD to that person, as explained below in Chapter 6. It also means that if the CD is payable to bearer, anyone in possession of the CD—even a thief—may be able to obtain the money represented by the CD from the bank, as explained below in Chapter 6.

F. Article 9 Instruments

One other type of "instrument" needs to be mentioned here, though it is primarily a creature of UCC Article 9 (which governs security interests in personal property) rather than Article 3. Because negotiable instruments are property, they can be used as a collateral for a loan. Article 9 sets out the rules governing such secured transactions and contains several specialized rules dealing with instruments. *See, e.g.,* UCC §§ 9-312(a), 9-313(a) (security interest in an instrument may be perfected by filing a financing statement or by taking possession of the collateral); UCC § 9-330 ("purchaser" of an instrument can get priority over a security interest in the instrument unless the secured party perfected its security interest by possession).

All of this would be relatively straightforward—once you master the general principles of UCC Article 9—if Article 9 simply adopted the Article 3 definition of "instrument." However, Article 9 has its own definition, which is both broader and narrower than the Article 3 definition discussed in Chapter 5:

> "Instrument" means a negotiable instrument [as defined in Article 3] *or any other writing that* evidences a right to the payment of a monetary obligation, is not itself a security agreement or lease, and is of a type that in ordinary course of business is transferred by delivery with any necessary indorsement or assignment. *The term does not include* (i) investment property, (ii) letters of credit, or (iii) writings that evidence a right to payment arising out of the use of a credit or charge card or information contained on or for use with the card.

UCC § 9-102(a)(47) (2003) (emphasis added).

The Article 9 definition is narrower than the Article 3 definition because it excludes "investment property," a term defined in UCC section 9-102(a)(49). Investment property that also meets the definition of a "negotiable instrument" under Article 3 is conceivable (though rare) in today's marketplace.

More importantly, the Article 9 definition of instrument is broader than the Article 3 definition. In addition to negotiable instruments defined in Article 3, so-called "Article 9 instruments" include "any other writing that evidences a right to the payment of a monetary obligation, is not itself a security agreement or lease, and is of a type that in ordinary course of business is transferred by delivery with any necessary indorsement or assignment." UCC § 9-102(a)(47). This means that something may be an Article 9 instrument based on the commercial practices of people who deal in such property, even though it would not qualify as a negotiable instrument under Article 3. Of course, the Article 9 definition of "instrument" only applies in Article 9. *See* UCC § 9-102(a) (initial phrase). Article 3 only applies to "instruments" that meet the definitions in Article 3. *See* UCC §§ 3-102(d) (1st sentence), 3-103(a) (initial phrase), 3 103(b) (cross-reference to definition of negotiable instrument), 3-104(a), (b) (Article 3 definition of "negotiable instrument" and "instrument").

G. "Acceptance," "Accepted," "Accept," etc. in Article 3

1. The Confusing UCC Definition of "Acceptance"

Many of the terms used in the UCC are unfamiliar, thereby signaling that you need to pay attention to the technical definition in order to understand the term's meaning. The word "acceptance" presents a different challenge: it's a familiar word used in ways that sometimes seem consistent with the familiar meaning. Even casebook authors and other law professors who should know better sometimes slip back into casual use of these terms when discussing transactions in negotiable instruments. (Citations omitted to protect the guilty.) However, this is a trap for the unwary, which can lead you astray. If you think someone has "accepted" a draft, you should double- and triple-check that belief.

For example, you might think that the electric company accepts the check you send each month to pay your electric bill. Or, you might think your bank accepts a check that you include in a deposit. *In both cases, you would be wrong.* Even worse, your incorrect assumption that the check was "accepted" will lead you to erroneous conclusions about the parties rights and obligations with respect to the check. In those two examples, the electric company and the bank "take" the check; they *do not* "accept" it.

As the term is used in Article 3 of the UCC, acceptance can only occur in one particular way, which occurs only rarely: "'Acceptance' means the drawee's signed agreement to pay a draft as presented." UCC § 3-409(a). If you are tempted to say someone "accepted" a check or other draft, in most cases you should say instead that the person "took" it.

Let's consider further the two brief examples above: When you pay your electric bill, the electric company cannot "accept" your check, because the electric company is not the drawee. The drawee of the check is your bank, i.e., the bank where you maintain your checking account, whose name is printed on your check forms. The electric company may sign the check to deposit it in a bank, but that signature is an indorsement, not an acceptance. *See* UCC §§ 3-204(a), 3-409(a).

When you deposit a check payable to you at your bank, two possibilities exist: either the check is drawn on the bank where you deposit it, or it is drawn on another bank. In neither case does the bank "accept" the check as that term is defined in UCC Article 3. If your bank is not the drawee, your bank can't "accept" the check because a check can only be accepted by the drawee. UCC § 3-409(a). If your bank (where you deposit the check) happens also to be the drawee of the check, your bank typically won't sign the check, it will simply charge it against the drawer's account.

2. Appropriate Use of "Acceptance": Certified Checks and Bankers' Acceptances

Only rarely is a check "accepted" within the narrow and technical meanings given to that and related terms in UCC Article 3. A certified check is one instance where you can properly say that the instrument is "accepted." Certified checks are discussed above in Section C of this chapter.

Another instance of acceptance occurs with "bankers' acceptances," which are drafts used as a financing mechanism. The parties usually agree in advance that the draft will be "accepted" (in the technical Article 3 sense) by the drawee upon satisfaction of specified conditions. This is usually important to the payee because these drafts—unlike checks and other demand drafts—are usually payable only after a certain period of time has elapsed after the draft is presented to the drawee. The term "bankers' acceptance" is not defined in the UCC, though Articles 8 and 9 contain occasional references to this type of instrument. These instruments are rarely encountered in law school courses.

You should also be alert to situations where the terms "accept" and "acceptance" are used in a more general sense. For example, Regulation CC (discussed more fully in Chapters 13 and 14 below) does not restrict its use of these terms to the peculiar UCC Article 3 definition. *See* Reg. CC §§ 229.15(a), 229.18(b), 229.19(c)(2)(i), 229.32(a), 229.33(c). UCC Article 4A has a different techical definition of "acceptance." *See* Section C of Chapter 19 below.

Checkpoints

- Cashier's checks and teller's checks are used for payment transactions where the payee insists on greater certainty of payment than an ordinary check or promissory note provides.

- "Acceptance" of a check or other draft can serve a similar function to cashier's checks and teller's checks, though the term "acceptance" can easily lead to confusion.

- Traveler's checks and certificates of deposit are negotiable instruments that serve particular, highly specialized functions.

- Some "instruments" that can be collateral under UCC Article 9 do not fit the UCC Article 3 definition of negotiable instrument.

Chapter 5

Characteristics of All Negotiable Instruments

Roadmap

- Definition of "negotiable instrument" is critical because it is the gateway to the special property rules of UCC Article 3
- A negotiable instrument must be
  - unconditional
  - a "promise" or "order"
  - for a fixed amount of money
  - payable to bearer or order
  - payable on demand or at a definite time
  - free of any nonmonetary undertaking or instruction
  - free of an election to opt out of UCC Article 3

As discussed in Chapters 3 and 4, UCC Article 3 encompasses several different types of negotiable instruments. The definitions discussed in the previous Chapters are important, because different types of negotiable instruments may be treated in different ways under Article 3.

However, an even more important definition in UCC section 3-104(a) establishes the dividing line between what is or is not a negotiable instrument. This dividing line is important—even though sometimes hard to apply in particular cases—because UCC Article 3 only applies to documents that fit this definition of a "negotiable instrument." *See* UCC § 3-102. The definition in section 3-104(a) is therefore the gateway to the special characteristics and powers that Article 3 grants to negotiable instruments.

A court may apply Article 3 by analogy even if it doesn't apply explicitly. *See* UCC § 3-104 Official Comment 2 (last paragraph). However, such instances will not concern us further here.

We will return to the definitions shortly. But first, what are those special characteristics and powers of negotiable instruments? Two of them are particularly important.

First, an Article 3 negotiable instrument doesn't merely serve as evidence of a payment order or promise. A negotiable instrument *becomes the embodiment of* the payment order or promise to which it relates. *See* UCC § 3-203 Official Comment 1 (3rd paragraph).

Even more important, only a negotiable instrument covered by UCC Article 3 may have a "holder in due course." This doctrine, discussed further in Chapter 7, is a major exception to the usual rules of property transactions, in that it sometimes allows the purchaser of a negotiable instrument to get more rights than his or her seller had.

Understanding the significance of the holder-in-due-course doctrine requires us to start with a fundamental common-law rule of property: generally, a purchaser only gets the rights that her seller had. This idea is often expressed by the Latin maxim, *nemo dat qui non habet,* or just *"nemo dat"* in short. In English, it's often referred to as the "rule of derivative title," because the purchaser's title is derived from the seller's title. An all-too-common example is the purchase of stolen goods. Even if the purchaser was totally innocent of any wrongdoing and paid the thief a fair price for the stolen goods, generally the purchaser gets only the title the thief had. If the true owner of the goods shows up, the defrauded purchaser will have to turn the goods over to the true owner. The purchaser has a remedy against the thief who sold her the goods, but of course the thief has usually disappeared without a trace by the time the true owner shows up. (For sales of goods, the defrauded purchaser's remedy against the thief is codified in UCC section 2-312(1), but having that remedy set out in a statute doesn't make it any more useful if the thief can't be found or is judgment-proof.)

The precise boundaries and implications of the holder-in-due-course doctrine are explored more fully below in Chapter 7, but this introduction should help you understand why we care about the boundaries of UCC Article 3 and the definition of "negotiable instrument." Only under Article 3 can someone achieve the status of a holder in due course, so we need to know whether the piece of paper we're concerned about is covered by Article 3. UCC section 3-102 provides that Article 3 applies (only) to negotiable instruments, so Article 3 will apply if and only if the piece of paper we're looking at qualifies as a negotiable instrument under the definition in section 3-104(a).

The definition of the term "negotiable instrument" in section 3-104(a) has seven parts: Section 3-104(a) provides that an aspiring negotiable instrument must:

(1) be "unconditional," UCC § 3-103(a), first sentence;

(2) be a "promise" or "order" to pay, *id.*;

(3) for a "fixed amount of money," *id.*;

(4) be "payable to bearer or to order," UCC § 3-104(a)(1);

(5) be "payable on demand or at a definite time," UCC § 3-104(a)(2);

(6) be free of any nonmonetary "undertaking or instruction," UCC § 3-103(a)(3), with limited exceptions in UCC § 3-103(a)(3)(i), (ii), and (iii); and

(7) not opt out of UCC Article 3, UCC § 3-104(d).

Each of these items is discussed below. To understand why these requirements exist, it's helpful to remember two general things about negotiable instruments. First, as discussed above, the law is designed to avoid the surprises that could result from people creating negotiable instruments unintentionally. Therefore, the boundaries are carefully drawn so that usually a negotiable instrument only results if the parties so intend. Second, the concepts governing negotiable instruments developed many years ago, when communication over distances was slower and more difficult. Decisions about the value of negotiable instruments often had to be made without the opportunity to obtain other documents, ask questions of distant parties, etc., so a negotiable instrument was most useful if it contained all the relevant information on the face of the instrument itself. As you work through the rules below, think about which of these objectives the rule was designed to advance, and how modern practices and developments have led to a softening of the basic rule.

A. Unconditional

A negotiable instrument must be "unconditional." Section 3-106 explains what "unconditional" might mean in this context. Probably the least surprising way a particular piece of paper might fail this test is by stating on its face that it is conditional. UCC § 3-106(a)(i). The piece of paper is also conditional if you have to look somewhere else to determine essential terms. UCC § 3-106(a)(ii) and (iii).

However, some terms are so commonly included in negotiable instruments that they do not destroy negotiability even if they might fit into the general criteria described in the preceding paragraph for making an instrument conditional. A negotiable instrument can still be "unconditional" even though it refers elsewhere (perhaps to a security agreement governed by UCC Article 9) for "rights with respect to collateral, prepayment, or acceleration," or says that it may only be paid from "a particular fund or source." UCC § 3-106(b).

Last, and probably least, two special rules appear at the end of section 3-106. Subsection (c) provides a special rule that allows traveler's checks to be unconditional negotiable instruments even though they require a countersignature before they can be paid. (The term "traveler's check" is defined in section 3-104(i); the term "countersignature" is not defined in the UCC beyond the explanation provided in sections 3-106(d) and 3-104(i). Traveler's checks are discussed further in Chapter 4 above.) Finally, subsection (d) provides a special rule to conform the UCC Article 3 rules for negotiable instruments used in certain kinds of consumer transactions to the Federal Trade Commission's Holder-In-Due-Course regulations, 16 CFR Part 433. This regulation is discussed further in subsection C 4 of Chapter 7.

B. Promise or Order

As discussed above in Chapter 3, notes and drafts are the two basic types of negotiable instruments. A *note* represents a *promise* to pay money, and a *draft* represents an *order* to pay. The definitions of "promise" and "order" appear in UCC section 3-103(a)(12) and (8). Those definitions require the signature of the person promising or ordering payment, and both definitions require a writing. Electronic transactions are more and more important in commercial law, and Article 3 sometimes refers to a "record," which is defined in UCC section 1-201(b)(31) to include electronic media. However, the current version of UCC Article 3 intentionally does not allow negotiable instruments themselves to be in electronic form; a negotiable instrument must, itself, be written on paper.

C. Fixed Amount of Money

Because the fundamental purpose of a negotiable instrument is to facilitate the payment of money, it's important to determine the amount of money involved. The simplest way for this to occur would be to require that the instrument state that it is for "X dollars" without any possibility of adjustment. However, the practical realities of commercial practices require a few adjustments, and negotiable instruments are made more useful for actual transactions by accommodating those adjustments.

Interest is the most significant thing that keeps the amount of money from being truly "fixed." Because of the time value of money, a dollar received today is worth more than a dollar to be received in the future. Consequently, someone who agrees to receive payment in the future typically insists on receiving interest to compensate for the delay.

UCC section 3-104(a) provides that the fixed amount of money stated in a negotiable instrument may be "with or without interest or other charges described in the promise or order." This may require a calendar and some calculations to determine the actual amount of money payable on the negotiable instrument, but it more-or-less preserves the idea that all the essential terms appear on the instrument's face. Calendars and arithmetic have been available for centuries, so if an instrument recites an amount of "one thousand dollars plus interest at six percent per year" from the date of the instrument, calculating the amount owed has always been easy.

In the past few decades, the availability of computers and virtually instantaneous worldwide communication has facilitated more complicated ways to calculate interest. Perhaps the most common example is the variable interest rate, which allows the rate of interest to adjust to market conditions.

A variable-rate loan typically involves an "index" and a "margin," though neither of those terms is defined in the UCC. The *index* is a rate determined by market forces or otherwise widely announced. Common choices for the index are the "prime rate" (set by individual banks, though banks tend to change their Prime rates together based on market conditions), the "London Inter-Bank Offered Rate," or "LIBOR" (set daily by the British Bankers' Association based on bank rates for certain very low-risk loans), or the rate of interest on a U.S. Treasury security (for example, "90-day T-bill" or "5-year T-note"). The *margin* is the number of percentage points added to (or perhaps subtracted from) the index to arrive at the rate the borrower will pay. A low-risk loan might have a variable interest rate of "LIBOR + 1," meaning that each time the interest rate is to be adjusted under the terms of the loan, the rate will be set at the publicly announced LIBOR rate plus one percentage point. A higher-risk loan might have a variable interest rate of "Bank of America's Prime Rate + 6," meaning that the interest rate will always be equal to the prime rate announced by the Bank of America plus six percentage points.

Of course, calculating the interest due on a note with a variable interest rate requires more than just the note, a calendar, and arithmetic. You also have to know the index values for the relevant period. Prior to the last major revision of UCC Article 3, completed in 1990, this created some uncertainty as to whether variable rate notes qualified as negotiable instruments. The current version of UCC section 3-112(b) resolved those questions in the most practical way: a negotiable instrument may have a variable interest rate or otherwise require looking beyond the face of the instrument to determine the amount of interest, without interfering with coverage as a negotiable instrument under UCC

Article 3. This moves us away from the historical requirement of not needing to look beyond the instrument itself, but modern communications technology makes information about various interest rate indexes almost as accessible as calendars and arithmetic.

In determining whether a purported negotiable instrument specifies a "fixed amount of money," we must also consider the boundaries of what is "money." UCC section 1-201(b)(24) defines that term to include not only U.S. dollars, but also money issued by foreign governments (e.g., the pesos issued by the Mexican government) and intergovernmental organizations and agreements (e.g., the euros used as the money of certain member countries in the European Union). As a result, specifying the amount to be paid in Canadian dollars, euros, francs, guilders, pesos, yen, yuan, or another currency will not destroy negotiable instrument status. Section 3-107 provides that if an instrument "states the amount payable in foreign money," it is payable in either that foreign money or "an equivalent amount in dollars." Section 3-107 goes on to specify the method for determining that equivalent amount. (The term "dollar" is not defined in the UCC. It is commonly understood to mean U.S. dollars, and that inference is strengthened by the reference to United States dollars in the Official Comment to section 3-107. However, some people might tend to assume otherwise if they live in Australia, Canada, Hong Kong, Jamaica, New Zealand, Singapore, Zimbabwe, or another country that issues "dollars" as its national currency.)

D. Payable to Bearer or to Order

The requirement in UCC section 3-104(a)(1) that a negotiable instrument must be "payable to bearer or to order" is probably the most formalistic of all the requirements. Qualification as a negotiable instrument requires certain magic words, as explained more fully in UCC section 3-109. The absence of those magic words generally prevents Article 3 from applying.

If you are writing a check, the magic words "Pay To The Order Of" are helpfully printed on the form supplied by your bank. If you are writing a note that you want to be a negotiable instrument, you need to be sure to include the appropriate magic words if you want Article 3 to apply. The appropriate choice of wording depends on whether you intend the instrument to be payable to a particular person or to anyone in possession.

If you intend your negotiable instrument to be payable to John Doe, you have two choices set out in UCC section 3-109(b)(i) and (ii): you can write either "pay to the order of John Doe" or "pay to John Doe or order." Either phrasing meets the "payable ... to order" requirement. The resulting instrument is referred to as being "payable to order" or "payable to an identified person." Both of those latter two phrases mean essentially the same thing.

If you intend your negotiable instrument to be payable to anyone who happens to be in possession of the instrument, you will meet the requirement of section 3-104(a)(1) by making the instrument "payable to bearer." The standard phrases are "pay to bearer" or "pay to cash." It's also OK, but not necessary, to write "pay to the order of bearer" or "pay to the order of cash." Section 3-109(a) indicates that other phrases can also work, but there's rarely if ever any benefit in creative writing for this purpose. The standard phrases will accomplish your desired result without creating any risk of uncertainty.

One exception to this magic-words requirement appears in section 3-104(c). If an instrument meets all the requirements to be a "check" except that it lacks the magic words "bearer or order," that instrument still qualifies as both a check and a negotiable instrument. An example would be a check that says "pay to Sam Smith" (instead of "pay to *the order of* Sam Smith"). The reason for this special rule is the practical realities of the check-collection system. As discussed more fully below in Part Two of this book, enormous numbers of checks are processed each day. The system for dealing with them is highly mechanized, with little scrutiny of the face of each check. If every document that looks like a check had to be carefully scrutinized for subtle omissions or modifications of words that are usually printed on the form, it would slow the collection process down substantially with little if any corresponding benefit.

E. Payable on Demand or at a Definite Time

UCC section 3-108 provides guidance for determining whether a purported negotiable instrument meets the requirement in section 3-104(a)(2) that it be "payable on demand or at a definite time." These two possibilities implicitly create two additional sub-categories of negotiable instruments: "demand" instruments and "time" instruments.

A demand instrument is payable when payment is demanded. UCC section 3-108(a)(i) also mentions the term "at sight," which is a synonym for "on demand" and describes the moment at which draft is presented for payment. UCC section 3-108(a)(ii) also provides that an instrument is payable on demand if it "does not state any time of payment." All checks are payable on demand. UCC § 3-104(f)(i). However, other types of drafts may be either demand instruments or time instruments.

A time instrument explicitly grants the right to defer payment. Perhaps the most common examples are promissory notes stating that payment is due, e.g., "90 days from the date of this note" or "in 47 equal monthly payments of $483.47 each beginning on July 1, 2007, with the entire remaining principal and interest due and payable on June 1, 2011." The latter example is the usual form for repayment of a modern installment loan. Both of these alternatives are "payable at a definite time" as required by UCC sections 3-104(a)(2) and 3-109.

Section 3-108(b) also suggests that a time instrument might be "payable on elapse of a definite period of time after sight or acceptance." "Sight" is generally synonymous with "demand," and refers to the moment at which a draft is presented for payment. "Acceptance" is a technical term that often confuses law students and lawyers, because its meaning in the negotiable instrument context is far narrower than its common usage; these issues are discussed above in Section G of Chapter 4.

F. Free of Any Non-Monetary Undertaking or Instruction

The primary purpose of a negotiable instrument is the payment of money. The usefulness of instruments for that purpose could be diminished by loading them up with other provisions that are not essential to the primary monetary purpose. For example, if fulfillment of a contract term were a condition to payment being made, you would have to assess whether the contract term had been fulfilled in order to gauge the value of the payment obligation.

Consequently, UCC section 3-104(a)(3) prohibits negotiable instruments from containing "any other undertaking or instruction by the person promising or ordering payment to do any act in addition to the payment of money." However, section 3-104(a)(3) then goes on to permit specific types of non-monetary conditions that have commonly been included in negotiable instruments, particularly in promissory notes.

G. No Opt-Out from UCC Article 3

Even if a particular piece of paper meets all the requirements of a negotiable instrument in UCC Article 3, the parties to the instrument still have the opportunity to opt out of negotiable instrument treatment. Section 3-104(d) provides that (unless it qualifies as a "check") a piece of paper is "not an instrument if, at the time it is issued or first comes into possession of a holder, it contains a conspicuous statement, however expressed, to the effect that the promise or order is not negotiable or is not an instrument governed by [Article 3]." In other words, if the parties don't want their piece of paper to be a negotiable instrument, all they have to do is say so—conspicuously—on that piece of paper.

Checks are excluded from the section 3-104(d) opportunity to opt out of negotiable instrument coverage, for the same practical reasons that led the drafters of section 3-104(a)(1) to eliminate the "bearer or order" magic-words requirement for checks. Check processing is extensively mechanized. There are few points at which a human being even looks at a check, and even fewer (sometimes none) at which careful consideration is given to all the writing on the check. Little if any benefit would result from allowing a check's status as a negotiable instrument to be destroyed by a notation on the check that normally isn't scrutinized. Requiring the check-processing system to scrutinize every check for such notations would substantially increase the cost of processing checks, with little or no corresponding benefit.

Checkpoints

- A negotiable instrument can usually be classified as either a *promise* or an *order* to pay money.

- A negotiable instrument (other than a check) must contain the magic words stating that it is "payable to bearer or to order."

- The parties to a negotiable instrument may choose to opt out of the negotiable instrument rules and consequences by clearly indicating their intent to do so on the instrument.

- Other formal requisites of negotiable instruments (unconditional, fixed amount of money, payable on demand or at a definite time, and free from nonmonetary undertaking or instruction) are subject to extensive definitional rules reflecting the historical evolution of negotiable instrument practices.

Chapter 6

Issue, Transfer, and Negotiation of Negotiable Instruments

Roadmap

- Issue
- Transfer
- Negotiation
- Holders and other persons entitled to enforce
- Types and functions of indorsements
  - Blank
  - Special
  - Restrictive
  - Anomalous
- Loss and theft

A. Issue

The law governing negotiable instruments (Article 3 of the Uniform Commercial Code (UCC)) distinguishes between the initial delivery of a negotiable instrument and its subsequent movement from one person to another. The initial creation and delivery of an instrument is referred to as "issue." UCC § 3-105(a). Not surprisingly, the person or entity who issues the instrument is called the "issuer." UCC § 3-105(c). The issuer of an instrument is also referred to as the "maker" if the instrument is a note, or the "drawer" if the instrument is a draft. *Id.*; UCC § 3-105(a)(7) and (5).

B. Transfer and Negotiation

Negotiable instruments often change hands again (and again and again) after they are initially issued. For example, if you issue a promissory note to a car dealer to buy a car, the car dealer typically will sell that note to a financial institution. This sale benefits the car dealer by giving it cash that it can use to buy another car for its inventory. The financial institution (usually a bank or finance company) will then collect the monthly payments from you over the term of the note. (Banks are good at this, and often better at it than car dealers.) As another example, when you issue your check to the power company to pay your monthly electric bill, the power company will take that check to its bank to begin the process of collecting the check. Here again, the receipt of the negotiable instrument is simply an intermediate step in the overall objective of getting actual money from buyer to seller.

These expected movements of a negotiable instrument after it has been issued are referred to as "transfer" or "negotiation," which are defined in UCC sections 3-203 and 3-201, respectively. We will return in Part Two below to the specialized rules in UCC Article 4 that govern the collection of checks. For now we focus on the general rules of Article 3 that govern transfer and negotiation.

The terms "transfer" and "negotiation" have particular and technical meanings in UCC Article 3. A transfer of a negotiable instrument is similar enough to other transfers of property that the colloquial definition of the term won't lead you too far astray. However, negotiation is a term that UCC Article 3 defines in a peculiar and counterintuitive way. You will be confused, not aided, by trying to analogize the negotiation of an instrument to the negotiation with your roommate or spouse over who has to clean up the kitchen tonight.

A "transfer" occurs when a person gives up a negotiable instrument and intends that the recipient have the right to enforce the instrument. UCC § 3-203(a). A person who transfers a negotiable instrument gives certain warranties by operation of law; those warranties are discussed in Chapter 15 below. A transfer also generally gives the transferee the rights of the transferor that the transferee would expect to get in an ordinary property transaction. See UCC § 3-203(b). This is commonly referred to as the "Shelter Rule," and is discussed further in Section E of Chapter 7.

A "negotiation" is a particular type of transfer, in which the recipient becomes a "holder." UCC § 3-201(a). Negotiation of a bearer instrument requires only a transfer of possession. See UCC § 3-201(b). This reflects the fact that only possession is required to be a holder of a bearer instrument. See UCC § 1-201(b)(21)(A). However, negotiation of an instrument payable to an identified person generally requires an indorsement in addition to the transfer of possession. *See* UCC § 3-201(b).

C. Holders

Understanding the difference between a transfer and a negotiation requires understanding the additional term, "holder." The rules for becoming a holder of a negotiable instrument are fundamental to negotiable instrument transactions and intersect with many of the other important concepts. Perhaps most important, one must first be a holder in order to achieve the coveted status of "holder in due course," which is discussed in Chapter 7 below.

The term "holder" is defined in UCC section 1-201(b)(21)(A). The definition is a bit hard to read, but it sets out two different ways to become a holder, depending on whether the instrument is payable "to bearer" or "to an identified person." (Paragraphs (B) and (C) of UCC section 1-201(b)(21) provide additional definitions, but those are for UCC Article 7 on Documents of Title, not for Article 3.) Every instrument will be *either* payable to bearer or payable to an identified person when it is created. An instrument may move between those two categories, depending on how it is indorsed. The types of indorsements, and their effects, are discussed in Section E of this Chapter. The question of whether an instrument is payable to bearer or to an identified person was introduced above in Chapter 5, and is discussed further below in Chapter 7.

If an instrument is payable to bearer, all that's required to be a holder of the instrument is physical possession of the instrument: "'Holder' means (A) the person in possession of a negotiable instrument that is payable ... to bearer." UCC § 1-201(b)(21)(A). On the other hand, if an instrument is payable to an identified person, being a holder requires that you *both* have physical possession of the instrument *and* be the identified person to whom the instrument is payable: "'Holder' means (A) the person in possession of a negotiable instrument that is payable ... to an identified person that is the person in possession." *Id.*

D. Persons Entitled to Enforce

Being a holder is itself a significant status under Article 3. In addition, being a holder is the most common way to become a "person entitled to enforce" an instrument. UCC § 3-301(i). You will see a number of provisions in Article 3 that give various rights to a person entitled to enforce an instrument. Anyone who is a holder gets those rights, so "holder" is synonymous with "person entitled to enforce" in most cases.

You should also note the additional ways to become a person entitled to enforce an instrument besides being a holder. You can be a person entitled to enforce even if you don't qualify as a holder on your own but can claim the rights of a holder via the Shelter Rule (discussed in Section B of this Chapter above, and Section E of Chapter 7 below). UCC § 3-301(ii). You can also be a person entitled to enforce an instrument that was lost, destroyed, or stolen, though the requirements may be cumbersome. UCC § 3-301(iii).

E. Indorsements

To understand transfer and negotiation fully, it's also important to understand one more thing about the distinction between instruments payable to bearer and instruments payable to an identified person: Whether the instrument was initially payable to bearer or payable to an identified person can be changed by the way the instrument is "indorsed." The terminology for indorsements appears in UCC sections 3-204, 3-205, and 3-206.

1. Blank Indorsements

You have probably cashed a check or deposited it in your account at your bank. (When you did, you *transferred* and *negotiated* the check.) In connection with that transaction, you probably signed your name on the back of the check. Your signature on the back of the check was an "indorsement." UCC § 3-204(a). If you just signed your name, your indorsement is further classified as a "blank indorsement." UCC § 3-206(a).

The effect of a blank indorsement on an instrument is to make the instrument payable "to bearer." *Id.* When you indorse a check in blank by simply signing your name on the back, anyone who subsequently gets physical possession of the check becomes a holder of the check. If the check was already payable to bearer (e.g., if it was payable to "Cash"), your indorsement doesn't change the check's status as a bearer instrument. However, if the check was originally payable to you (or more precisely, "to your order"), your blank indorsement converts the check from being payable to an identified person to being payable to bearer.

2. Special Indorsements

Conversely, an indorsement can convert an instrument payable to bearer into an instrument payable to an identified person. This type of indorsement is a "special indorsement," defined in UCC section 3-205(a). If you are in possession of an instrument check payable to bearer (either because it was originally issued that way or because it was validly indorsed in blank), you can make it payable to an identified person by writing "pay to Floyd Michaels" on the back and signing your name. (Note that the magic words "to the order of" are not required for indorsements, as they are for the designation of the original payee.) After you specially indorse the instrument, only Floyd Michaels can be a holder of it (*if* Floyd Michaels also has possession) unless and until Floyd Michaels indorses it. If Floyd Michaels subsequently indorses the check in blank, it will be converted back into a bearer instrument, so that anyone in possession may be a holder. On the other hand, if Floyd Michaels puts a special indorsement on the check, only the person identified in that special indorsement can be a holder (and that person will also have to get possession or further indorse the check in order for anyone else to be a holder).

3. Restrictive Indorsements

Blank and special indorsements are the most common classifications of indorsement, but Article 3 recognizes other special categories. The one you are most likely to have seen is the "restrictive indorsement." If you add the words "for deposit" or "for collection" to your indorsement, the bank will face potential liability for conversion if you don't get the money represented by that check. UCC §3-206(b). (Conversion is a tort with particular application in the negotiable instrument context; *see infra* Section F of Chapter 16.) This means that a bank usually won't cash a check with a special indorsement and will typically require that you deposit any specially indorsed check into your account. Using a special indorsement is a good idea for checks that you plan to deposit in your account.

4. Anomalous Indorsements

Understanding "anomalous indorsements" requires you to remember that indorsements have dual functions in Article 3. First, as discussed above, they are typically a part of the process of transferring and negotiating negotiable instruments from one person or entity to another. Second, the person or entity who indorses an instrument typically becomes liable on the instrument if it isn't paid. We have focused on the first function of indorsements in this Chapter. The second function of indorsements is discussed below in Chapter 8. The classification of "anomalous indorsement" in section 3-205(d) relates to this second, liability-related, function of indorsements.

F. Loss and Theft

Transfer and negotiation don't exhaust all the possible ways a negotiable instrument can change hands, but they cover the typical cases. Other ways that an instrument might change hands include loss and theft. Usually those are neither a transfer nor a negotiation, because they both lack the intent that the transferee get the right to enforce the instrument.

If an instrument is payable to bearer, even a thief becomes a holder, because nothing more than physical possession is required for holder status. UCC § 1-201(b)(21)(A) Therefore, acquisition of an instrument by a thief constitutes a "negotiation." UCC § 3-201 and Official Comment 1. However, acquisition by a thief does not constitute a "transfer," because there is no "deliver[y] ... for the purpose of giving to the person receiving delivery the right to enforce the instrument." UCC § 3-203(a). Consequently, a thief of a bearer instrument gets the right to enforce the instrument under the rules of Article 3, but does not succeed to the owner's property rights in the instrument. *See* UCC § 3-203 Official Comment 1 (second paragraph).

Checkpoints

- Issue is the "birth" of a negotiable instrument.
- Transfer and negotiation are the movement of the instrument from one person to another.
- Indorsement is essential to the negotiation of an instrument payable to an identified person.
- An indorsement also imposes liability on the indorser.
- Being a holder is the typical way to become a person entitled to enforce an instrument.
- Holder status always requires physical possession.
  - Only possession is required to be holder of a bearer instrument.
  - Both possession and being the person identified are required to be holder of an instrument payable to an identified person.

Chapter 7

Holders, the Holder-In-Due-Course Doctrine, and the Shelter Rule

---

Roadmap

- Benefits of being a holder
  - Holder is a person entitled to enforce
  - Must be a holder to be a holder in due course
- Requirements to be a holder
  - Possession
  - Bearer instrument or person identified in order instrument
  - Effect of indorsement
- Requirements to be a holder in due course
  - Instrument appears normal
  - Value
  - Good faith
  - No notice of problems
- Benefits of being a holder in due course
  - Freedom from claims
  - Freedom from most defenses
    - Personal defenses
    - Not real defenses
  - Freedom from claims in recoupment
- Shelter doctrine

As we saw above in Chapter 6, UCC Article 3 carefully prescribes the status of "holder" and the process of negotiation that leads to that status. Being a holder of a negotiable instrument is important in itself, because a holder is a "person entitled to enforce" the instrument. UCC § 3-301. But becoming a holder is also important as a waypoint on the path to becoming a "holder in due course." This status and its consequences are perhaps the most remarkable feature of negotiable instruments law. A holder in due course gets more rights than the typical property transaction confers on the typical buyer of property, so understanding the significance of holder-in-due-course status requires a brief review of some basic property concepts.

Normally when you buy a piece of property, you only get the rights to that property that your seller had. This idea has long been recognized in the common law by the Latin maxim *"nemo dat qui non habet,"* or just *"nemo dat"* for short. In English it's also called the "rule of derivative title," which captures its essence: In most property transactions you only get the property rights of the person you got the property from, and nothing more. One consequence of *nemo dat* is that if you buy property from a thief, in the usual case you get only the thief's rights to the property—i.e., generally no rights at all. If the true owner of the property shows up, he or she will be able to demand the return of the stolen property. You as buyer will be left with a claim against the thief, who is typically long gone. (UCC section 2-403(2) provides a limited exception to this rule in particular contexts, but it's an exception; the general rule of nemo dat is reflected in section 2-403(1).)

UCC Article 3 doesn't take away the normal property rights for negotiable instruments. It provides that the transferee of a negotiable instrument gets the rights that his or her seller had, consistent with nemo dat. This is commonly referred to as the "shelter rule" or "shelter doctrine"—the transferee can take shelter in the rights of the transferor—and it is codified in section 3-203(b). This idea is discussed further in Section E of this Chapter below. The remarkable thing about Article 3, though, is that it gives some people—called "holders in due course"—important additional rights, on top of the normal derivative rights that a purchaser gets from a seller.

Becoming a holder in due course first requires becoming a "holder." We first consider the benefits and requirements of being a holder. Then we will turn to the benefits and requirements of being a holder in due course.

A. Benefits of Being a Holder

Being a holder is the usual way that someone becomes a "person entitled to enforce" an instrument. *See* UCC § 3-301(i). You will notice a number of provisions that give rights to a person entitled to enforce an instrument. *See* UCC

§§ 3-412 (last sentence), 3-413(a)(1) (last sentence), 3-414(b) (last sentence), 3-415(a) (last sentence), 3-416(a)(1), 3-417(a)(1), 4-207(a)(1), 4-208(a)(1).

Being a holder is also a necessary step along the way to becoming a holder in due course, as discussed in Section D of this Chapter.

B. Requirements to Become a Holder

UCC section 1-201(b)(21) defines a "holder" as "the person in possession of a negotiable instrument that is payable either to bearer or to an identified person that is the person in possession." This definition requires us to consider two things: First, who is in possession of the instrument? Second, to whom is the instrument payable?

1. Possession

Physical possession is *always* required to be a holder of an instrument. If someone doesn't have physical possession of an instrument, that person cannot be a holder of the instrument in his, her, or its own right. (There are a few special rules that allow someone to exercise someone else's rights as a holder or a holder in due course; these are discussed in Section E of this Chapter. However, those rules simply allow the exercise of another's rights; they don't make someone a holder, or a holder in due course, without meeting the qualifications for that status.)

2. Payable to Bearer or to the Person in Possession

However, possession alone may not be sufficient. We must also consider whether the *right person* is in possession. This requires understanding two different categories of instruments.

As we saw in Chapter 5, a negotiable instrument must be either "payable to bearer or to order." UCC § 3-104(a)(1). This suggests that some instruments are "payable to bearer," (also referred to as "bearer instruments"), and other instruments are "payable ... to order" (also referred to as "order instruments"). *Id.* Becoming a holder has different requirements depending upon which type of instrument is involved.

a. Instruments Payable to Bearer

An instrument may be issued "payable to bearer" (also called a "bearer instrument") in a variety of ways. UCC § 3-109(a), (c). One common way is to make the instrument "payable to the order of cash." UCC § 3-109(a)(3). Other possibilities include making it "payable to bearer or to the order of bearer." UCC § 3-109(a)(1). (An instrument may also become a bearer instrument as the result of an indorsement, as discussed below.)

If an instrument is payable to bearer, possession is all that is required to become a holder. UCC § 1-201(b)(21)(A). Possession makes even a thief a holder of a bearer instrument.

b. Instruments Payable to Order (i.e., to an Identified Person)

Usually someone who issues a negotiable instrument intends a particular person to get the money. As a result, instruments are usually payable "to order" or "to an identified person." Both of these phrases mean essentially the same thing. An instrument payable to an identified person is often referred to as an "order" instrument (to distinguish it from a "bearer" instrument).

An instrument is made payable to order by writing on it that it is "payable (i) to the order of an identified person or (ii) to an identified person or order." UCC § 3-109(b). An example of the former would be a check that says "Pay to the order of John Smith." (You may have noticed that checks have the words "Pay to the order of" printed on the form next to the line for the name of the payee.) An example of the latter would be "Pay to John Smith or order." (An instrument may also become an order instrument as the result of an indorsement, as discussed below.)

If an instrument is payable to an identified person, only that identified person may be a holder, unless that person indorses it. UCC § 1-201(b)(21)(A).

c. Effect of Indorsements

Determining whether an instrument is payable to bearer or to order also requires examination of the indorsements on the instrument. Two types of indorsements are relevant here, *blank* indorsements and *special* indorsements.

A "special indorsement" is one that identifies a particular person as being the person to whom the instrument is payable. UCC § 3-205(a). The person identified in a special indorsement becomes the person to whom the instrument is payable, whose signature is required to negotiate the instrument further. *Id.*

For example, suppose you receive a check payable to you (or more precisely, to your order). If you write "Pay to John Jones" on the back of the check and sign your name, the check will thereafter be payable to John Jones. Until John Jones indorses the check, only he may then be a holder of the check (and only while he is in possession).

Any indorsement that does not fit the definition of a special indorsement is a "blank indorsement." UCC § 3-205(b). The most common type of blank indorsement is a signature by itself. A blank indorsement causes the instrument to be payable to bearer; anyone in possession is a holder. *Id.*

For example, suppose again that you receive a check payable to you, but this time you merely sign your name on the back without writing anything else. You have indorsed that check in blank, and anyone who gets possession of the check will be a holder.

C. Benefits of Being a Holder in Due Course

The benefits of being a holder in due course are set out in UCC sections 3-305 and 3-306. A holder in due course is protected from most, though not quite all, *claims* and *defenses* that might otherwise interfere with enforcing the instrument. These claims and defenses come in various guises. First we consider the types of defenses and claims that are available to an obligor of an instrument who doesn't want to pay, and to someone who claims superior rights to the instrument. Then we consider the protections of a holder in due course against those claims and defenses.

Of course, the benefits to a holder in due course may cause corresponding burdens to someone who has to give up defenses or claims. If you gave someone a negotiable instrument in a transaction but didn't get what you bargained for in return, you will not be happy if you have to pay a holder in due course despite your complaints about not getting what you paid for. We consider these tensions in this Chapter, below.

1. Defenses

The term "defense" is not precisely defined in the UCC, though a catalog of possible defenses to payment of an instrument appears in UCC section 3-305(a). Each of the defenses is a legally-recognized basis for denying responsibility to pay on an instrument. Section 3-305(a) divides defenses into three categories: *real defenses*, UCC § 3-305(a)(1) and UCC § 3-305 Official Comment 1; *personal defenses*, UCC § 3-305(a)(2); and *claims in recoupment*, UCC § 3-305(a)(3). A holder in due course is not subject to personal defenses and claims in recoupment. UCC § 3-305(b). However, anyone, including a holder in due course, is subject to the real defenses. *Id.*

The terms "real defense," "personal defense," and "claim in recoupment" are not explicitly defined in the UCC, but are widely used.

a. Real Defenses

The "real defenses," which are good even against a holder in due course, are such significant problems with a transaction that no one is permitted to overcome them. As you might suspect, problems of this magnitude are relatively rare. Moreover, some of the categories are narrower than they might initially appear.

The first real defense is *"infancy."* UCC § 3-305 (a)(1)(i). Article 3 imports the idea from contract law that a valid obligation can only be made by a person who has reached legal age, and includes that limitation in the real defenses. Article 3 also looks to contract law to determine whether infancy will be a defense on particular facts. Unlike the second group of defenses, discussed in the next paragraph, infancy is a defense under Article 3 whether contract law would make the transaction void or merely voidable. *See* UCC § 3-305 Official Comment 1 (second paragraph).

The second real defense is actually a group of defenses: *"duress, lack of legal capacity, or illegality of the transaction...."* UCC § 3-305(a)(1)(ii). Like infancy, these are circumstances surrounding a transaction that can prevent enforcement of a contract. Also like infancy, Article 3 looks to other law outside the UCC to determine whether one of these problems will be available as a defense on the particular facts. However, *un*like infancy, these problems are only available as a defense if the other law would make the transaction null and void. If the problem would merely make the transaction voidable, but not automatically void, the defense does not qualify as a real defense.

For example, if someone signed a contract or note because a gun was pointed at his head, that level of duress would make the transaction void in most states, creating a real defense. However, if the level of duress was a lesser threat, such as a threat to prosecute the signer's relative, and this lower level of duress would make the transaction merely voidable at the option of the signer under the applicable state law, the duress will not qualify as a real defense. *See* UCC § 3-305 Official Comment 1 (third and fourth paragraphs).

The third real defense often seems much broader to law students than it actually is: *"fraud that induced the obligor to sign the instrument with neither knowledge nor reasonable opportunity to learn of its character or essential terms."* UCC § 3-305(a)(1)(iii) (emphasis added). This is a very, very narrow subset of fraud, sometimes referred to as "real fraud" or "fraud in the factum" (as contrasted with "ordinary fraud" or "fraud in the inducement," which is *not* a real defense). For example, suppose a completely blind person signs a promissory note because her father, who she had no reason to distrust, told her that she was signing a letter. This could qualify as a real defense. However, if the signer could have read the letter with the aid of eyeglasses or a magnifying glass, but chose not to go to that trouble, or if there were circumstances that made it unreasonable to rely on her father's assertions, the signer may not be able to avail herself of this real defense.

The last real defense is "*discharge of the obligor in insolvency proceedings.* UCC § 3-305(a)(1)(iv). Most cases would probably reach the same result without having this real defense in the UCC, because bankruptcy law, which comprises most insolvency law, is all federal law. As you know from Constitutional Law, federal law preempts conflicting state law. *See* U.S. Const. Art. I, § 8; Art. VI. A few relatively minor state laws still apply to certain methods for dealing with insolvency that are outside the bankruptcy laws, such as receivership, composition, extension, and assignment for the benefit of creditors. However, those are specialized issues addressed in the bankruptcy context. For commercial law purposes, the UCC's explicit deferral to a bankruptcy discharge protects debtors from having to make constitutional supremacy arguments to preserve the benefit of the discharge. Because this is a real defense, it is good even against a holder in due course.

b. Personal Defenses

Most defenses are "personal" defenses, a term widely used but not explicitly defined in the UCC. Some personal defenses are defined in the UCC, and those are summarized in Official Comment 2 to section 3-305. (Official Comment 4 to section 3-203 also has some helpful examples.) Article 3 also imports from contract law the defenses "that would be available if the person entitled to enforce the instrument were enforcing a right to payment under a simple contract." UCC § 3-305(a)(2).

The numerous personal defenses are good against someone who does not qualify as a holder in due course. However, they do *not* prevent a holder in due course from enforcing the instrument. UCC § 3-305(b).

Defenses based on fraud appear in both the real defenses of paragraph 3-305(a)(1) and the personal defenses of paragraph 3-305(a)(2). It's important to recognize that many types of fraud count as defenses to payment of an instrument; however, as discussed above, *only* the particular type of "real fraud" or "fraud in the factum" described in subparagraph 3-305(a)(1)(iii) qualifies as a real defense good against a holder in due course. *Other types of fraud are merely personal defenses,* to which a holder in due course is not subject.

c. Payment and Other Means of Discharge

Payment and other forms of discharge are not listed as real defenses (except discharge in insolvency proceedings). However, you shouldn't simply lump them in with the personal defenses, either, because in some cases a defense based on payment or another kind of discharge may be good even against a holder in due course. A special rule provides that, even though payment and discharge are defenses to having to pay again, a holder who takes an instrument with notice of a payment or discharge is not prevented from becoming a holder in due course. UCC § 3-302(b). That same special rule goes on to say that even a holder in due course is subject to a payment or discharge of which the holder in due course had notice. *Id.*

2. Claims in Recoupment

A claim in recoupment is a particular type of defense that is treated separately in UCC section 3-305(a). A detailed explanation appears in Official Comment 3 to section 3-305, which offers a typical example of a claim in recoupment: a warranty claim for a problem with equipment purchased by a buyer in exchange for a negotiable instrument. In the usual case, such a warranty claim would not give the buyer the right to avoid any payment on the instrument, because the seller performed the contract by providing the equipment to the buyer. However, the buyer would have the opportunity to offset the amount of the warranty claim to reduce the total amount owing on the instrument, as long as the instrument is not held by a holder in due course. Claims in recoupment were treated simply as defenses under the pre-1990 version of Article 3, but the current version treats them separately, as further explained in Official Comment 3 to section 3-305.

Like personal defenses, claims in recoupment are not available against a holder in due course, but are available against persons who do not qualify for holder-in-due-course status.

3. Claims to a Negotiable Instrument

As with any piece of property, more than one person may have rights to a negotiable instrument. Someone with a negotiable instrument may be subject to the possibility that someone else may show up with a better claim of possession or ownership. That same issue exists with respect to negotiable instruments, with an important exception: A holder in due course is not subject to competing claims to the instrument. UCC § 3-306. However, persons who do not qualify as a holder in due course do not get this protection. *Id.*

4. Other Special Rules Relating to Defenses, Claims, and Holders in Due Course

Article 3 provides various other specialized rules governing defenses to negotiable instrument liability. One such rule governs the ability of an accommodation party to assert defenses. UCC §3-305(d). This provision is discussed in Subsection B 3 of Chapter 10.

Special rules also apply to consumer transactions. Article 3 explicitly defers to law outside the UCC that may provide additional protections in consumer transactions. UCC §3-305(f).

A more specific but harder-to-understand rule for consumer transactions appears in section 3-305(e). Understanding this provision requires background on the Federal Trade Commission (FTC) Holder-in-Due-Course regulation.

Suppose you agree to buy a set of encyclopedias. If the seller fraudulently fails to deliver the encyclopedias as promised, you would have a defense to your obligation to pay under the contract. *See* UCC §2-711(4). This defense would be a defense to paying the seller even if you signed a negotiable promissory note in exchange for the seller's promise to deliver the encyclopedias. *See* UCC §3-305(a)(2).

Your defense is a personal defense, *not* a real defense. UCC §3-305(b). Your defense remains good against the seller of the encyclopedias: because the seller took the note with notice of your defense, he could not be a holder in due course. UCC §3-302(a)(2)(vi). However, the defense would not be good against a holder in due course. UCC §3-305(b). Therefore, if the seller negotiates the note to someone who qualifies as a holder in due course, you would have to pay the amount due on the note for the encyclopedias, even though you never got the encyclopedias. Your remedy would be to get a refund from the seller, but it's usually much harder to get a refund than it is to refuse to pay in the first place. Often the seller will have disappeared with your money, or may be judgment-proof.

Before the FTC promulgated its rule, courts struggled to craft doctrines to prevent overly harsh application of the holder in due course rule, particularly in consumer transactions. Courts developed various doctrines to deal with this problem.

Courts were sometimes willing to deny holder-in-due-course status to a purchaser of the debt obligation was too "closely connected" to the seller of the encyclopedias. However, the unhappy buyer/debtor could only obtain this result via litigation, which is always expensive and usually subject to uncertainty. Another problem with this approach was that sellers and their related financers developed alternative techniques that didn't rely on holder-in-due-course status but achieved the same result. One such approach was to include a "waiver of defenses" clause in the promissory note, in which the buyer/debtor agreed not to assert any defenses to payment against a purchaser of the note. Another approach was to require the buyer to obtain financing directly from the lender, who would provide cash to the seller and could collect the debt without being hampered by the buyer/debtor's complaints about the ostensibly independent sale transaction for the goods or services.

The FTC put a stop to these end runs around defenses in consumer transactions, with the Holder-In-Due-Course regulations. *See* 12 C.F.R. §§ 433.1, 433.2. These regulation require a legend (the FTC HDC legend) in all "consumer credit contracts" that subjects any holder to "all claims and defenses which the debtor could assert against the seller of goods or services obtained." 12 C.F.R § 433.2(a), (b) (emphasis omitted). This is the "statement" referred to — somewhat mysteriously — in UCC sections 3-106(d) and 3-305(e).

The FTC HDC legend does not make the note conditional so as to prevent the application of UCC Article 3. UCC §§ 3-106(d), 3-104(a). However, no one can be a holder in due course of an instrument that contains the FTC HDC legend. UCC § 3-106(d).

Furthermore, any negotiable instrument that is required to contain the FTC HDC legend is deemed to include it, even if the legend does not actually appear on the face of the instrument. UCC § 3-305(e). Consequently, there is no incentive for a seller to omit the FTC HDC legend in the hope of avoiding its application. Omitting the legend creates a violation of the FTC Act, but does not create any corresponding benefit to a seller or financer.

Incidentally, you might wonder why the Holder-In-Due-Course regulations focus on the "seller" of goods or services rather than on the lender who is denied holder-in-due-course status or its equivalent. The reason is that the FTC doesn't have jurisdiction over banks and savings and loan associations. *See* 15 U.S.C.A. § 45(a)(2). Therefore, the FTC had to regulate these transactions via its authority to regulate other types of "persons, partnerships, [and] corporations." *See id.*

D. Requirements to Become a Holder in Due Course

The basic requirements to become a holder in due course are set out in UCC section 3-302(a). Various rules for interpreting the basic requirements appear in sections 3-302(b)–(g), 3-303 and 3-304.

A prospective holder in due course must meet five requirements. The first is meeting the requirements for becoming a holder. UCC § 3-302(a). Second, the instrument must not be obviously forged, altered, or otherwise suspicious-looking. UCC § 3-302(a)(1). Third, the holder must have taken the instrument for *value*. UCC § 3-302(a)(2)(i). Fourth, the holder must have taken the instrument in *good faith*. UCC § 3-302(a)(2)(ii). Finally, the prospective holder in due course must have taken the instrument *without notice* that the instrument has certain types of problems. UCC § 3-302(a)(2)(iii), (iv), (v), and (vi).

The first requirement is discussed above in Section B of this Chapter, and in Section C of Chapter 6. The second requirement is straightforward, although highly fact-intensive; the range of situations in which a negotiable instrument might be "so irregular or incomplete as to call into question its authenticity," UCC § 3-302(a)(1), is limited only by the imagination. The third, fourth, and fifth requirements need additional explanation, to which we now turn.

1. Value

A holder who seeks to become a holder in due course must take the instrument "for value." UCC § 3-302(a)(2)(i). The UCC provides more than one definition of this term, and it's important to recognize that fact and to understand how to apply each definition in the appropriate context.

The general UCC definition of value appears in section 1-204. Like other Article 1 definitions, it applies to many situations governed by various Articles of the UCC. However, it does *not* apply to Articles 3 or 4. UCC § 1-204 (initial clause). The *Article 3* definition of "value" appears in section 3-303.

The major difference between these two definitions arises in connection with executory contracts. If the holder of a negotiable instrument received the instrument in exchange for entering into a contract, but no performance occurs under the contract, sections 1-204 and 3-303 reach different results as to whether the holder gave "value." Under the Article 1 definition, giving consideration for a contract—even a peppercorn—is sufficient to constitute "value." UCC § 1-204(4). However, the Article 3 definition provides that if the holder took the instrument "for a promise of performance," that consideration constitutes value only "to the extent the promise has been performed." UCC § 3-303(a)(1).

The definition of value in Article 3 includes situations where "the transferee acquires a security interest or other lien in the instrument...." UCC § 3-303(a)(2). This form of value is primarily of interest in the check collection context. A collecting bank (defined in section 4-105) gives value "to the extent that it has a

security interest...." UCC § 4-211. The rules for a collecting bank to get a security interest in a check require that the bank actually part with money; here,
again, a peppercorn of consideration is not sufficient. *See* UCC § 4-210(a).

2. Good Faith

A holder who seeks to become a holder in due course must also take the instrument "in good faith." UCC § 3-302(a)(2)(ii). The UCC definition of good
faith has a complex history.

Prior to the 1990 revision of UCC Articles 3 and 4, the Article 1 definition
of good faith applied throughout the UCC. That definition provided simply that
good faith was "honesty in fact in the conduct or transaction concerned." UCC
§ 1-201(19) (2000). This definition was purely subjective, focused on the state
of mind of the actor. As long as the actor was not intending to be dishonest,
it didn't seem to matter what the custom of others might be.

When UCC Articles 3 and 4 were revised in 1990, one of the innovations
was the addition of an arguably *objective* element to the definition of good
faith. (Though there's lots to argue about. *See* James J. White & Robert S. Summers, Uniform Commercial Code § 14-6 (5th ed. 2000).) The new definition
of good faith was "honesty in fact and the observance of reasonable commercial standards of fair dealing." UCC § 3-103(a)(6). That new definition was incorporated into UCC Article 1 in 2001, applicable to all of the UCC except
Article 5. See UCC § 1-201(b)(20).

Some states kept the old definition of good faith when they adopted the
1990 revisions to Article 3. *See* 2 U.L.A. 39–40 & Supp. 4–5 (2004 & Supp.
2007). The expanded definition of good faith has met similar resistance as
states have adopted the 2001 revisions to Article 1. *See* 1 U.L.A. 24–25 & Supp.
9–10 (2004 & Supp. 2007).

The primary resistance to the objective definition of good faith seems to be
from financial institutions concerned that the newer definition creates greater
risk of liability for their actions. It appears likely that good faith will have different statutory definitions in different states for the foreseeable future.

However, even courts limited to the old subjective-only definition of good
faith have the power to interpret what "honesty in fact" should mean. Historically, some courts have been willing to find violations of good faith, at least
in egregious cases, based on reading in an objective component to the meaning of honesty in fact. *See* James J. White & Robert S. Summers, Uniform
Commercial Code § 14-6 at 521–525 (5th ed. 2000). Such interpretive exercises are likely to continue, and the precise boundary between good faith and
bad faith will probably remain somewhat elastic.

3. No Notice of Problems with the Instrument

The last hurdle to becoming a holder in due course is actually a group of hurdles, though they are often grouped together. This requirement is that "the holder took the instrument without notice" of various problems that might adversely affect the holder's ability to get the value represented by the instrument. UCC § 3-302(a)(2)(iii), (iv), (v), (vi). As we will see below, these problems may not prevent a holder in due course from collecting on the instrument, though all the requirements of holder-in-due-course status must be met before learning of the problem. The protections of holder-in-due-course status are most clearly appropriate in cases where the person attempting to enforce the instrument took it without knowledge of any problems. Because someone who knows of problems before giving value for an instrument has the opportunity to decline the transaction, the substantial power of holder-in-due-course status is limited to persons who don't know of the problems in advance.

In order to become a holder in due course, the holder must (in addition to meeting the requirements discussed above) take the instrument:

> (iii) without notice that the instrument is overdue or has been dishonored or that there is an uncured default with respect to payment of another instrument issued as part of the same series, (iv) without notice that the instrument contains an unauthorized signature or has been altered, (v) without notice of any claim to the instrument as described in Section 3-306, and (vi) without notice that any party has a defense or claim in recoupment described in Section 3-305(a).

UCC § 3-302(a)(2). We consider each of those requirements in order below.

One other definitional point is necessary for understanding the "without notice" elements of section 3-302(a): *Notice* is a broader category than *knowledge.* See UCC § 1-202. "Knowledge" requires "actual knowledge," i.e., a subjective state of mind. *See* UCC § 1-202(b). "Notice" includes cases of actual knowledge, as well as cases where a person "received a notification" but did not understand or remember it, or should have known something even though he or she didn't actually know it. UCC § 1-202(a)(1)-(3).

a. Overdue, Dishonored, or Affected by Uncured Defaults

A holder who takes the instrument with notice that its terms have been violated will be denied holder-in-due-course status. If an obligation is not being paid as agreed, that suggests that something may have gone wrong with the transaction. For example, the obligor may be refusing to pay because the payee didn't deliver what was promised. Holder-in-due-course status is only provided for instruments where the payment obligations are current. Determining whether a note is overdue is relatively easy. Moreover, the price paid for a note should generally be less than the total amount originally owed on the note, to reflect the usual expectation that payments due in the past have already been paid. Such calculations are relatively simple with the aid of a financial calculator, though they require some understanding of the time value of money, discussed in Section C of Chapter 5.

Additional rules for determining whether a note is overdue are set out in UCC section 3-304. Understanding those rules requires an understanding of the difference between notes payable *on demand*, and notes payable *at a definite time*, discussed above in Section E of Chapter 5. Rules for notes payable on demand appear in subsection (a) of Section 3-304, and for notes payable at a definite time in subsections (b) and (c).

Subsection 3-304(c) emphasizes a point that is implicit in subsection 3-304(b): an instrument is made overdue by failure to pay principal when due, but not by failure to pay interest. In the typical modern installment loan, this distinction rarely matters, because each installment is allocated partly to interest and the remainder goes to pay principal. Therefore, failure to pay an installment on time will make the note overdue, except in unusual cases. Nevertheless, this formalistic, historically-based distinction remains a part of the law.

This distinction probably reflects the fact that interest is often a small amount compared to principal, so a lender who agrees to receive only interest for a period of time might be less concerned about precise dates for collecting that interest than for the much-larger payment of principal owed. This is arguably an artificial distinction, because a late payment of interest may indicate as much cause for concern about the ultimate collection of the loan as a late payment of principal.

For example, suppose you sold a car to Buyer, who gave you a negotiable promissory note for $10,000.00, to be repaid in equal monthly installments over four years with six percent interest per year. The monthly payment on such a note would be $234.85; each payment would go first to pay interest, with the remainder reducing the principal. If you sold this note for cash to a finance company before the first installment is due, the finance company would not have to worry about overdue payments (although even then a careful finance company would want to know about the debtor's compliance with other terms, such as the obligation to provide insurance on the car). However, the finance company would not be able to achieve holder-in-due-course status if it had notice that a payment is overdue or if there is any other default in the terms (e.g., failure to insure the car) that has not been cured. If the sale of the note took place after the due date of one or more installments, a prudent finance company would almost certainly want to know whether the installments have been paid as agreed. If you told the finance company about an outstanding overdue payment and the finance company bought the note anyway, the finance company could not be a holder in due course because it would have notice (and knowledge) of the overdue payment. If the finance company failed to ask about defaults, it might still be denied holder-in-due-course status if the court determines that the finance company should have asked and would have found out the situation if it had asked.

b. Unauthorized Signatures or Alterations

As discussed in Section A of Chapter 16, an alteration on an instrument may limit the extent to which it may be enforced. As discussed in Section A of Chapter 8, a signature that appears valid, but was unauthorized, will not make the instrument enforceable against the purported signer. A holder in due course may be protected from some of these problems, as discussed above in Section C of this Chapter. However, a holder who takes the instrument with notice that it has one of these problems will be denied holder-in-due-course status.

For example, suppose a friend sells you a negotiable promissory note that calls for repayment of $150,000.00 in principal at the end of the year. Suppose further that the maker had left the amount blank, based on an agreement with your friend that the amount would be approximately $150.00 and would not exceed $200.00, and your friend filled in the larger amount in violation of that agreement. (Your friend has made an "alteration" on these facts. See UCC § 3-407(a)(ii).) If you have no reason to suspect your friend's misbehavior (such as a sloppy job of filling in the blank or similar bad experience with your friend in the past), the alteration will not prevent your becoming a holder in due course. But if you know of the alteration, or should have known, you cannot be a holder in due course of this note.

Suppose instead that Bill Gates' signature appears on the front of the note as maker, and the note was originally payable to Warren Buffett, whose indorsement appears on the back of the note. If one of those signatures is a forgery, you cannot be a holder in due course of the note if you know that the signature on the note doesn't look like the genuine signature should look, or if you know that your friend couldn't possibly have had any dealings with Bill Gates or Warren Buffett. However, if you know that your friend knows Bill and Warren well, the signatures on the note look just like the real thing, and there is nothing else to make you suspicious about the validity of the note, the forgery of one of the signatures will not prevent your becoming a holder in due course. Of course, even as a holder in due course you will not be able to enforce the note against anyone whose actual or authorized signature does not appear on it. *See* UCC §§ 3-401, 3-402 and Section A of Chapter 8.

c. Claims to the Instrument

Someone who asserts ownership, possessory, or other property rights to an instrument is said to make a "claim" to the instrument. UCC § 3-306 Official Comment. As noted in Section C of this Chapter, a holder in due course takes free of conflicting claims to an instrument. UCC § 3-306. However, if a holder takes with notice of a claim to the instrument, that holder will not be a holder in due course. UCC § 3-302(a)(2)(v).

For example, suppose you buy a promissory note that turns out to have been stolen. If you had no way of knowing of the theft before you bought the note, and you meet the other requirements for being a holder in due course, you are not subject to the true owner's claim to regain the note. UCC § 3-306. However, if you knew or should have known that you were buying a stolen instrument, you cannot be a holder in due course of the note and you will be subject to the true owner's claim.

d. Defenses and Claims in Recoupment

Similarly, as we saw in Section C of this Chapter, a holder in due course is protected from ordinary defenses and claims in recoupment. However, if a holder has notice of a defense or claim in recoupment before meeting the requirements for holder-in-due-course status, that holder will not become a holder in due course. Notice of *any* such problem prevents the holder from avoiding the effect of *all* such problems.

E. Exercising Someone Else's Rights as Holder or Holder in Due Course: The Shelter Rule

We noted at the beginning of this Chapter that the special powers of a holder in due course are exceptions to the usual property rules of derivative title or *nemo dat*. We also noted that the normal property rights apply even to negotiable instruments. Most of the time, someone who can establish rights as a holder or holder in due course has all the rights needed from the special UCC rules. However, occasionally someone unable to be a holder or holder in due course in their own right may be able to exercise someone else's rights.

If you are a "transferee" of an instrument you get the rights of your transferor. UCC § 3-203(b). This means that if your transferor was a holder or a holder in due course, you get to enforce those rights even if you don't qualify for them on your own. This is often referred to as the "shelter rule," although that term is not defined in the UCC.

For example, suppose you bought a promissory note from the payee, and the payee delivered it to you but neglected to indorse the instrument. If the instrument was an order instrument payable to the stated payee, you cannot be a holder of the instrument unless the payee indorses it. However, as transferee you will be able to enforce the rights that the payee had. UCC § 3-203(b). If the payee was a holder, you can enforce those rights. If the payee was a holder in due course, you can enforce those rights as well. *Id.* (You also get the right to insist on the transferor's indorsement if you gave value. *See* UCC § 3-203(c).)

Two limitations apply to the rights discussed in the preceding paragraph. First, someone who is denied holder-in-due-course status because of his or her fraud or illegal acts cannot use the shelter principle to get the benefit of holder-in-due-course status by transferring the instrument to a holder in due course and receiving the instrument back by transfer. UCC § 3-203(b) (last clause). Second, these rights only accrue on "transfer" of an instrument as defined in UCC § 3-203(a). Therefore, a thief does not get to enforce a transferee's rights, even though a thief may be a holder of a bearer instrument. *See* UCC § 3-203 Official Comment 1 (second paragraph).

Checkpoints

- Being a holder is the typical way to become a person entitled to enforce a negotiable instrument.

- Only a holder can become a holder in due course.

- To become a holder, a person must have physical possession, and the instrument must be either payable to bearer or payable to the person in possession.

- Indorsement can make an instrument payable to a different person, or to bearer.

- A holder who is not a holder in due course is subject to claims, defenses, and claims in recoupment.

- A holder in due course is free from claims, personal defenses, and claims in recoupment.

- Even a holder in due course remains subject to real defenses, though they are narrowly defined and rare.

- To become a holder in due course, the instrument must not appear obviously suspicious, and the holder must take for value, in good faith, and without notice of problems with the instrument.

- The purchaser of a negotiable instrument may also be able to enforce the seller's rights as holder or holder in due course, under the shelter doctrine.

Chapter 8

Basic Liability Rules for Negotiable Instruments

In analyzing the liability of a party to a negotiable instrument, you should ask two initial questions: First, does a valid signature of that party appear on the instrument? Second, what type or types of liability does the party have? This chapter considers each of those questions in turn.

If you initially find a basis for liability, you need to ask a third question: Has the liability been discharged? That question is addressed in Chapter 9.

This Chapter focuses on the liability created under UCC Article 3 on the negotiable instrument itself. Additional issues related to liability on negotiable instruments are addressed in Chapter 7 (defenses to liability and the effect of holder-in-due-course status), Chapter 10 (secondary liability), Chapter 11 (underlying obligations), and Part Two of this book (liability in the check collection system).

A. Signatures on Negotiable Instruments

The most basic rule governing liability on a negotiable instrument is the signature requirement: No one is liable on a negotiable instrument unless his, her, or its signature is on the instrument. UCC section 3-401(a). Of course, it's not entirely that simple; otherwise, this discussion would be very short. Nevertheless, in assessing whether a person or entity is liable on an instrument, it's always good to start with the question, "Is there a valid signature of that person on the instrument?"

1. Signatures by Agents

One complicating factor about signatures is that you don't actually have to hold the pen in your hand and touch it to the paper yourself to become liable on an instrument. If your authorized representative signs the instrument on your behalf, and is clear about what he or she is doing, that counts as your signature on the instrument under the rules set out in UCC sections 3-401(a)(ii) and 3-402. The typical instance of a signature by a representative on a negotiable instrument involves a corporation or other juridical person, which is simply incapable of signing anything except by getting a living, breathing human being to act for it. This set of rules also applies to situations where someone (an ill or injured parent, for example) authorizes you to sign a check or note for them in lieu of their actually signing it themselves. However, the latter examples are relatively unusual cases.

The rules under which one person may sign a negotiable instrument and bind someone else are set forth in UCC section 3-402. The UCC adopts the general rules of agency law (i.e., rules outside the UCC itself) as applicable to the parties' intentions to determine whether the signature by a representative is authorized. UCC §§ 1-103(b), 3-402(a), and Official Comment 1 to § 3-402.

If the signature by an agent is authorized, you must analyze whether the signature should bind the principal, the agent, or both. This question is addressed generally in section 3-402(b), with specialized rules for particular situations in sections 3-402(c) and 3-403.

You would usually expect someone who signs as agent to want to (a) bind the principal on the instrument, and (b) avoid being liable himself or herself. If the person who signs as agent is authorized to do so, the general rule in section 3-402(b) gives the agent the opportunity to accomplish both of these objectives; the agent's success in binding the principal and avoiding personal liability is governed by how clearly the agent expresses the intention to sign as agent on behalf of the principal. If that intention is clear from looking at the instrument, the authorized agent escapes liability, and the principal is bound. UCC § 3-402(b)(1).

As an example, suppose that George Jetway is signing a note as representative for Intergalactic Corporation, and George is authorized to do so. One simple way for George to avoid personal liability and bind Intergalactic Corporation on the note is to use the following format:

Signed,
INTERGALACTIC CORPORATION

By: _____
George Jetway, Treasurer

This makes it clear that when George writes his name on the blank line, he is intending to sign on behalf of Intergalactic Corporation and does not intend to be personally liable.

A more complicated set of rules deals with situations where the agent is authorized to sign on behalf of the principal but does not clearly express that intention on the instrument. *See* UCC §§ 3-402(b)(2), 3-402(c). If the instrument is being enforced by a holder in due course (a person with the coveted super-plaintiff status discussed in Chapter 7 above), the agent who fails to indicate the agency arrangement clearly on the instrument will be liable unless the holder in due course who took the instrument had notice that the agent shouldn't be liable. UCC § 3-402(b)(2) (first sentence). However, as against anyone other than a holder in due course, the agent gets the opportunity to prove that the original parties did not intend for him or her to be liable. UCC § 3-402(b)(2) (second sentence).

Another special rule protects agents who sign checks on others' accounts. *See* UCC § 3-402(c) As long as the principal is identified on the check and the agent is authorized, the agent escapes liability even if the agent simply signs his or her own name.

The rules in the preceding paragraphs apply to cases where the agent is actually authorized to sign on behalf of the principal. As noted above, this question is determined by rules of agency law outside the UCC. UCC § 3-402(a). A different set of rules in UCC section 3-403 applies to cases where the agent is *not* authorized to sign on behalf of the purported principal. In those cases, the agent is bound by his or her signature, and the principal has no liability. So, in the corporation example above, if George Jetway is not authorized to sign on behalf of Intergalactic Corporation, George's signature will make George liable but will not bind Intergalactic Corporation.

2. Forged Signatures

Another common situation in which these rules apply is forged signatures. If Britney Darts signs Paris Marriott's name to a negotiable instrument, but Britney is not authorized to sign as Paris's agent, the signature will result in *Britney* being liable, but will not impose any liability on Paris. UCC § 3-403(a). Notice that in cases like this, liability will be imposed on Britney even though there is no signature in Britney's name. Notice also that the instrument looks as if Paris signed it, but Paris will not be liable.

3. Other Signature Rules

Additional special rules deal with situations where multiple signatures are required to bind a corporation or similar organization. *See* UCC § 3-403(b). The UCC also defers to other laws that may seek to punish someone who signs without the authority to do so. UCC § 3-403(c).

It's important to remember that even though almost all checks have printed on them the name of the bank on which the check is drawn, this does *not* make the bank liable on the check. The bank, like anyone else, has no liability on a negotiable instrument it has not signed, and only very rarely does a bank actually sign a check. Cashier's checks and teller's checks, discussed in Chapter 4 above, are the most common examples of checks on which a bank takes liability by signing the check.

Certified checks are another example, though they are rare in modern practice. Certified checks are said to be "accepted" by the drawee bank; *this is a peculiar, confusing, narrow, and technical use of that term which often leads students astray.* These issues are discussed more fully in section G of Chapter 4 above, but you should remember that it is very, very unusual and rare for anyone to "accept" a check or another type of draft in the UCC sense. See UCC §§ 3-409, 3-408.

B. Types of Liability: Issuer (Maker or Drawer), Indorser, or Acceptor

The liability that someone incurs from signing a negotiable instrument depends on the signer's role with respect to the instrument. Once the fact of liability is established, the next step is to classify the type of signature and analyze the nature of the liability created. UCC Article 3 provides that someone who signs an instrument (either personally or via an authorized agent, as discussed above) may have three types of liability: as "issuer" of a note or cashier's check (also referred to as "maker" of a note, see Official Comment 1 to UCC § 3-412 (second sentence)); as "drawer" of a draft other than a cashier's check; or as "indorser" of either a draft or a note. A fourth type of liability, as "acceptor," is discussed in Section G of Chapter 4. As discussed below, when you write a check, you typically sign as "drawer" of that check, which is a type of draft.

1. Issuers (Makers and Drawers) in General

The "issuer" of an instrument is the person who first delivers the instrument with the intention to make it enforceable. UCC § 3-105(c) and (a). Although these provisions of the UCC talk about delivery, not signatures, they also note that an "issuer" is either "a maker or drawer of an instrument." UCC § 3-105(c). Whether someone is a maker or drawer depends on the nature of the instrument. It's important to keep in mind that a maker of a note and a drawer of a draft may also be referred to as an "issuer," and vice-versa, because Article 3 uses all three terms in defining the nature of the resulting liability.

When you borrow money and sign a note in connection with the transaction, you typically sign as "maker" of the note. The precise definition of "maker" appears in UCC section 3-103(a)(7), and says, "'Maker' means a person who signs or is identified in a note as a person undertaking to pay." In other words, the person who signed as maker (or authorized someone else to sign on the maker's behalf) is the person who is expected to pay the note. Usually that's the person who borrowed the money.

When you sign a draft instructing your bank to pay money to someone out of your account at that bank, you are signing as "drawer" of that draft (and the draft is typically a "check"). The precise definition of "drawer" says "'Drawer' means a person who signs or is identified in a draft as a person ordering payment." UCC § 3-103(a)(5). In other words, the drawer of a draft is the person ordering someone else to make payment. In the common example of checks, the drawer is ordering his, her, or its bank to pay the check out of the drawer's funds on deposit at that bank.

2. Issuers of Notes and Cashier's Checks

Both makers of notes and drawers of drafts are included in the term "issuer": "'Issuer' applies to issued and unissued instruments and means a maker or drawer of an instrument." UCC § 3-105(c). In other words, the issuer is making the promise to repay (in the case of a note) or the order to repay (in the case of a draft). The second and third sentence of Official Comment 1 to section 3-412 make clear that the same rules apply to the "maker" of a note (a term defined in section 3-103(a)(7)) and to the issuer of a cashier's check, who signs as drawer (a term defined in section 3-103(a)(5)). Essentially, the issuer or maker is required to pay the instrument if it is presented by either "a person entitled to enforce the instrument" (i.e., a holder; see Chapter 6 above) or "an indorser who paid the instrument under Section 3-415." UCC § 3-412. In short, the issuer or maker of a note or cashier's check should expect to pay it.

Subsections (i) and (ii) of section 3-412 include some special rules for dealing with the occasional case where the note or cashier's check is altered after it is issued, or was issued with blanks that are filled in later. The issuer is not bound by unauthorized alterations. UCC § 3-412(i). However, the issuer often *will be* bound by the filling-in of blanks. UCC § 3-412(ii). The moral of this story is that you should be very cautious about signing a negotiable instrument that isn't completely filled out. Alterations and completions of incomplete instruments are discussed further in section C of this Chapter below.

3. Drawers of Drafts

The liability of the drawer of a draft is set out in UCC section 3-414. This set of rules is more complicated than the rules for the issuer of a note. This additional complexity reflects the fact that a draft is a three-party instrument, and therefore creates more relationships than a two-party note.

First, the drawer is not liable unless and until the draft is "dishonored." The rules for dishonor of a draft are set forth in UCC section 3-502(b), (c), and (e), and are discussed below in Section D of Chapter 11. You'll notice that these UCC provisions apply to an "unaccepted" draft; this is usually the case. Rules for the relatively rare cases in which a draft has been "accepted" are set forth in section 3-414(c) and (d); these rules are discussed in Section G of Chapter 4 above.

Once a draft is dishonored, the basic rules in section 3-414(b) governing the drawer's liability are essentially the same as the rules discussed above for the issuer/maker of a note: The drawer has to pay. Section 3-414(b) also includes some special rules similar to those in section 3-412(i) and (ii) (discussed above) for dealing with the occasional case where the draft is altered after it is issued, or was issued with blanks that are filled in later. The drawer is not bound by unauthorized alterations. UCC § 3-414(b)(i). However, the drawer often *will be* bound by the filling-in of blanks. UCC § 3-412(b)(ii). The moral of this story is, again, that you should be very cautious about signing a negotiable instrument that isn't completely filled out.

UCC section 3-414(e) provides a way that a drawer of a draft may avoid the liability that ordinarily results from signing as drawer. This is accomplished by placing the words "without recourse" or a similar disclaimer on the draft. (As discussed below, indorsers have a similar opportunity to avoid liability on their indorsements.) However, this disclaimer of liability by the drawer is only effective for certain types of drafts; it does not apply to checks, as stated in the last sentence of section 3-414(e). Official Comment 5 to section 3-414 explains this limitation: "There is no legitimate purpose served by issuing a check on which no one is liable." (Remember that your bank is not liable to the payee on the checks you write, as discussed above in Section A of this Chapter.)

4. Indorsers

If you sign a negotiable instrument and you don't sign as issuer, maker, drawer, or acceptor, you are an indorser. The precise definition of an indorser is "a person who makes an indorsement." UCC § 3-204(b). That by itself is not very helpful until we also see that:

> "[i]ndorsement" means a signature, other than that of a signer as maker, drawer, or acceptor, that alone or accompanied by other words is made on an instrument for the purpose of (i) negotiating the instrument, (ii) restricting payment of the instrument, or (iii) incurring indorser's liability on the instrument, but regardless of the intent of the signer, a signature and its accompanying words is an indorsement unless the accompanying words, terms of the instrument, place of the signature, or other circumstances unambiguously indicate that the signature was made for a purpose other than indorsement."

UCC § 3-204(a). In other words, if you can't otherwise classify a particular signature on an instrument, it's probably an indorsement.

Like we saw above for issuers (i.e., drawers and makers), liability on an instrument is also created by signing as an indorser. This liability is set forth in UCC section 3-415(a), and is similar to the liability of the drawer of a draft. The indorser is obligated to pay a person entitled to enforce the instrument, but only if the instrument is dishonored.

5. Acceptors

The acceptor of a draft takes on liability similar to that of a drawer or indorser. *See* UCC § 3-413. *This is a peculiar, confusing, narrow, and technical use of "accept," "acceptance," etc., which often leads students astray.* These issues are discussed more fully in Section G of Chapter 4 above, but you should remember that it is very, very unusual and rare for anyone to "accept" a check or other type of draft in the UCC sense. *See* UCC §§ 3-409, 3-408.

C. Liability for Altered Instruments

Most negotiable instruments ultimately result in payment of the right amount to the right person. However, the law must also deal with the occasional case where someone along the way changes the amount payable or the identity of the payee. UCC section 3-407 deals with this group of problems, called "alterations."

The effect of an alteration will differ depending on whether the instrument was completed, or was an "incomplete instrument" because it had blank spaces when it was signed. *See* UCC § 3-115(a). The rules in UCC Article 3 protect parties against alterations of completed instruments, but require parties to an incomplete instrument to bear the risk of leaving blanks, as explained below.

1. Incomplete Instruments

Suppose your sister asks you to pick up her dry cleaning and wants you to pay for it with one of her checks. Suppose further that she thinks the amount will be approximately $40.00, but isn't sure of the exact amount. Your sister might write (or "draw" in the UCC parlance) a check on her checking account payable to the dry cleaner, but with the spaces for the dollar amount left blank. You and she agree that you will fill in the exact amount, approximately $40.00.

When your sister signs the check with the amount left blank and gives it to you, she is issuing an "incomplete instrument." UCC § 3-115(a). If you take the check to the dry cleaner, fill in the amount as $39.75, and exchange it for your sister's clothing, everything is fine. Your sister's checking account will be charged for the amount she intends, the dry cleaner will get its money, and everyone will be happy. (We'll ignore the possibility that the dry cleaner might have damaged your sister's clothing.) However, if you fill in the amount as $539.75, get the extra $500.00 in cash from the dry cleaner, and disappear, the loss of the $500.00 must fall on either the dry cleaner, your sister, or one of the banks that handles the check. (Your sister will also be upset if you take her clothing with you, but we'll leave that issue aside, too.)

The loss from unauthorized completion is clearly allocated to the issuer of an incomplete instrument (e.g., your sister in the hypothetical above): "A payor bank or drawee paying a fraudulently altered instrument or a person taking it for value, in good faith and without notice of the alteration, may enforce rights with respect to the instrument ... (ii) in the case of an incomplete instrument altered by unauthorized completion, according to its terms as completed." UCC § 3-407(c). As long as the dry cleaner met the "for value, in good faith, and without notice" requirement, the loss falls entirely on your sister. *See id.* She took the risk of your potential dishonesty by issuing an incomplete instrument.

2. Completed Instruments

Modifying the hypothetical above, suppose instead that your sister knew that the dry cleaning charge would be $39.75, and completed the check for that amount. Suppose further that you skillfully alter the amount of the check to be $539.75, get the extra $500.00 in cash from the dry cleaner, and disappear. Once again we have the same candidates to bear the loss: the dry cleaner, your sister, or one of the banks that handles the check. However, the analysis is considerably different. The ultimate result may (or may not) be different.

First, the rule we saw above for incomplete instruments no longer applies. The applicable rule now — initially, at least — puts the loss on the dry cleaner: "A payor bank or drawee paying a fraudulently altered instrument or a person taking it for value, in good faith and without notice of the alteration, may enforce rights with respect to the instrument (i) according to its original terms." UCC § 3-407(c). The dry cleaner may initially be able to get the full $539.75 for the check. However, once all the facts are known, section 3-407 will limit the dry cleaner and the banks to enforcing the check for only the original amount of $39.75.

Of course, if your sister promptly learned of the alteration and alerted the dry cleaner and her bank of the problem, her bank (the drawee or payor bank) would be able to dishonor the check and return it to the dry cleaner under the rules discussed in Chapter 14. The dry cleaner could then enforce the check against your sister for the original $39.75. UCC § 3-407(c)(i).

Typically, though, the check would be paid and charged against your sister's account for the full $539.75. The issue then becomes how each of the affected parties can fix the problem for themselves and shift the loss to someone else. The full analysis of that process potentially involves: (a) settling up for the breach of the transfer and presentment warranties (UCC §§ 3-416(a)(3), 4-207(a)(3), 3-417(a)(2), 4-208(a)(2), discussed in Chapter 15); (b) apportioning the loss between your sister, the dry cleaner, and the banks if your sister was negligent, such as by writing the check in pencil or leaving you ample space to alter the check without the alteration being apparent (UCC § 3-406(a) and (b), discussed in Chapter 16); and (c) apportioning the loss between your sister and her bank if you had pulled a similar trick before and your sister failed to recognize that on a prior bank statement (UCC § 4-406(d)(2) and (e), discussed in Chapter 16). You should also notice that if the check was paid by your sister's bank, indorser and drawer liability won't figure into the analysis, because those only arise if a check is dishonored. *See* UCC §§ 3-414(b), 3-415(a).

Checkpoints

- Signature is essential for liability on an instrument.
- Signature may be made by an agent.
  - For signatures by an agent, consider the potential liability of both the principal and the agent.
- A forged signature binds the forger, but does not bind the person whose name is forged.
- Issuer of a note signs as maker.
  - Maker has to pay person entitled to enforce.
- Issuer of a draft signs as drawer.
  - Drawer has to pay person entitled to enforce if the draft is dishonored.
- Indorser may sign to facilitate negotiation, or solely to take liability on the instrument.
  - Indorser has to pay person entitled to enforce if the instrument is dishonored.
- Drawer, maker, or indorser who signs an incomplete instrument takes the risk of unauthorized completion.
- Drawer, maker, or indorser who signs a completed instrument remains liable for the original terms despite the alteration.

Chapter 9

Payment and
Other Means of Discharge

Roadmap

- Payment as discharge
- To whom payment must be made
- Discharge by other methods
  - Cancellation
  - Renunciation
  - Surrender
  - Mutilation
  - Destruction

When you sign a note, a check, or another kind of draft, you usually intend only to pay once. Although there are certain limited circumstances where payment might be required more than once, as discussed in this Chapter, the law of negotiable instruments generally honors the usual expectation of parties that only one satisfaction will be required.

When someone's obligation is satisfied and may no longer be enforced, that obligation is said to be discharged. The term "discharge" is not precisely defined in the UCC; the closest Article 3 comes to defining it is in section 3-601, which refers us to the various ways discharge occurs in Article 3 and in contract law. Black's Law Dictionary defines discharge as "[a]ny method by which a legal duty is extinguished; esp., the payment of a debt or satisfaction of some other obligation," Black's Law Dictionary 495 (8th ed. 2004), and that definition works pretty well for our purposes.

In the usual case, discharge occurs because the money owed has been paid as agreed. In those usual, easy cases, everyone agrees that no one has any further obligation. Of course, if all the cases were easy, there would be no need for law to govern the harder cases where the parties don't agree about what liabilities are still owed, and by whom.

The most common way that discharge occurs is "payment." For most purposes, payment is a fairly simple idea, but the term has a surprisingly complex definition in UCC section 3-602. Once payment is appropriately made, the obligation is discharged. UCC § 3-602(c). Moreover, once a payment has been "tendered," that act discharges the obligation to pay interest beyond the due date on the amount tendered. The limitations relate to *who* may make a "payment," and *to whom* a "payment" must be made.

A. Who May Make Payment

UCC section 3-602(a) contains a limitation on who may make a payment that results in discharge, but the limitation is rarely significant in practice. Payment must be made "by or on behalf of a person obliged to pay the instrument." UCC § 3-602(a). Of course, it is the very rare case where anyone else pays an instrument. You would be very pleased if a stranger with no obligation to you decided to pay off your car loan; sadly, though, that almost never happens. Either you make the required payments yourself, or someone related to you (e.g., a parent or spouse) makes payments on your behalf. Both of these typical cases easily fit the requirement in the first sentence of section 3-602(a).

B. Who Must Receive Payment

The rules as to the recipient of a payment are more complex, and they matter in more cases. The complexities usually apply to notes as a practical matter, though they are written to apply almost equally to drafts as well.

1. Payment "to a Person Entitled to Enforce"

As we saw in Chapter 6, negotiable instruments are commonly transferred from one holder to another. The person obliged to pay (the issuer, maker, or drawer) may not know about the transfer. If you borrowed money from Acme Finance Company and signed a promissory note for that debt, you would naturally expect to pay Acme when the time comes for payment. But the law must deal with the situation where Acme sells the note you signed to Baker Bank. If you pay Acme after that sale and that discharges your obligation on the note, Baker may be disappointed in its expectation of collecting from you on the note. On the other hand, if your payment to Acme does *not* discharge your obligation on the note, Baker may be able to make you pay a second time, even though you already paid Acme.

The general rule is that payment must be made "to a person entitled to enforce the instrument." UCC § 3-602(a). When Acme sold and negotiated to Baker the note for the money you borrowed from Acme, Baker became the holder and therefore the person entitled to enforce the note. Therefore, the general rule would require you to pay Baker. The problem, of course, is that you may not know about the sale of the note, so you might pay Acme, and then risk having to pay Baker despite your already having paid.

The first sentence of section 3-602(b) deals with this problem on the basis of whether you get notice of the sale of the note from Acme to Baker: "a note is paid to the extent payment is made ... to a person that formerly was entitled to enforce the note [i.e., Acme] only if at the time of the payment the party obliged to pay [i.e., you] has not received adequate notification that the note has been transferred and that payment is to be made to the transferee [i.e., Baker]." UCC § 3-602(b). If you didn't know that Acme sold the note to Baker, you will get your discharge if you pay Acme. However, after you are notified that Acme sold the note to Baker, you risk having to pay Baker again if you continue to pay Acme.

The remainder of section 3-602(b), together with subsection (d), provide a mechanism for dealing with uncertainty about whether the note has actually been sold. If Baker claims that it has bought the note, but Acme denies that, there has to be a way for you to decide who to pay. You can require Baker to "furnish reasonable proof" that it is now the person entitled to enforce the note. UCC § 3-602(b). If Baker complies with your request, you must pay Baker; if Baker does not comply, you can get your discharge by paying Acme.

2. Conflicting Claims to the Instrument

UCC section 3-602 deals with situations where there are conflicting claims to an instrument. A claim to an instrument arises in situations where more than one person or entity asserts conflicting rights of ownership to the instrument, or other rights related to enforcing the instrument. Such situations are addressed generally in section 3-306. Some claims may arise in connection with a disputed transfer of the instrument, and may be dealt with as discussed above. However, conflicting claims may arise in other circumstances, such as alleged theft of the instrument or assertion of a security interest in the instrument.

Generally, a payment is effective and results in discharge "even though payment is made with knowledge of a claim to the instrument." UCC § 3-602(a) and (c) (last clause). A narrow set of exceptions to this general rule appears in section 3-602(e). These exceptions deny the discharge for payment in three circumstances. First, no discharge results from payment if the payor knows that a court has issued an injunction or similar prohibition against payment. UCC § 3-602(e)(1)(i). Second, discharge is denied to a payor who pays after accepting indemnification from the claimant. UCC § 3-602(e)(1)(ii). Third, discharge is denied to a payor who knows that the instrument was stolen and knowingly pays the thief or another wrongdoer. UCC § 3-602(e)(2).

C. Other Discharge Mechanisms

Payment is the normal and expected way that obligations on a negotiable instrument are discharged. In addition to that usual mechanism, there are other, specialized ways that obligations or obligors on an instrument may be discharged in particular circumstances.

1. Cancellation, Renunciation, etc.

An obligor who has paid an instrument may want clear and simple evidence to overcome any further claim for payment. Even if an obligation on an instrument is not paid, the parties may decide that one or more of the obligors should no longer be liable. Article 3 provides various methods by which this evidence of discharge may be provided, whether or not payment has been made. A person entitled to enforce an instrument may:

> discharge the obligation of a party to pay the instrument (i) by an intentional voluntary act, such as surrender of the instrument to the party, destruction, mutilation, or cancellation of the instrument, cancellation or striking out of the party's signature, or the addition of words to the instrument indicating discharge, or (ii) by agreeing not to sue or otherwise renouncing rights against the party by a signed record.

UCC § 3-604(a).

2. Drawers of Drafts

A special discharge rule is provided for drawers of drafts in limited circumstances:

> If (i) a check is not presented for payment or given to a depositary bank for collection within 30 days after its date, (ii) the drawee sus-

pends payments after expiration of the 30-day period without paying the check, and (iii) because of the suspension of payments, the drawer is deprived of funds maintained with the drawee to cover payment of the check, the drawer to the extent deprived of funds may discharge its obligation to pay the check by assigning to the person entitled to enforce the check the rights of the drawer against the drawee with respect to the funds.

UCC § 3-414(f). This rule protects the drawer in the unusual case where the payee delays in negotiating a check for more than 30 days, and then cannot get cash for the check because the drawee bank has failed.

"Acceptance" of a draft also discharges the drawer, because when a draft is "accepted," a bank becomes liable on the draft. As discussed in Section G of Chapter 4, you should remember that "acceptance" has a very narrow, technical, and counterintuitive meaning in UCC Article 3.

3. Indorsers

An indorser typically takes on liability on the instrument. UCC § 3-415(a), (b). However, an indorser may be only secondarily involved in the transaction that generated the instrument. An indorser may be able to qualify as a "secondary obligor" and gain the protections discussed in Chapter 10 of this book. Whether or not that avenue is available to a particular indorser, various special rules are available to indorsers generally.

Tender of the payment owed on any kind of instrument discharges the indorsers. UCC § 3-603(b). An indorser of a check is discharged if the check is not put into the bank collection process within 30 days after the indorsement is made. UCC § 3-415(e). An indorser of a draft is also discharged if the indorser was entitled to "notice of dishonor" and did not get that notice. UCC § 3-415(c). (Notice of dishonor and related procedural exercises are discussed in Section D of Chapter 11.)

An indorser of a draft is also discharged by subsequent "acceptance" of the draft. As discussed in Section G of Chapter 4, you should remember that "acceptance" has a very narrow, technical, and counterintuitive meaning in UCC Article 3.

4. Other Discharge Rules for Secondary Obligors

Obligors on an instrument who can establish their status as secondary obligors, guarantors, sureties, accommodation parties, etc., may be able to obtain a discharge via the "suretyship defenses" discussed in Chapter 10.

Checkpoints

- Payment is the typical method of discharging liability on an instrument.
- To be effective, a payment must be made by a person obliged to pay, though that is rarely a problem.
- Payment must be made to a person entitled to enforce the instrument.
  - Demanding to see the instrument before paying is an effective but cumbersome way to deal with this requirement.
- Notice that an instrument has been transferred requires the obligor to pay the transferee or perhaps risk having to pay a second time.
- Discharge may also be accomplished by other means such as cancelling, renouncing, surrendering, mutilating, or destroying the instrument.

Chapter 10

Secondary Obligors: Guarantors, Sureties, Accommodation Parties, and Other Secondary Sources of Repayment

---

Roadmap

- Primary and secondary sources of repayment
- Principal and secondary obligors
- Underlying and secondary obligations
- Secondary obligations may appear on a negotiable instrument
- Secondary obligations may also appear in a separate contract
- Guaranty of collection contrasted with guaranty of payment
- Joint and several liability
- Contribution contrasted with reimbursement
- Suretyship defenses
- Letters of credit
  - Documentary
  - Standby

A. Distinguishing Primary and Secondary Sources of Repayment

People to whom money is owed want assurance that they will be paid. As the amount of money goes up, so does the level of concern about payment. If your roommate owed you two dollars, you probably wouldn't worry too much about whether the money will be paid. Even if your roommate doesn't pay, the loss of the two dollars won't affect your financial situation all that much. Resolving never again to lend money to a deadbeat roommate is often a sufficient remedy for dealing with the loss of two dollars.

However, if—hypothetically for most of us—your roommate owed you two million dollars, you would be very concerned about payment. Unless you are very wealthy (and perhaps even if you are), you would have a big hole in your financial situation if you don't collect that money.

Our legal system has developed various mechanisms for increasing the creditor's assurance that money owed will be paid. Because increased formality comes at a cost, small transactions usually proceed using relatively inexpensive, informal mechanisms. For a two-dollar obligation, little formality or documentation is usually required; a brief verbal exchange (perhaps even without the minor formality of a handshake) will usually be enough. However, as the size of the transaction increases, the level of formality usually does, too. Having more money at stake makes the cost of formal mechanisms less significant to the overall transaction and makes the increased assurance of payment more valuable.

Negotiable instruments provide one mechanism for giving greater formality and certainty to a payment transaction. As you have seen in previous chapters, UCC Article 3 provides the holder of a note or a draft with a precisely defined set of legal remedies if the money owed is not paid as agreed. These negotiable instrument remedies supplement and enhance (and, as we will see in Chapter 11, may suspend or discharge) the legal remedies inherent in the underlying transaction for which the negotiable instrument is issued. Writing down the payment terms agreed upon also clarifies those terms for both parties, thus reducing the risk that the parties will remember the terms differently.

However, preparing and signing a negotiable instrument still may not, by itself, be enough assurance of payment. The instrument gives legally enforceable rights against any person or entity who signs the instrument, but those rights are only as good as the financial strength and availability of the signer or signers and their assets. If you want to buy a tube of toothpaste at your local store, but don't have enough cash, the shopkeeper may be willing to take a negotiable instrument—usually a check, perhaps a note—as assurance that cash will be forthcoming. (Even in this small transaction, relying on your signature on a negotiable instrument may be acceptable only if the shopkeeper knows you and is confident that you will make good on the obligation.) For a larger transaction, such as the purchase of a car, a house, a large piece of equipment, or a business, a creditor will usually require additional mechanisms for assuring repayment beyond the obligations reflected in a note or draft. These additional mechanisms are sometimes referred to as "secondary sources of repayment," reflecting the fact that the obligation reflected in the note or draft is expected to be the primary source of repayment.

One typical secondary source of repayment is *collateral*. In larger transactions, the debtor often gives the creditor special rights in some or all of the debtor's property; if the debtor doesn't pay as agreed, the creditor has the right to seize this property of the debtor and sell it to satisfy the debt. These arrangements are very common, and are covered in law school courses with names like Secured Transactions (which usually focuses primarily on transactions involving personal property, governed by UCC Article 9) and Real Estate Finance (which focuses on transactions involving real property, governed primarily by state laws outside the UCC). Collateral arrangements go by various names. "Security interest" is the usual term for personal property collateral transactions governed by the UCC, and that term is often extended to include real property transactions as well. However, real property collateral transactions are governed by varied state laws outside the UCC and go by various names: mortgage, security deed, deed to secure debt, deed of trust, and others. With that brief overview, we leave the rest of the law of security interests to the other courses and books devoted to that subject.

This chapter focuses on another secondary source of repayment, called *suretyship*, *guaranty*, and various other names. These arrangements consist of one or more persons or entities — in addition to the primary parties to the transaction — agreeing to become obligated to pay the amount owed. One common situation is the student who wants to buy a car on credit but has not yet established a credit history of his or her own. As mentioned above, lenders who finance the purchase of cars routinely require a security interest in the car financed, but even adding a security interest in the car may not be enough for the lender if the borrower has a troubled credit history, or no credit history at all. A common solution to this problem is for the buyer of the car to persuade a parent or other relative with an established credit history — often called a "cosigner," also referred to as a "surety," "guarantor," and various other terms — to add his or her commitment to the repayment obligation. The remainder of this chapter explores the various mechanisms for accomplishing this and similar types of transactions, and the legal protections afforded to persons who provide this additional credit strength to others' transactions.

Suppose you bought a car on credit and your grandmother agreed to be a secondary obligor on your car loan. Car loans routinely call for the borrower to give the lender a security interest in the car purchased. Your grandmother's agreement to be a secondary obligor on your loan and the obligee's security interest in the car are both often called "secondary sources of repayment." The *primary* source of repayment is—in theory and usually in practice—your paying the monthly payment each month, as you agreed to do. The secondary sources of repayment—the lender's options to make your grandmother pay, or seize the car and sell it—increase the lender's assurance that it will actually be able to collect the amount owed on the loan.

Despite the functional similarity of these two secondary sources of repayment, though, they are subject to very different legal rules. Issues related to your grandmother's obligation are governed primarily by UCC Article 3, so we explore them in some detail in this chapter. Issues related to the security interest in the car, on the other hand, are governed primarily by UCC Article 9; they are addressed in the Secured Transactions course and in the volume in this series, *Mastering Secured Transactions (UCC Article 9)*.

B. Terminology

As in much of commercial law, terminology is important. Unfortunately, the definitions of some of the terms in this area are neither precise nor universally followed. Consequently, you must be exceptionally alert to the possibility that someone else may define terms differently than you do. These problems are particularly acute with respect to the terms "guarantor" and "surety" (and the corresponding terms "guaranty" and "suretyship"), which have various meanings depending largely on who is using the terms. The remainder of this Chapter follows the Restatement in generally avoiding the use of those terms. Instead, the term "secondary obligor" denotes one who agrees to lend credit support to the debt of another. *See* Restatement (Third) of Suretyship and Guaranty § 1 Comment d. (1996). Continuing the example above of the grandmother who "cosigns" a grandchild's debt for the purchase of a car, the grandmother would be a "secondary obligor" taking on a "secondary obligation" to pay; the grandchild would be the "principal obligor" on the "underlying obligation." Finally, the lender—the bank, finance company, or car dealer to which both the secondary obligation and the underlying obligation are owed—would be the "obligee." *See* UCC § 3-103(a)(11), (17); Restatement Third, Suretyship and Guaranty, § 1 Comments c. and d. (1996).

Calling the parties principal and secondary obligors avoids some of the confusion in the various definitions of guarantor, surety, etc. However, this terminology is not perfect either. As we will see, often the "secondary" obligor may be called upon to pay whether or not the obligee proceeds first against the "principal" obligor. In order to understand those complications, though, we need to consider the ways in which someone typically becomes a secondary obligor in a transaction involving a negotiable instrument.

C. Secondary Obligations on the Instrument Itself

The simplest mechanism for a secondary obligor to provide his or her assurance of payment is to sign the instrument that evidences the debt. In those cases, UCC Article 3 provides a ready-made structure governing the rights and obligations of the affected parties.

1. Classifications of Signatures on the Instrument

A secondary obligor who takes liability by signing the negotiable instrument for the underlying obligation is referred to as an "accommodation party," and is said to have signed the instrument "for accommodation." UCC § 3-419(a). The first step in analyzing an accommodation party's liability is similar to the analysis of a principal obligor's liability, discussed above in Chapter 8: Like a principal obligor, a secondary obligor may sign as issuer (maker or drawer), indorser, or acceptor, and takes on the same type of liability as that signature would give a principal obligor. UCC § 3-419(b).

The analysis is relatively easy if the principal obligor signs as maker or drawer, and the secondary obligor signs as indorser. In those easy cases, the rights and obligations of the parties may be determined by the rules defining the liability of issuers (i.e., makers), drawers, and indorsers, as discussed in Chapter 8. See UCC §§ 3-412 (last sentence), 3-414(b) (last sentence), 3-415(a) (last sentence). (These relatively simple cases are discussed further below.) However, things may not be that simple.

It may not be possible to tell from the face of the instrument itself whether a particular signature was made for accommodation; section 3-419(c), (d), and (e) provides ways (discussed further below) that accommodation parties may choose to identify themselves as such, but those are not required and do not change the accommodation party's obligation to pay. Adding even more potential confusion, in some cases the accommodation party and the principal obligor may sign the instrument in the same capacity (i.e., as co-makers, co-indorsers, etc.). Thus, additional evidence may be necessary to determine whether someone signed an instrument as a principal obligor or as an accommodation party. This distinction typically does not affect the obligee's right to demand payment from the obligor, but it will affect claims among the parties obligated to pay as they sort out how they will share the ultimate cost of payment.

a. Joint and Several Liability

In many cases, a holder or other person entitled to enforce an instrument may demand that the accommodation party pay, without proceeding against anyone else. In those cases, the main difference between being a principal obligor and an accommodation party usually occurs as the various parties liable on the instrument settle up among themselves after one of them has paid the amount due. That settling-up process is discussed below in this Chapter.

One way that principal and secondary obligors may take on the same liability on the instrument is by both signing in the same capacity, most commonly as co-makers of a note. In that case, they have "joint and several" liability. UCC § 3-116(a). That is, the obligee may demand payment from any of them, and each of them will be required to pay the full amount to the obligee. *See* Black's Law Dictionary 854 (8th ed. 2004) (definition of "joint and several").

b. Principal and Secondary Liability

Alternatively, the principal and secondary obligors may sign the instrument in different capacities. One arrangement is for the principal obligor to sign as maker (i.e., issuer) of a note, with the secondary obligor signing as indorser. Indorsers, unlike makers of a note, are only required to pay "if an instrument is dishonored." *See* UCC §§ 3-415(a), 3-412. Therefore, the obligee will be required to proceed first against the principal obligor (the maker of the note), and can only demand payment from the secondary obligor after the note is dishonored. "Dishonor" is defined in UCC section 3-502. The procedural boundaries of dishonor in sections 3-502, 3-503, 3-504, and 3-505 are important in some cases, and they are discussed more fully in Chapter 11 of this book. For most purposes it's sufficient to consider a note or draft dishonored if it was not paid as agreed.

The indorsement made for the purpose of taking liability on the instrument, and not for the purpose of negotiating the instrument (*see supra* Chapter 6) is referred to as an "anomalous indorsement." *See* UCC § 3-205(d).

Even if the secondary obligor signs in the same capacity as the principal obligor (as maker, drawer, indorser, acceptor, etc.), the secondary obligor has the opportunity, when initially signing a negotiable instrument, to require the obligee to demand payment first from the principal obligor, and only proceed against the accommodation party if that is unsuccessful. The formula for imposing this limitation is to add "words indicating unambiguously that the [accommodation] party is guaranteeing collection rather than payment." UCC

§ 3-419(d). If the secondary obligor does not clearly impose this limitation, the obligee can require the secondary obligor to pay the instrument as if he or she were a principal obligor. UCC § 3-419(c) and (e).

2. Sorting Out the Ultimate Cost of the Debt

The difference between being a principal obligor and being a secondary obligor or accommodation party comes into play after someone has paid the instrument, as the parties obligated on the instrument work out the sharing of their expenditures. At this stage of the process, an accommodation party or secondary obligor has the potential to come out far better than a principal obligor. There are three rules to choose from in this situation:

(1) a party who shares the same obligation with other obligors (i.e., a case of multiple principal obligors or multiple secondary obligors) is entitled to "contribution" to equalize the outlays among the parties with the same obligation;
(2) an accommodation party (secondary obligor) who has paid an instrument is entitled to "reimbursement" from the principal obligor; and
(3) a principal obligor who pays is not permitted to recover from a secondary obligor.

a. Contribution

UCC section 3-116(b) (read together with section 3-116(a)) sets out the rule that a party with joint and several liability who pays an instrument is generally entitled to "contribution" from the other parties who share the same obligation on the instrument. The term "contribution" is not defined in the UCC. A helpful general definition of "contribution" is "the right that gives one of several persons who are liable on a common debt the ability to recover ratably from each of the others when that one person discharges the debt for the benefit of all." Black's Law Dictionary 352–53 (8th ed. 2004). The rules of contribution are applied to negotiable instrument transactions "in accordance with applicable law," which must be found outside the UCC. See UCC §§ 3-116(b), 1-103(b).

Suppose Ashley, Britney, and Catherine are in business together as equal partners in a partnership, and they want to buy a machine on credit for the partnership. All three sign the note as co-makers, and they agree that each should have one-third of the liability for the $300,000.00 debt. As a result, Ashley, Britney, and Catherine are all principal obligors on the note, and they have joint and several liability for this debt. UCC § 3-116(a). This means that the obligee of the note may require any one of the three partners to pay the entire amount.

If Catherine pays the entire $300.000.00, she is entitled to contribution from her co-makers. UCC § 3-116(b). Catherine will be entitled to collect $100,000.00 each from Ashley and Britney, which will put the three co-makers in the same position as if each had initially paid $100,000.00 of the total debt.

Of course, Catherine's rights are subject to the same uncertainties in practice as those of any other creditor. If Ashley and Britney are judgment-proof or cannot be found, Catherine may be stuck with the entire $300.000.00 payment. The rules of joint and several liability and contribution benefit the creditor, by giving it multiple ways to recover the amount owed and shift the loss to the solvent co-debtor unwise or unlucky enough to share liability with insolvent or deadbeat co-debtors.

b. Reimbursement

A party entitled to reimbursement can come out better in the settling-up process than one entitled to contribution. This is good news for secondary obligors, because secondary obligors are generally entitled to reimbursement, not just contribution.

UCC section 3-116(b) notes that its rule is subject to section 3-419(f), which provides that "[a]n accommodation party who pays the instrument is entitled to reimbursement from the accommodated party and is entitled to enforce the instrument against the accommodated party." The term "reimbursement" is not defined in the UCC; an applicable general definition is "[r]epayment." Black's Law Dictionary 1312 (8th ed. 2004). *See also* Restatement (Third) Suretyship and Guaranty §§ 22–25 (1996).

Modifying the example above, suppose Ashley and Britney, only, are in business together as equal partners in a partnership, and they buy a machine on credit for the partnership. Suppose further that the two of them can't get the loan based on their own credit, but their friend Catherine agrees to co-sign the loan. All three of them (Ashley, Britney, and Catherine) sign as co-makers on the note, though everyone (including the lender) agrees that Catherine is an accommodation party.

Just as in the "contribution" example above, Catherine will have joint and several liability along with Ashley and Britney. The holder of the note may require Catherine (or Ashley or Britney) to pay the entire amount. UCC §§ 3-116(a), 3-419(c) (last sentence), 3-419(e). (The reference in section 3-419(c) to section 3-605 invokes the "suretyship defenses," which are discussed below.)

However, if Catherine pays the entire $300,000.00, on these facts she will be entitled to *reimbursement* from Ashley and Britney, not just contribution. Catherine will be entitled to get her entire $300,000.00 back. UCC § 3-419(f).

Ashley and Britney, as principal obligors, are still entitled to contribution from each other. If one of them pays the entire $300,000.00, she may recover $150,000.00 from the other. UCC § 3-116(b).

Once again, though, Catherine's rights are subject to the same uncertainties in practice as those of any other creditor. If Ashley and Britney are judgment-proof or cannot be found, Catherine may be stuck with the entire $300.000.00 payment. Similarly, if Ashley has to pay more than her $150,000.00 share, she will only get reimbursement from Britney if Britney can be found with available assets. The rules of joint and several liability, contribution, and reimbursement again benefit the creditor, by giving it multiple ways to recover the amount owed and shift the loss to the solvent co-debtor unwise or unlucky enough to share the liability of insolvent or deadbeat co-debtors.

c. No Recovery by Principal Obligors against Secondary Obligors

The last sentence of UCC section 3-419(f) (to which section 3-116(b) is expressly subject) is the source of our third general rule that accommoda*ted* parties (i.e., principal obligors) cannot recover from accommoda*tion* parties (i.e., secondary obligors). Someone who agrees merely to lend additional credit strength to someone else's transaction should not have to pay the principal obligor back for payments she makes.

Continuing the previous example where Catherine is an accommodation party (secondary obligor) and Ashley and Britney are accommodated parties (principal obligors), neither Ashley nor Britney is entitled to recover anything from Catherine. UCC § 3-419(f) (last sentence). If Ashley or Britney pays, each is limited to recovering on her right of contribution from the other.

3. Suretyship Defenses

An accommodation party who is called upon to enforce an obligation on an instrument is permitted to assert any of the defenses that would be available to the accommodated party, *except* "discharge in insolvency proceedings, infancy, and lack of legal capacity." UCC § 3-305(d). Defenses to enforcement of an instrument are discussed in Chapter 7 above.

Secondary obligors provide their credit to someone else's obligation, so they don't benefit directly from the transaction like the principal obligor does. This disadvantageous situation of secondary obligors has led the law to protect them, and courts have often been quick to release or reduce the secondary obligation when the underlying obligation is changed. These protections for secondary obligors—which developed at common law, but now also appear in statutes—are commonly referred to as the "suretyship defenses."

UCC section 3-605 codifies suretyship defenses in negotiable instrument transactions. Since its modification in 2002, this provision is reasonably consistent with the law of suretyship defenses outside the UCC. Nevertheless, section 3-605 does not contain all the myriad twists and turns of suretyship law, and Official Comment 1 to section 3-605 explains how the law of suretyship outside the UCC can apply to a particular transaction. The Third Restatement of Suretyship and Guaranty (1996), cited in Official Comment 1 to section 3-605, is the leading recent compendium of the applicable rules.

Of course, while the Restatement does a good job of collecting and summarizing the law in the various states, it is not itself authoritative law in any state. The authoritative law for a particular transaction is found in the statutes and cases of the jurisdiction or jurisdictions whose law governs the transaction. Generally that law will correspond to the general principles reflected in the Restatement, though the possibility of idiosyncratic local variations adds even more complexity to this mix.

Making a secondary obligor pay after other parties change the deal probably seems intuitively wrong to you, if you have thought about it. As in many areas of the law, intuition is a good guide to part of the rule. It is the basis of the *general rule* that a modification of terms or risk *may* result in releasing the secondary obligor, if the secondary obligor doesn't agree to the change. However, again as in many areas of the law, intuition only gets you part of the way down the path. We will see important exceptions to the general rule, some of which may be harder to reconcile with your intuitive sense of justice.

UCC section 3-605 identifies four categories of modification to the underlying obligation that can result in discharge or reduction of the secondary obligor's liability: (1) release of a principal obligor, § 3-605(a); (2) extension of time for payment, § 3-605(b); (3) modification of the principal obligor's obligation other than release, § 3-605(c); and (4) impairment of collateral, § 3-605(d). Each of these categories follows the general rule in part, but three of the four incorporate important exceptions or limitations to the secondary obligor's release.

Because UCC section 3-605 is exceptionally hard to read, Appendix A to this Chapter provides a chart that lays out the corresponding language in each subsection.

a. Impairment of Collateral

The simplest and most straightforward of the rules in section 3-605 applies to cases where the value of collateral is impaired. Collateral can be a valuable and important source of repayment. The loss of collateral available to repay a loan, therefore, can have an enormous adverse effect on a secondary obligor's risk.

If the value of a collateral interest is "impaired" by a "person entitled to enforce the instrument" (i.e., by the obligee, *see* section D of Chapter 6), the secondary obligor is discharged to the extent of the impairment. UCC § 3-605(d) (first sentence). The statute goes on to provide a detailed definition of when "[t]he value of an interest in collateral is impaired." UCC § 3-605(d) (second and third sentences). Common examples of such impairments include the obligee's allowing the collateral to be freed of the security interest without getting other collateral, failure to maintain the perfection of the security interest, or allowing the collateral to be sold in violation of the rules in UCC Article 9 and in other law. *See* UCC § 3-605(d) (second and third sentences).

These rules are discussed in Official Comment 7 to UCC § 3-605.

b. "Other" Modifications

The next-least-complex of the four rules in UCC section 3-605 is in subsection (c) of that section. With two exceptions, this provision deals with modifications of a principal obligor's obligations on a negotiable instrument. The two exceptions carved out of subsection 3-605(c) are particular types of modifications: release of a principal obligor and extension of time to pay. The special rules for those two cases in UCC section 3-605 (a) and (b) are discussed below. We will refer to the subsection 3-605(c) modifications as "other" modifications, to distinguish them from the particular types of modifications addressed in subsections (a) and (b) of section 3-605 and discussed below.

If the obligee agrees to an "other" modification of a principal obligor's obligation, the secondary obligor has *the opportunity* to be discharged from the remaining obligations, but the discharge is not always complete or guaranteed. The secondary obligor is only discharged "to the extent that the modification would otherwise cause the secondary obligor a loss." UCC § 3-605(c)(2). In other words, if the "other" modification increases the amount the secondary obligor has to pay, the secondary obligor is discharged to the extent of that increase. However, the secondary obligor remains on the hook for the exposure that already existed before the "other" modification.

As to that remaining exposure, the secondary obligor gets to choose whether to perform under the original terms of the deal or the terms that reflect the "other" modification. UCC § 3-605(c)(3).

So far we have focused on the secondary obligor's obligation to the obligee. Another set of rights and duties obligates the secondary obligor to reimburse the secondary obligor for the latter's payments. If the secondary obligor made payments before the "other" modification took place, the principal obligor's duty to reimburse for those payments remains the same. UCC § 3-605(c)(1) (first sentence). However, the principal obligor's obligation to reimburse for the secondary obligor's post-modification payments is modified in the same way as the principal obligor's obligation to the debtor. UCC § 3-605(c)(1) (second sentence).

The rationale for this set of rules appears in Official Comment 6 to UCC section 3-605, with examples of their application in Cases 8 and 9 of that Comment.

c. Extension of Time

Extension of the principal obligor's time for payment has long been a basis for the secondary obligor to obtain a discharge. In many cases, of course, extension of time for payment *increases* the chances that the principal obligor will pay as agreed. However, the long-accepted rationale for this portion of the suretyship defenses focuses on the secondary obligor's reasonable expectation that the secondary obligation will cease on the due date originally agreed upon: it's a nasty surprise for a secondary obligor to discover that the obligation has been extended (for a month, a year, a decade, etc.) when the debt was due yesterday.

UCC section 3-605(b) codifies the effect on the secondary obligor of extensions of time granted to the principal obligor. As with the "other" modifications discussed above, the secondary obligor isn't discharged automatically upon extension. An extension of time for a principal obligor to pay a negotiable instrument only discharges the secondary obligor to the extent that "the extension would otherwise cause the secondary obligor a loss." UCC § 3-605(b)(2). The secondary obligor gets a discharge only to the extent that the modification increases the amount the secondary obligor has to pay.

The rules for extension of time add a layer of complexity beyond the rules for "other" modifications discussed above. An obligee giving an extension of time, unlike the "other" modifications, may "retain[] the right to enforce the instrument against the secondary obligor as if the time for payment had not been extended." UCC § 3-605(b)(3). In other words, the obligee may insist on collecting from the secondary obligor on the original schedule while giving the principal obligor an extension. A related rule allows "the terms of the extension [to] preserve the secondary obligor's recourse." UCC § 3-605(b)(1). If the extension incorporates both of these options, i.e., if the extension preserves both the rights of enforcement against the secondary obligor and the secondary obligor's rights against the principal, the extension of time may be illusory. Even though the obligee agrees to give the principal obligor more time, if the obligee demands payment from the secondary obligor on the original schedule, and the secondary obligor exercises its (preserved) rights to be reimbursed on the original schedule, the principal obligor will not enjoy any actual extension of time for payment (unless the secondary obligor successfully claims a "loss," thereby taking the analysis into paragraphs 3-605(b)(2), via the initial phrase of paragraph 3-605(b)(3)).

Otherwise, the rules for extension of time are the same as those discussed above for "other" modifications.

The rationale for this set of rules appears in Official Comment 5 to UCC section 3-605, with examples of their application in Cases 5, 6, and 7 of that Comment.

d. Release

The rules governing release of principal obligors add three possible effects on secondary obligors, in addition to those already discussed above.

First, the secondary obligor may be discharged without any necessity to show a loss if the release does not preserve the obligee's rights against the secondary obligor. UCC § 3-605(a)(2) (first sentence). Carefully drafted forms used by sophisticated lenders typically preserve the obligee's rights against the secondary obligor. In those cases, the secondary obligor may still be discharged on a showing of loss, as in the other rules discussed above. UCC § 3-605(a)(3) (last clause).

Second, a special rule for checks provides that secondary obligors whose liability is based on an indorsement are always discharged by release of a principal obligor. UCC § 3-605(a)(2) (second sentence). The classification of signatures is discussed in Chapter 6.

Third, if the principal obligor gives consideration for being released, the secondary obligor is also discharged to the extent of that consideration. UCC § 3-605(a)(3).

The rationale for this set of rules appears in Official Comment 4 to UCC section 3-605, with examples of their application in Cases 1, 2, 3, and 4 of that Comment.

e. Other Limits on Release, Modification, etc.

Further opportunities to keep a secondary obligor on the hook appear in UCC section 3-605(f). The secondary obligor is not discharged by the release of a principal obligor "if the secondary obligor consents to the event or conduct that is the basis for the discharge, or the instrument or a separate agreement of the party provides for waiver of discharge...." UCC § 3-605(f). In other words, if the secondary obligor either consents to the specific discharge, or has generally waived the right to claim the suretyship defenses, the secondary obligor remains bound. Consequently, sophisticated parties routinely require waivers of the suretyship defenses, and also get secondary obligors to consent to any release of a principal obligor whenever this is possible.

Some comfort may be provided to the secondary obligor by the preservation of his, her, or its recourse against the principal obligor. UCC § 3-605(g). All too often, though, this is cold comfort. In many cases, if there were any realistic prospect of collecting from the principal obligor, the secondary obligor would not have to pay in the first place.

D. Secondary Obligations in a Separate Guaranty Agreement

1. The Nature of the Transaction

The previous section of this Chapter dealt with obligations of secondary obligors that arise from a signature on the negotiable instrument for the principal obligation. Alternatively, secondary obligors frequently sign separate guaranty agreements to establish their obligations. (The nouns "guaranty" and "guarantee" mean essentially the same thing, though the former spelling is often used by sophisticated parties in banking and finance transactions to signal their sophistication. *See* Black's Law Dictionary 723 (8th ed 1004) (definition of "guarantee"). This is like using the spelling "indorse" rather than "endorse.")

One important practical advantage of a separate guaranty agreement is administrative convenience. An extension of credit may be evidenced by a succession of different notes (or sometimes drafts) due to refinancing, renewal, increase, etc. If the secondary obligation is evidenced by a signature on the note (or draft) for the principal obligation, the obligee will need to get the secondary obligor's signature on each and every note. That can be inconvenient and is easy to forget.

Having a separate guaranty agreement can avoid this problem. Such agreements are commonly drafted to cover all obligations of the principal obligor to the obligee, whether or not they exist yet when the guarantee is signed. Of course, the secondary obligor who doesn't want such open-ended liability should be careful about the terms of the guaranty agreement.

2. Waivers

Guaranty agreements also give obligees the opportunity to get various waivers from the secondary obligors. As we will see in Chapter 11, UCC Article 3 provides for various procedural formalities for enforcing a negotiable instrument: presentment, dishonor, notice of dishonor, etc. These formalities are commonly waived in promissory notes, and guaranty agreements also routinely contain waivers of these requirements by the secondary obligor.

Guaranty agreements also routinely provide that the secondary obligor waives some or all of the suretyship defenses. As we have seen throughout this Chapter, the law has created a number of opportunities for a secondary obligor to be discharged if the principal obligor and the obligee change their agreement without the secondary obligor's consent. Obligees usually want to keep secondary obligors on the hook for whatever the principal obligor may owe to the obligee, even if the obligee releases the principal obligor, extends the time for payment, releases collateral, etc. Such events can discharge a secondary obligor via the suretyship defenses, but that discharge will not be available if the secondary obligor has waived those rights.

3. Governing Law

When a secondary obligation is created by a separate guaranty agreement rather than a signature on a note, the UCC does not govern the secondary obligation. The legal source of the rules is state law outside the UCC. The Third Restatement of Suretyship and Guaranty (1996) provides a comprehensive collection and discussion of the various state laws on this subject. Many of the rules are similar or identical to the UCC rules discussed in this Chapter, and the UCC rule is often a useful first approximation, at least, of what the applicable state suretyship law will be. However, you should be alert to the possibility that a particular state's law may vary significantly from the UCC rules discussed in this Chapter.

E. Letters of Credit

Letters of credit can serve many of the same purposes as guaranty and suretyship arrangements. Although the law of letters of credit is quite distinct from that of suretyship, enough overlap exists to warrant a brief treatment of letters of credit in this Chapter. Like a surety or guarantor's obligation, a letter of credit offers a mechanism for one or more banks to lend their financial support to a transaction and thereby give primary parties who know and trust the banks, but not each other, sufficient confidence to enter into a transaction.

Letters of credit come in two basic types: "Documentary" letters of credit (also called "trade" or "commercial" letters of credit) are used primarily in international trade transactions. "Standby" (or "guaranty") letters of credit more closely resemble the guaranties and suretyship arrangements that are the focus of this chapter. Both types of letters of credit are used to provide an extra layer of security for the party expecting payment. However, documentary letters of credit are more integral to the underlying transaction, whereas standby letters of credit usually more closely resemble the guaranty standing alone behind a separate transaction.

1. Governing Law

Letters of credit are governed by a body of law primarily found in UCC Article 5 and two important private-ordering regimes promulgated by the International Chamber of Commerce (ICC). The ICC has published two important books in this area: *Uniform Customs and Practices for Documentary Credits* (ICC 500) (1993) and *International Standby Practices* (ISP98) (1998). As the titles suggests, the former focuses on documentary letters of credit, and the latter on standby letters of credit. Each provides detailed rules for interpreting letters of credit, and one or the other of these sets of rules is often incorporated by reference in a particular letter of credit when issued.

You should note that when Article 5 of the UCC outlines the rights, obligations, and liabilities created in a letter of credit transaction, it applies to both documentary and standby letters of credit and does not distinguish between the two. *See* 50 Am. Jur. 2d Letters of Credit §9 (2004). The distinction between these two types depends largely upon the intent of the parties to the underlying contract rather than the law; it's usually easy to classify a particular letter of credit into one of the two types.

2. Basic Terminology and Mechanics

Documentary and standby letters of credit share the same terminology and basic mechanics, in addition to sharing the governing law in UCC Article 5. An "applicant" for a letter of credit requests a bank to serve as "issuer" of the letter of credit for the benefit of the "beneficiary." *See* UCC §5-102(a)(2), (9), (3). The letter of credit provides that upon presentation of specified documents by the beneficiary, the issuer will pay money to the beneficiary. *See* UCC §5-102(10). This promise by the issuer is given in the expectation that it will get the money back from the applicant.

Those three parties are all that is essential for a letter of credit transaction. If both the applicant and the beneficiary are comfortable with one bank, the three parties can get the job done on their own. However, in international transactions there may be no one bank that has the confidence of both the applicant and beneficiary, and a fourth party may be added. In those cases, the issuer is commonly the applicant's bank, and the beneficiary's bank (which is familiar and comfortable with the issuer's reputation and financial strength) participates to give the beneficiary additional confidence in the transaction.

The beneficiary's bank may serve as "adviser," "nominated person," or "confirmer." *See* UCC §5-102(a)(1), (11), (4). An adviser has the least responsibility, and agrees merely to pass information along. *See* UCC §§5-102(a)(1), 5-107(c). A nominated person is authorized to make payment under the letter of credit, but is not obligated to. *See* UCC §§5-102(a)(11), 5-107(b). A confirmer takes the highest level of responsibility, and therefore typically charges the highest fee. A confirmer is obligated on the letter of credit, as if it were the issuer. *See* UCC §§5-102(a)(4), 5-107(a).

Much like a bank presented with a check drawn on the bank by one of its customers, an issuer (which is typically a bank) presented with a letter of credit makes the decision to honor or dishonor the letter. After the beneficiary presents the required documents to the issuer, the issuer has seven business days to do one of three things: honor the letter, defer its obligation to a later date, or give notice to the beneficiary of some discrepancy in the presentation of the necessary documents. UCC 5-108(b). Also like a check payment situation, the beneficiary makes certain warranties to the issuer and the applicant when she presents a letter of credit for payment. UCC 5-110(a), (b). The issuer is liable to the other parties in the transaction for wrongfully dishonoring the letter of credit. *See* UCC §5-111. That liability may still be enforceable even if documents presented are forged or fraudulent. *See* UCC §5-109(a)(1), (b). (The analogy to check payments will be clearer after you have read Part Two of this book.)

3. Documentary Letters of Credit

In a documentary letter of credit, often the applicant is the buyer of goods, and the beneficiary is the seller of goods. The terms of a documentary letter of credit typically provide that the issuer will pay the beneficiary upon presentation of precisely-specified documents that evidence that the beneficiary has shipped goods conforming to the contract between the beneficiary and the applicant. Usually those documents include a bill of lading or other document necessary for the applicant to pick up the goods from the shipper. The issuer will then provide the documents to the applicant in exchange for reimbursement.

Note that in a documentary letter of credit transaction, a drawing against the letter of credit is a normal part of the transaction, and is entirely expected. This is perhaps the biggest difference in the dynamics of documentary and standby letter of credit transactions.

4. Standby Letters of Credit

A standby letter of credit is more like a guaranty. Usually a standby letter of credit will only be drawn against if something has gone wrong in the underlying transaction.

Recall that a person seeking a loan will often seek a close family member or friend to serve as secondary obligor, and thereby provide extra security to the creditor. When no family or friend is willing or able to provide that security to the creditor's satisfaction, the prospective borrower might seek a standby letter of credit from a financial institution to serve the same purpose.

A standby letter of credit does not function as a payment mechanism like documentary letters of credit do. Rather, it functions like a guaranty, in that it provides a safety net for contracting parties should the underlying transaction go badly. In other words, the holder of a standby letter of credit may only seek payment from the issuer if she cannot get payment from the applicant, perhaps due to the failure of a contract or a default on a debt repayment. At this point, the beneficiary seeks payment from the issuer of the letter of credit much like a creditor seeks payment from a secondary obligor. One important difference is that the recovery on the letter of credit is governed by UCC Article 5, instead of UCC Article 3 or the law of suretyship and guaranty.

Checkpoints

- Suretyship and guaranty obligations serve as a secondary source of repayment for financial obligations.

- A secondary obligor may sign the negotiable instrument that reflects the principal obligation, or the secondary obligor may sign a separate guaranty agreement.

- A Secondary obligor may have joint and several liability with the principal obligors for the debt, but the secondary obligor who pays the debt is entitled to reimbursement (not just contribution) from the principal obligors.

- If a secondary obligor wants to require the obligee to proceed first against the principal obligor, the secondary obligor needs to clearly establish that he, she, or it is guaranteeing "collection rather than payment."

- The suretyship defenses protect secondary obligors from changes to the obligation to which the secondary obligors do not agree.

- A letter of credit can serve similar functions to suretyship and guaranty obligations.

Appendix: Section 3-605 Subsection Comparison

(a) [Release]	(b) [Extension of time]	(c) [Modification other than release or extension of due date]	(d) [Impairment of collateral]
(1) Any obligations of the principal obligor to the secondary obligor with respect to any previous payment by the secondary obligor are not affected.	(1) Any obligations of the principal obligor to the secondary obligor with respect to any previous payment by the secondary obligor are not affected.	(1) Any obligations of the principal obligor to the secondary obligor with respect to any previous payment by the secondary obligor are not affected.	
Unless the terms of the release preserve the secondary obligor's recourse, the principal obligor is discharged, to the extent of the release, from any other duties to the secondary obligor under this article.	Unless the terms of the extension preserve the secondary obligor's recourse, the extension correspondingly extends the time for performance of any other duties owed to the secondary obligor by the principal obligor under this article.	The modification correspondingly modifies any other duties owed to the secondary obligor by the principal obligor under this article.	
(2) Unless the terms of the release provide that the person entitled to enforce the instrument retains the right to enforce the instrument against the secondary obligor, the secondary obligor is discharged to the same extent as the principal obligor from any unperformed portion of its obligation on the instrument. If the instrument is a check and the obligation of the secondary obligor is based on an indorsement of the check, the secondary obligor is discharged without regard to the language or circumstances of the discharge or other release.			

Appendix: Section 3-605 Subsection Comparison *continued*

(3) If the secondary obligor is not discharged under paragraph (2), the secondary obligor is discharged to the extent of the value of the consideration for the release, and to the extent that the release would otherwise cause the secondary obligor a loss.	(2) The secondary obligor is discharged to the extent that the extension would otherwise cause the secondary obligor a loss.	[T]he obligation of the secondary obligor is discharged to the extent of the impairment.
(3) To the extent that the secondary obligor is not discharged under paragraph (2), the secondary obligor may perform its obligations to a person entitled to enforce the instrument as if the time for payment had not been extended or, unless the terms of the extension provide that the person entitled to enforce the instrument retains the right to enforce the instrument against the secondary obligor as if the time for payment had not been extended, treat the time for performance of its obligations as having been extended correspondingly.	(2) The secondary obligor is discharged from any unperformed portion of its obligation to the extent that the modification would otherwise cause the secondary obligor a loss.	[Definition of impairment of collateral follows, but is omitted here.]
	(3) To the extent that the secondary obligor is not discharged under paragraph (2), the secondary obligor may satisfy its obligation on the instrument as if the modification had not occurred, or treat its obligation on the instrument as having been modified correspondingly.	

Chapter 11

Underlying Obligations: Suspension and Discharge

Rights and obligations arise from issuing and negotiating a negotiable instrument. The rights and obligations that flow from signatures on the negotiable instrument itself were the focus of Chapters 8, 9, and 10.

In addition to those matters, it's important to understand that another set of rights and obligations is usually affected by negotiable instrument transactions. A negotiable instrument is almost always issued in connection with some other transaction involving a body of law beyond negotiable instruments law. The term "underlying obligations" is shorthand for the legal consequences of that other transaction. Often, the underlying obligations relate to a sale of goods governed by UCC Article 2. As you probably learned in your Contracts course, when a buyer accepts goods, the buyer becomes obligated to pay the price under the contract. *See* UCC §§ 2-301, 2-607. Similarly, when one person borrows money from another, the borrower is obligated to repay the loan.

In both the sale of goods example and the loan example, law beyond the specific law of negotiable instruments creates the underlying obligations. The details of those underlying obligations may be complicated, of course, but we happily leave those additional complications to the other bodies of law. The important point for our purposes is that negotiable instrument transactions affect both the obligations on the negotiable instrument itself *and* the underlying obligations.

Usually the parties expect that both the obligations on the instrument and the underlying obligations will be discharged, typically as the result of money being paid as agreed. Along the way, the underlying obligations may be suspended. And if things go wrong, both the obligations on the instrument and the underlying obligations may (or may not) be available for enforcement. The details of all that are discussed below.

A. The Simple Case with Specialized Instruments: Certified Checks, Cashier's Checks, and Teller's Checks

Certain specialized negotiable instruments are usually as good as cash. Consequently, UCC section 3-310(a) provides when someone takes one of these specialized types of instruments, the underlying obligation is *discharged*. That is, the only remaining obligation is the obligation on the negotiable instrument itself.

This dramatic effect is generally limited to three types of negotiable instruments: certified checks, cashier's checks, and teller's checks. UCC § 3-310(a). The common characteristic of these three types of checks is that they are signed by a bank, so the bank is liable on the instrument. *See* UCC §§ 3-104(g) and (h), and 3-409(d) and (a), as well as the discussion of "acceptance" in Section G of Chapter 4. (Remember that ordinary checks have the name of a bank printed on them, but that doesn't make the bank liable on the check, as discussed in Chapter 8; the drawee bank is only liable to its depositor if the bank signs the check.)

Of course, sometimes there is a problem with collecting on one of these specialized instruments. The bank that signed the draft may fail. However, this concern is alleviated somewhat by the fact that the Federal Deposit Insurance Corporation, which insures bank deposits, extends its insurance coverage (to a maximum of $100,000.00) to certified checks, cashier's checks, and teller's checks. *See* 12 U.S.C.A. § 1813(*l*)(1), (4).

Subsection (c) of section 3-310 also applies the rule of subsection (a) to other types of negotiable instruments on which a bank is liable, but those are even rarer than the certified checks, cashier's checks, and teller's checks that are directly covered in subsection 3-310(a).

B. The Usual Case: Notes and Non-Specialized Checks

The rule discussed in section A of this Chapter is relatively simple, but it only applies to a narrow class of negotiable instruments. For all the other types of instruments, we have the more complicated rule of UCC section 3-310(b). This rule provides for *suspension* of the underlying obligation during the period when the parties don't know whether the instrument will be paid or not. UCC § 3-310(b). If the instrument is ultimately paid, the underlying obligation is then discharged. UCC § 3-310(b)(1) (for checks) and (2) (for notes). If the instrument is dishonored (a term discussed further in Section D of this Chapter), the suspension of the underlying obligation typically ends. UCC § 3-310(b)(3). The person owed the money generally gets the choice of enforcing the rights on the instrument or enforcing the underlying obligation. *Id.*

The rules discussed so far apply to the usual case where the same person who is owed the underlying obligation is the person who can enforce the negotiable instrument. For example, when a buyer buys goods from a seller, the seller usually gets the check or promissory note, payable to the seller, and the seller is also owed the underlying obligation for payment. Other, more complicated cases sometimes arise, which are addressed by a qualification to section 3-310(b)(3), and by section 3-310(b)(4).

Section 3-310(b)(3) is limited to cases where "the obligee of the obligation for which the instrument was taken [i.e., person who is owed the underlying obligation] is the person entitled to enforce the instrument." UCC § 3-310(b)(3). Most of the time that is the case. However, in some cases the seller of the goods may not be entitled to enforce the instrument. The seller may have sold the instrument, or may have lost it, or a thief may have stolen it. The limitation in the first sentence of UCC section 3-310(b)(3), together with UCC section 3-310(b)(4), deal with these possibilities.

Continuing our example, if the seller of goods took an instrument for the price of goods and then sold that instrument, the seller of goods has presumably gotten the money for the goods. If the instrument is subsequently dishonored, the right to recover belongs to the buyer of the instrument, not the seller of the goods. If the seller of the goods were permitted to sue the buyer for the price after dishonor of the negotiable instrument, the buyer might have to pay twice—once on the underlying obligation to the seller of goods, and a second time on the instrument to the buyer of the instrument. The limitation discussed in the preceding paragraph solves this problem by eliminating the revival of the underlying obligation in these circumstances. (Official Comment 3 to section 3-310 suggests that this will be the result whenever a seller of goods receives a negotiable instrument in exchange for goods and then sells the instrument to a third party. It's possible that the purchaser of the instrument might also purchase the underlying contractual right to payment and thereby be able to enforce it, but this would be governed by law outside UCC Article 3. *See* UCC § 1-103(b).)

If the person who is owed the underlying obligation no longer has the negotiable instrument because it was "lost, stolen, or destroyed," the underlying obligation is not revived. UCC § 3-310(b)(4). Only the instrument itself may be enforced, and that may be difficult or impossible. Section 3-309 provides a limited and cumbersome mechanism for enforcing lost, destroyed, or stolen instruments. Someone who seeks to enforce such an instrument must first run the gauntlet of subsection (a) and the first sentence of subsection (b) of section 3-309. Even if that is successful, though, as a practical matter the claim may not have any real value due to the requirement of providing "adequate protection" for the person required to pay. Like most attempts to prove a negative, it's often impossible to prove that a lost, destroyed, or stolen instrument will not show up in the hands of someone (perhaps a holder in due course; see Chapter 7) who could require payment on the instrument. Consequently, the cost of providing the adequate protection required by section 3-309(b) may be as much as the amount of the instrument itself.

C. Payment

Payment is the usual method of discharging the obligation on a negotiable instrument. Payment and its consequences are discussed in Chapter 9 above.

D. Presentment, Dishonor, Notice of Dishonor

Part 5 of UCC Article 3 (sections 3-501, 3-502, 3-503, 3-504, and 3-505) provides a formalized set of rules for the ritual dance between the person seeking to enforce a negotiable instrument and the obligor on the instrument. Checks and other drafts are usually presented formally, but many of these formalities are routinely waived in modern promissory note forms. The formalities may also be excused for either a draft or a note as provided in UCC § 3-504. Nevertheless, understanding the meaning of presentment, dishonor, etc. remains important, even if the formalities themselves are waived. You need to understand what you're waiving.

1. Presentment

Presentment is essentially a formal demand for payment. *See* UCC § 3-501(a). (Presentment may also be a demand "to accept a draft," UCC § 3-501(a)(ii), though the term "accept" has a very narrow, technical, and counterintuitive meaning in Article 3, as explained in Section G of Chapter 4 above.) Detailed rules governing presentment appear in section 3-501(b). However, the details of those rules aren't necessary to an understanding of the basic concept.

The concept of presentment is significant because it triggers the obligation to either pay or dishonor (or "accept") the instrument, if presentment is required. Presentment is usually required for drafts, but less commonly required for notes, and may be excused for either drafts or notes. *See* UCC § 3-504(a).

2. Dishonor

Dishonor is essentially the failure or refusal of an obligated person to pay an instrument when it should be paid, though it is defined elaborately in the UCC. *See* UCC § 3-502. As discussed above in this chapter, dishonor terminates the suspension of the underlying obligation for which the instrument was taken. Dishonor is also required to enforce the obligation of a drawer or indorser. UCC §§ 3-414(b) (last sentence), 3-415(a) (last sentence).

Failure or refusal to "accept" a draft may also constitute dishonor. This alternative turns on the narrow, technical, and counterintuitive meaning of "accept," "acceptance," etc., in Article 3, which is discussed in Section G of Chapter 4.

Dishonor in the check collection context is discussed in Chapter 14.

3. Notice of Dishonor

Notice of dishonor is a formal requisite to the enforcement of indorsers' and drawers' liability. UCC § 3-503(a). Like presentment, notice of dishonor is commonly waived. *See* UCC § 3-504(b).

Checkpoints

- Taking a certified check, cashier's check, or teller's check results in discharge of the underlying obligation for which the instrument was taken.

- Taking another type of negotiable instrument results in suspension of the underlying obligation for which the instrument was taken.

  - If the instrument is paid, the underlying obligation is discharged.

  - If the instrument is dishonored, the suspension ends, and either the underlying obligation or the negotiable instrument may be enforced.

- If an instrument is lost, stolen, or destroyed before it is paid or dishonored, the suspension of the underlying obligation continues; UCC section 3-309 provides a cumbersome mechanism for enforcement of the instrument in such cases.

- Presentment, dishonor, and notice of dishonor are the ritual steps in an unsuccessful collection attempt on a negotiable instrument.

  - Dishonor ends the suspension of the underlying obligation and subjects drawers and indorsers to the possibility that they may have to pay.

  - Presentment and notice of dishonor are formal requisites for demanding payment, but they are often waived.

Part Two

Check Collection (UCC Article 4 and Related Federal Law)

Chapter 12

Forward Collection, Presentment, and Final Payment

Roadmap

- Draft
- Item
- Payor bank
- Collecting bank
- Depositary bank
- Intermediary bank
- Customer
- Expedited Funds Availability Act
- Regulation CC
- Transaction-planning phase
- Litigation phase
- Presentment
- Settlement
  - Provisional
  - Final
- Final payment
- Midnight deadline
- Extension of time for afternoon receipt
- Properly payable
- Overdraft
- Forged drawer signature
- Forged indorsement

- Stop-payment order
- Postdated check

A. Parties and Terminology

UCC Article 4 provides specialized rules for check collection by banks. Checks are negotiable instruments, as are most other things subject to Article 4. Therefore, the terminology of Article 3 usually still applies. UCC §4-104(c). However, the term "draft" is defined differently in Article 4 to include payment orders handled by banks, whether or not they qualify as negotiable instruments. *See* UCC §4-104(a)(7).

UCC Articles 3 and 4 also use different terms to identify some of the same things. UCC Article 4 applies to the collection of *items*, focusing on the practices of banks rather than on qualification as a negotiable instrument. *See* UCC §4-102(a). An "item" is defined as "an instrument or a promise or order to pay money handled by a bank for collection or payment." UCC §4-104(a)(9). In this Chapter we will generally refer to "checks," because that is the most common and most familiar type of "item."

UCC Article 4 refers to the drawee of a check as the "payor bank." UCC §4-105(3). The other banks that participate in collecting a check are (unsurprisingly) called "collecting banks." UCC §4-105(5). The collecting bank where the check is initially deposited is the "depositary bank." UCC §4-105(2). The collecting banks other than the depositary bank are called "intermediary banks." UCC §4-105(4). The drawer of the check being collected is the "customer" of the payor bank, and the payee who deposits a check at his, her, or its bank is the "customer" of the depositary bank. *See* UCC §4-104(a)(5).

B. Applicable Law: The Complex Intersection of State and Federal Rules

Historically the study of check collection was a study of UCC Article 4, because it contained the applicable rules. Starting around the 1980s, however, Congress began enacting federal laws that encroach substantially on the UCC framework. The federal statutes authorize administrative regulations to flesh out the statutory provisions.

Some of these federal laws and regulations conflict with, and therefore preempt, the UCC provisions. Other federal rules leave the UCC provisions intact but add a layer of analysis on top of the existing UCC framework. Worst of all, the boundaries between the UCC and the federal law are not always precise, so that uncertainty lingers when we try to classify some of the federal statutes into one or the other of these two categories.

Full consideration of the relationship between particular provisions of UCC Article 4 and corresponding federal law is far beyond the scope of this concise treatment of fundamental rules. For the most part, in this book we will explore the structure of the rules in both the UCC and federal regimes, without worrying too much about the vagaries of whether a particular UCC rule is preempted by federal law.

It's important to recognize that a lawyer may advise a client as to either of two very different stages of a transaction: (1) the *transaction-planning* phase, in which you're analyzing how to comply with the law as to events that haven't yet occurred, or (2) the *litigation* phase, at which the events have occurred and the analysis focuses on the legal significance of those events. If you're at the transaction-planning phase, the safe course is to assume that all the rules are effective, and you make sure you comply with each and every one of them. On the other hand, if you're at the litigation stage, you must take the facts as given and explore all possible interpretations of the applicable law. You hope to find a supportable interpretation that gives your client a favorable result. The possibility that an inconvenient UCC rule might be preempted by federal law usually becomes more important at the litigation stage; that analysis is often extremely detailed.

C. The Normal Path of a Check

The usual check collection process—in which you have probably participated—is that a *customer* (the payee) deposits a check in his, her, or its account at the *depositary bank*. The depositary bank then *presents* the check (the subject of Section D of this Chapter) to the *payor bank*, either directly or via one or more *intermediary banks*. If the payor bank's customer (the drawer of the check) has sufficient funds on deposit and the check is "properly payable" (the subject of Section F of this Chapter), the payor bank will "pay" the check and deduct the amount paid from the drawer's account at the payor bank. The surprisingly complex meanings of "pay" and related terms are discussed in Section E of this Chapter and in Chapter 9.

In the overwhelming majority of cases, everything goes just fine: the check is paid, the money moves (via the banks) from the drawer to the payee as intended, and each bank gets back all the money it disbursed. Things do occasionally go wrong, though, and the law provides mechanisms—discussed in Chapters 14 through 16—for dealing with those problem situations.

D. Presentment

The definition of "presentment" appears in UCC Article 3. *See* UCC §§ 3-501, 4-104(c); *see also* Section D of Chapter 11 above. The full definition in section 3-501(a) and the related rules in section 3-501(b) are complex; for most purposes you can think of presentment as simply a demand for payment of a check or other item. The "presenting bank" is defined such that presentment is made to the payor bank, but the payor bank does *not* "present" the check to its customer (the drawer). *See* UCC § 4-105(6). Historically, presentment has been made by delivering the actual check to the payor bank, though recent federal legislation provides a mechanism for presenting checks electronically. *See* UCC § 4-110. *See also* Section C of Chapter 14 below.

E. Settlement and Payment

In a course that is often called "Payment Systems," it's no surprise that terms like "payment," "pay," etc. have various meanings and come up in a variety of contexts. However, when you work with UCC Article 4, you risk getting confused if you say that anyone other than the payor bank "pays" a check. Other parties involved in collecting a check may give money or other value in exchange for the check, but you should be very careful if you're describing such an act by someone other than the payor bank. Almost always, you will do better if you say the other party "takes," "receives," "settles for," or "collects" a check. *See* UCC § 4-104, Official Comment 10. (The terms "accept," "acceptance," etc. create similar confusion, as discussed above in Section G of Chapter 4.) And even in the case of the payor bank, final payment only occurs in particular circumstances. Once the payor bank makes final payment, a number of significant legal consequences result.

We look first at the provisional settlements given by each bank as a check works its way through the system. We then consider the ways that the payor bank makes final payment; this occurs most often when the payor bank retains the check past its "midnight deadline," though there are other alternatives. Then we consider the legal consequences of final payment.

1. Provisional Settlement

When you deposit a check in your account at your bank, you expect the bank to record the related funds as an increase in your account balance. In the terminology of UCC Article 4, your bank is said to "settle" for that check. *See* UCC § 4-104(a)(11). Similarly, when your bank sends that check to another collecting bank or the payor bank, the recipient will settle for the check. *See id.* As noted in the last sentence of the definition of "settle," a settlement "may be either provisional or final." *Id.* Any settlement given by a collecting bank is presumed to be provisional, prior to the time final payment is made by the payor bank, unless the parties clearly express their intent to the contrary. *See* UCC § 4-201(a). As long as the settlement remains provisional, the bank that gave that settlement retains the right to revoke it if the check isn't paid. UCC § 4-214(a). When the payor bank makes final payment, generally that causes the provisional settlements given by the depositary bank and other collecting banks to become final. UCC §§ 4-215(d), 4-214(a) (last sentence).

A provisional settlement is said to "firm up" as a synonym for "become final," though the phrase "firm up" appears only a few times in UCC Official Comments. *See* UCC §§ 4-201 Official Comment 4 (2nd paragraph); 4-215 Official Comment 9. Those Official Comments also address the relatively rare cases in which final payment by the payor bank may *not* firm up the provisional settlements by collecting banks. *See id.*

You will occasionally see references to "midnight of the banking day of receipt" as the deadline for giving settlement. *See* UCC §§ 4-301(a), 4-302(a)(1). This is potentially confusing, because this is *not* the "midnight deadline" whose passing usually results in final payment, as discussed below. Banks routinely give provisional settlement each day for items they received that day. This is simply an accounting function. This settlement may or may not immediately result in funds being made available to the depositor; that issue requires an additional line of analysis, discussed below in Chapter 13.

2. Final Payment

a. The Midnight Deadline Rule

As discussed more fully below in Subsection 3 and in Chapters 2, 13, and 14, federal law has encroached on payment systems law, which was once the exclusive province of the UCC. Along with the federal law have come questions of whether particular UCC provisions are preempted by the related federal law. Many of those questions remain quite messy, so the best strategy for understanding these rules—and the approach followed by this book—is to focus on the internal structure of each statutory framework, leaving the intersection (or collision) of the competing frameworks to last.

In the UCC Article 4 framework, most checks are paid because the payor bank kept the check instead of returning it by the "midnight deadline." It is well established that a payor bank makes final payment of a check if it does not dishonor the check by its midnight deadline. However, the statutory language of the UCC does not state this rule clearly in any one place. Seeing the statutory authority requires you to read section 4-215(a)(3) together with section 4-301(a).

The first piece of the rule says that a payor bank makes final payment if it doesn't revoke a provisional settlement quickly enough: "An item is finally paid by a payor bank when the bank has ... (3) made a provisional settlement for the item and failed to revoke the settlement in the time and the manner permitted by statute...." UCC § 4-215(a)(3).

Second, in the UCC Article 4 framework the payor bank is permitted to revoke a provisional settlement given for a check if it returns the check before the payor bank's midnight deadline (assuming the normal case in which the payor bank hasn't made final payment in some other way): "If a payor bank settles for a demand item ... the payor bank may revoke the settlement and recover the settlement if, before it has made final payment and before its midnight deadline, it (1) returns the item [or, in limited circumstances, returns a substitute for the item]." UCC § 4-301(a). This suggests that if the payor bank *doesn't* return the check (or take appropriate alternative action, if permitted) by its midnight deadline, the payor bank loses the opportunity to revoke the settlement.

Putting those rules together: a payor bank can and must return a check by its midnight deadline, or it makes final payment on the check.

(A bank may also become "accountable" for a check without paying it. *See* UCC §§ 4-302(a)(1), 4-302 Official Comments 1 and 2, 3-502(b)(1) (last clause), 3-502 Official Comment 4 (second and third paragraphs). However, those provisions are for situations that occur infrequently, and are probably best omitted from your analysis as you seek an initial understanding of the system.)

b. Other Ways the Payor Bank Might Make Final Payment

Passage of the midnight deadline is the usual way that checks are finally paid by the payor bank. However, a payor bank may occasionally make final payment prior to the midnight deadline in one of two other ways.

First, final payment occurs immediately when the payor bank has "paid the item in cash." UCC § 4-215(a)(1). Notice that this requires the *payor* bank to hand over cash. Final payment does *not* occur if you get your bank to cash a check drawn on another bank. In this latter case, your bank is extending credit to you in the amount of the check; your bank expects that credit to be repaid either by collecting the check (i.e., presenting it to the payor bank), or by collecting from you if the check is dishonored by the payor bank.

Second, the payor bank makes final payment if it gives irrevocable settlement when it receives a check: "An item is finally paid by a payor bank when the bank has … (2) settled for the item without having a right to revoke the settlement under statute, clearing-house rule, or agreement." UCC §4-215(a)(2). The expectation of the Article 4 rules is that such irrevocable settlement is unusual; the custom assumed in the UCC is provisional settlement. (As discussed below, Regulation CC provides a contrary rule, which might be read to preempt the UCC rule. See Regulation CC §229.36(d); 12 CFR Part 229 Appendix E Commentary to §229.36(d); UCC §4-301 Official Comment 1. However, our focus here is on understanding the UCC structure before we explore the contrary federal rule.) Typically the requisite "right to revoke the settlement" is found in section 4-301(a), though a number of subtleties are possible. See UCC §4-215 Official Comment 4. Notice that the payor bank's rule for returning a check implies that settlement given by the payor bank is provisional unless the check is presented "for immediate payment over the counter." UCC §4-301(a). More important, notice again that only irrevocable settlement by the *payor* bank results in final payment.

c. Basic Definitions

The midnight deadline is defined (for both a payor bank and a collecting bank) as "midnight on its next banking day following the banking day on which it receives the relevant item or notice or from which the time for taking action commences to run, whichever is later." UCC §4-104(a)(10). "Banking day" is defined as "the part of a day on which a bank is open to the public for carrying on substantially all of its banking functions." UCC §4-104(a)(3).

Based on these definitions, you would think that if a check is received by a bank on Wednesday while it is open, its midnight deadline would be midnight the next day that the bank is open (usually Thursday, unless that Thursday is a holiday). Often you would be right, but there is one more wrinkle we need to address before turning to detailed examples.

d. Extension of Time for Afternoon Receipt

If you monitor your checking account very closely, you may have noticed that deposits you make in the late afternoon don't appear on your statement until the following day. A payor bank can treat checks received from collecting banks in the same way. When a bank receives checks after 2:00 p.m. on a banking day, UCC Article 4 allows the bank to treat those checks as if they had been received on the next banking day:

> (a) For the purpose of allowing time to process items, prove balances, and make the necessary entries on its books to determine its position for the day, a bank may fix an afternoon hour of 2 P.M. or later as a cutoff hour for the handling of money and items and the making of entries on its books.
>
> (b) An item or deposit of money received on any day after a cutoff hour so fixed or after the close of the banking day may be treated as being received at the opening of the next banking day.

UCC § 4-108. (A similar rule applies for calculating deadlines under the Expedited Funds Availability Act and Reg CC, which are discussed in Chapter 15 below. *See* 12 C.F.R. § 229.19(a)(5).)

So, in our example above, a bank may treat a check received after 2:00 p.m. on Wednesday as received at the opening of business on Thursday; as a result, the midnight deadline for that check is midnight on Friday (assuming that the bank is open on all three days).

e. Examples

To recap our example above: Suppose a payor bank receives a check on Wednesday morning, and the bank is open on that Wednesday, Thursday, and Friday. The midnight deadline will be midnight on Thursday. If the payor bank doesn't return the check by then, it has made final payment

However, if the bank receives the check at 4:00 p.m. on Wednesday, the bank can (and usually will) treat the check as being received at the opening of business on Thursday. The midnight deadline for that check will be midnight on *Friday.*

Suppose instead that the bank is open on Wednesday and the following Friday, but Thursday is a holiday when the bank is closed. The bank receives a check on Wednesday morning. The midnight deadline will be midnight on Friday.

Modifying the example in the preceding paragraph, suppose the check is received at 4:00 p.m. on Wednesday. Suppose further that Thursday is a holiday when the bank is closed, and the bank is also closed on Saturday and Sunday. The bank can (and usually will) treat the check as being received at the opening of business on Friday. If the bank is open on Wednesday, Friday, and the following Monday, the midnight deadline will be midnight on Monday.

3. Consequences of Making Final Payment

a. Consequences to the Payor Bank

As explained above, once a payor bank makes final payment on a check it will usually be stuck with liability for the amount of the check. For most cases, this general rule will suffice. The closest the UCC comes to actually stating this rule is, "the payor bank may revoke the settlement if, before it has made final payment and before its midnight deadline, it (1) returns the item...." UCC § 4-301(a). In other words, the payor bank loses the opportunity to revoke the settlement given for a check when its midnight deadline passes—which results in final payment under UCC § 4-215(a)(3)—or if it otherwise makes final payment before the midnight deadline.

If you seek a complete understanding of this and related rules, you should note at least three difficulties with the general rule in the preceding paragraph. First, understanding the statutory basis of the general rule requires you to read section 4-215, 4-301, and 4-302 together, along with the Official Comments to each of those sections. Second, there are circumstances in which a payor bank might recover even after final payment was made, under warranty, restitution, or fraud theories, as discussed in Chapters 15 and 16. Third, as mentioned above and discussed more fully below in Section B of Chapter 14, the additional rules in Regulation CC supplement the UCC rules, and sometimes preempt them, though the boundaries of that preemption are sometimes unclear. Further detail on these topics is available in more-detailed treatises. *See* Fred H. Miller and Alvin C. Harrell, The Law of Modern Payment Systems ¶¶ 8.02, 8.04 (2003 & Supp. 2006); James J. White & Robert S. Summers, Uniform Commercial Code §§ 17-2, 17-3, 17-4, and 17-5 (5th ed. 2000).

For our purposes in this book, however, the general rule is a useful approximation. Full exposition of all the twists and turns here risks creating more confusion than enlightenment. The most productive way to understand the rules, at least initially, is to examine the UCC and Regulation CC systems separately before trying to understand their interaction.

b. Consequences to Collecting Banks

In the UCC Article 4 framework, final payment by the payor bank doesn't just affect the obligations of the payor bank itself. It also causes the provisional settlements given by collecting banks to "firm up": "If a collecting bank receives a settlement for an item which is or becomes final, the bank is accountable to its customer for the amount of the item and any provisional credit given for the item in an account with its customer becomes final." UCC § 4-215(d). *See also* UCC § 4-214(a) (last sentence). Here again, Regulation CC, discussed below in Section B of Chapter 14, provides a supplementary and sometimes contradictory mechanism. (There's also an exception to this rule if the settlement is not made through a clearing house or by account entries between the banks. *See* UCC § 4-215 Official Comment 9.)

F. Is the Check "Properly Payable"?

A bank that gives money out is always concerned about getting it back, and the payor bank is no exception. When the payor bank makes final payment on a check, it does so expecting to be able to recover the money from its customer, the drawer of the check. Whether or not the payor bank will be successful in this quest turns on whether the check is "properly payable": "A bank may charge against the account of a customer an item that is properly payable from the account." UCC § 4-401(a).

1. The Meaning of "Properly Payable"

UCC Article 4 provides a rather cryptic definition of when a check is properly payable: "An item is properly payable if it is authorized by the customer and is in accordance with any agreement between the customer and bank." UCC § 4-401(a). Understanding and applying that definition can be difficult in the abstract. The best way to give it meaning is to consider various things that may (or sometimes, surprisingly, may not) prevent a check from being properly payable.

2. Overdrafts

You might assume—perhaps based upon a bad experience or two with your own bank account—that a check is not properly payable if there's not enough money in the account to cover the check. However, the UCC explicitly gives the bank the option in such circumstances: "A bank *may* charge against the account of a customer an item that is properly payable from the account *even though the charge creates an overdraft*." UCC § 4-401(a) (emphasis added). *See also* UCC § 4-401 Official Comment 1. However, the bank is not *obligated* to pay checks that overdraw an account. *See* UCC § 4-402(a) (last clause). So, if a bank doesn't want to pay a check that creates an overdraft it doesn't have to. On the other hand, if the bank *wants* to pay the check (perhaps because of a strong relationship with the drawer and confidence that the drawer will make good on the overdraft), the analysis shifts to other factors to determine whether the check is properly payable.

One other rule is worth mentioning with respect to overdrafts: While generally you can expect your bank to demand that you pay for any overdraft from your account, your liability may be limited in particular circumstances: "A customer is not liable for the amount of an overdraft if the customer *neither* signed the item *nor* benefited from the proceeds of the item." UCC § 4-401(b) (emphasis added). This provision is applicable in cases of joint accounts or other accounts where more than one person has authority to sign checks. It partially reflects the general rule that signing an instrument is fundamental to having liability on it. However, the focus of this provision is on liability for the *overdraft*, which can be imposed if the non-signer was benefitted, even though that person would not be liable on the *check*.

3. Forgeries

A forgery or a missing signature is a fundamental defect in a check. No one is liable on a check or other negotiable instrument unless that person's valid signature is on the instrument. UCC § 3-401.

Although not critical to the analysis here, it's useful to form the habit of distinguishing two categories when you speak of "forgeries" related to checks: a forgery may be either a forged drawer's signature, or a forged indorsement. The legal consequences differ, so you should always precisely describe the nature of a particular forgery.

Whichever type of forgery is involved, though, the rule is clear: "An item containing a forged drawer's signature or forged indorsement is not properly payable." UCC § 4-401 Official Comment 1. The presence of either prevents a check from being properly payable.

If the drawer's signature is forged, the check is not valid as an order for payment. However, indorsers may still be required to make good on their liability as indorsers if the check is dishonored, as discussed in Chapter 8. *See* UCC § 3-415(a).

If an indorser's signature is forged, the check may still represent a valid order for payment. However, there may be no "person entitled to enforce" the check because it is payable to someone not in possession. These rules and their consequences are discussed further in Chapter 15.

4. Stop Payment Orders

UCC Article 4 gives bank customers a broad right to stop payment on checks. UCC § 4-403(a). However, there are important limitations. The customer must describe the check with "reasonable certainty," a highly fact-specific analysis. *Id.*

The bank must receive the stop-payment order "at a time and in a manner that affords the bank a reasonable opportunity to act on it...." *Id.* Also, stop-payment orders are only effective for a limited time: 14 days for oral orders, and six months for written orders, though written stop-payment orders may be renewed before they expire. UCC § 4-403(b).

Moreover, even if a bank erroneously pays a check despite a valid stop-payment order, the bank may still be able to charge the customer's account for the amount paid if the customer was obligated to make the payment to the payee. UCC Article 4 gives the payor bank a subrogation right in cases where that is necessary to prevent the customer from being unjustly enriched. UCC § 4-407.

For example, suppose Boris Badunov bought a diamond from Rocky. Ever wanting to believe the best about people, Rocky delivered the diamond and took Boris' personal check in exchange. Boris promptly went to his bank and filled out a valid stop-payment order, even though he knew he was obligated to pay for the diamond.

If Boris's bank erroneously paid his check when presented two days later, this would violate the stop-payment order. The check was not properly payable, so Boris' bank could not charge the check to Boris's account under UCC section 4-401. *However,* the bank would be authorized to charge Boris's account by subrogation of Rocky's right to be paid. UCC § 4-407(2). The bank made a payment that Boris was obligated to make, and Boris would be unjustly enriched if he got to keep both the diamond and the $2,000.00. (Of course, Boris' bank may have practical difficulties collecting if Boris has emptied his account at the bank and disappeared.)

5. Postdated Checks

Generally a negotiable instrument is not payable before the date stated on the instrument. *See* UCC §§ 3-113(a) (last sentence); 3-108. If not for the special rule for postdated checks discussed below, this could prevent a postdated check from being properly payable before the date on the check.

Because the date of a check is not encoded in magnetic ink on the bottom edge of a check, the check collection system cannot easily keep track of check dates. Requiring human intervention to check the date of a check would increase costs and be subject to error. Moreover, relatively few checks are postdated. To deal with this problem, UCC Article 4 treats a postdated check as if it were properly payable, regardless of its date, *unless* the drawer "has given notice to the bank of the postdating describing the check with reasonable certainty." UCC § 4-401(c). The rules for these notices are similar to the rules for stop payment orders. This extra notice calls the attention of the bank to the prospect of a postdated check coming through the account. Thus, the bank can set up a mechanism to watch for the postdated check without having to examine the dates on the multitude of checks that are not postdated.

If the bank pays a postdated check even though the drawer has timely provided an effective notice that the check was postdated, the bank may be liable for damages, including the damages for wrongfully dishonoring checks that would have been paid if the postdated check had not been paid. UCC § 4-401(c) (last two sentences). As discussed in Section A of Chapter 14, these damages can be substantial.

Checkpoints

- UCC Article 4 governs the collection of "items" by banks.

- The most common type of item is a check.

- Only the payor bank "pays" or makes "final payment" of a check.

- The "depository bank" and other "collecting banks" participate in "collecting" a check.

- "Intermediary banks" may also participate in check collection, helping move the check from the depository bank to the payor bank.

- The UCC was once the main source of law for check collection; however, federal law such as the Expedited Funds Availability Act and the related Regulation CC have encroached on the area, and raise potentially difficult preemption issues.

- Collecting banks and the payor bank typically give initial "provisional settlement," when they receive a check.

- Once the payor bank makes final payment, the provisional settlements become final ("firm up") and can no longer be revoked.

- Final payment usually occurs as the result of the payor bank keeping the check and not dishonoring it by the "midnight deadline."

- UCC Article 4 permits banks to treat checks received after 2:00 p.m. as if they were received on the next banking day.

- The payor bank may only charge a "properly payable" check to the drawer's account.

- An overdraft does not prevent the payor bank from charging a check to the drawer's account; the payor bank has the option whether or not to pay a check that results in an overdraft.

- Forgeries, stop payment orders (subject to limitations) and postdated checks (also subject to limitations) prevent a check from being properly payable.

Chapter 13

Funds Availability to Depositors

Roadmap

- Expedited Funds Availability Act (EFAA)
- Regulation CC
- Paying bank
- Returning bank
- Banking day
- Business day
- Local check
- Nonlocal check
- Availability schedule
- Adjustment for risk factors

A. UCC Rules

The UCC Article 4 rules are lenient toward banks as to when funds from a deposited check must be made available to the depositor. In the relatively rare cases where the depositary bank is also the payor bank, the funds must be made available "at the opening of the bank's second banking day following receipt of the item," unless the item was dishonored. UCC § 4-215(e)(2). In the more common situations involving more than one bank, the general rule is that the depositary bank is not required to make funds from a deposit available to the depositor until after it "has had a reasonable time to receive return of the item and the item has not been received within that time." UCC § 4-215(e)(1). Other rules require collecting banks to use "reasonably prompt method[s]" for sending checks and prohibit collecting banks from holding on to checks for a long period of time before sending them. *See* UCC §§ 4-204, 4-

202. However, the UCC system is subject to the possibility of delays, especially when the payor bank is a great distance from the depositary bank. In addition, the UCC provides neither affirmative notice to a collecting bank that a check has been paid, nor any specific maximum time by which a check must be paid or returned to the depositary bank. Therefore, prior to the Expedited Funds Availability Act, cautious banks focused on the elasticity of what might be a "reasonable time to receive return" of a check, and imposed significant delays — often a week or more — on deposit availability.

B. Expedited Funds Availability Act/ Regulation CC Rules

Congress acted to correct the shortcoming it perceived in the UCC's availability rules, and enacted the Expedited Funds Availability Act, now codified at 12 U.S.C.A. 4001–4010 (the "EFAA"). (A few states also have their own availability statutes, but those are beyond the scope of this book. *See* 12 C.F.R. Part 229 Appendix F (preemption determinations with respect to state availability requirements.) The EFAA authorizes the Board of Governors of the Federal Reserve System to issue regulations to help accomplish the goals of the statute. 12 U.S.C.A. § 4008. Those regulations appear at 12 C.F.R. Part 229. The regulations are commonly referred to as "Reg. CC," reflecting the convention of assigning letters to Federal Reserve Board regulations explained in Chapter 2.

The EFAA and Reg. CC are difficult to read, but they provide a useful exercise in statutory and regulatory interpretation. (Any similarity here to the advice, "Eat your vegetables; they're good for you!" is, of course, purely coincidental.) Our focus will be on Reg. CC, which contains the detailed rules that banks must follow. This regulation is divided into four subparts. Subpart A provides general definitions. Subpart B prescribes the schedules on which funds from deposits must be made available to depositors. Subpart C imposes stricter deadlines than the UCC on the timeliness of check collection and return, in order to make the availability requirements of Subpart B feasible without imposing undue additional risks on banks. Subpart D was added to accommodate the rules to the Check Clearing for the 21st Century Act discussed in Section C of Chapter 14 below. The Federal Reserve Board of Governors' interpretations of various provisions in Reg. CC appear as "Commentary" at 12 C.F.R. Part 229 Appendix E.

Because the EFAA and Regulation CC are federal law, they preempt conflicting state law, including the UCC. However, the interaction of the EFAA and Reg. CC with the UCC rules is complex and sometimes uncertain. Therefore, the safest assumption for a bank to make is that it must comply separately with both the UCC and EFAA/Reg. CC rules, except in the few instances where a UCC rule is clearly preempted. Similarly, the best strategy for a student or lawyer trying to understand these rules is to examine each system separately and consider how a particular fact pattern would be treated under each system individually, leaving analysis of the interaction between the systems for last. Preemption is addressed in 12 U.S.C. § 4007, and 12 C.F.R. §§ 229.20, 229.41, and 229.59. Some guidance as to preemption is also provided in 12 C.F.R. Part 229 Appendix F, though it focuses primarily on state-specific statutes beyond the UCC and is not exhaustive as to the UCC rules. The Federal Reserve Board's Commentary to sections 229.10 and 229.20 also provide some limited guidance as to preemption. *See* 12 C.F.R. Part 229 Appendix E.

1. Subpart A of Reg. CC: Definitions

Reg. CC contains an extensive set of definitions. *See* 12 C.F.R. § 229.2. Reg. CC incorporates the UCC definitions for terms that do not have a specific Reg. CC definition. 12 CFR § 229.2 (first sentence).

Most of the EFAA and Reg. CC definitions are similar to the UCC Article 3 and 4 definitions, though it's always a good idea to review the definition of any term important to your analysis. Reg. CC uses the term "paying bank" instead of the UCC Article 4 term "payor bank," and the focus of each definition differs, but both terms will usually identify the same bank in any particular transaction. *See* 12 C.F.R. § 229.2(z); UCC § 4-105(3). Reg. CC also uses the term "returning bank" instead of "intermediary bank" for banks other than the payor/paying and depositary bank that participate in returning a check. *See* C.F.R. § 229.2(cc); UCC § 4-105(4). For this discussion, you should particularly note that a "returning bank" in Reg. CC has a special and potentially counterintuitive definition. Neither the paying bank nor the depositary bank is a returning bank. Reg. CC § 229.2(cc). A returning bank corresponds to an "intermediary bank" under Article 4, though "returning bank" is used only for banks handling dishonored checks in the return process. By contrast, an intermediary bank may participate in either the forward collection process or the return process. *See* UCC § 4-105(4).

A few definitions are potentially troublesome. In order to count the days correctly to determine when funds from a deposit must be made available to the depositor, it's critical to understand the definitions of "banking day" and "business day." A "business day" is defined as weekdays other than federal holidays. 12 C.F.R. § 229.2(g). A "banking day" is defined as a business day when a bank office "is open to the public for carrying on substantially all of its banking functions." 12 C.F.R. § 229.2(f). The tricky part is this: a Saturday, a Sunday, or a holiday can *never* be a banking day for Reg. CC purposes, *even if the bank is open on that Saturday, Sunday, or holiday,* because "banking day" is defined as a subset of "business day," and Saturdays, Sundays, and holidays are never business days under Reg. CC. This is made even more confusing because Articles 3 and 4 of the UCC define "banking day" simply by reference to whether the bank is open or not. *See* UCC §§ 4-104(a)(3), 3-103(c). Consequently, if a bank is open on a Saturday, Sunday, or holiday, that day counts as a banking day for counting days under the UCC, but not under Reg. CC.

You will also need to know the difference between "local checks" and "nonlocal checks." These terms are defined based upon whether the paying bank and the depositary bank are located in the same "check processing region" defined as "the geographical area served by an office of a Federal Reserve Bank for purposes of its check processing activities. 12 C.F.R. § 229.2(r), (s), (v), (w), (m). If the depositary bank and paying bank are located in the same city, the check should be a local check. If the depositary bank is in New York and the paying bank is in San Francisco, you can safely assume that the check is nonlocal. In between those extremes, being certain requires careful study of the Federal Reserve Check Processing Regions to determine whether the paying bank and receiving bank are in the same region or different regions. A list of Federal Reserve Bank offices appears in 12 C.F.R. Part 229 Appendix A, though you need the routing and transit number identifying each bank (which appears in the MICR line on the check) for close cases.

In working through the rules of Subpart B below, you should note that "next day" availability is a useful shorthand, but determining *which* is the next day is always qualified by the definition of banking days and business days. The precise formulation of next day availability is "not later than the business day after the banking day" of deposit. *See* 12 C.F.R. § 229.10(a), (b), (c). Similar phrases such as "second-day availability," "fifth-day availability," etc. are useful but subject to corresponding limitations.

2. Subpart B of Reg. CC: Availability Rules

The general effect of the Subpart B rules in Reg. CC is to impose deadlines by which banks must make deposited funds available to the depositor. The specific deadline varies depending on how risky the type of deposit is. We start with the general availability schedule found in the initial parts of Reg. CC sections 220.10 and 229.12. However, you need to remember that those general rules are only the starting point, and you must adjust them for various risk factors such as withdrawals by cash rather than by check, ATM deposits, new accounts, large deposits, and other factors that increase the likelihood that the depositary bank may have a problem collecting the deposited items.

a. The General Availability Schedule

Cash deposits and types of checks that typically impose little risk on the bank generally get next-day availability (or more precisely, as noted above, "not later than the business day after the banking day" of deposit). 12 C.F.R. § 229.10(a), (c). Funds deposited by "electronic payment" also generally get this same next-day availability. 12 C.F.R. § 229.10(b). In addition, the first $100.00 of any deposit gets next-day availability. 12 C.F.R. § 229.10(c)(1)(vii).

Most checks, however, don't qualify for next-day availability. The general availability schedule for such higher-risk checks depends on whether a particular check is a "local check" or a "nonlocal check." Generally, the depositary bank must make funds from the deposit of a *local check* available to the depositor "not later than the *second* business day following the banking day on which funds are deposited." 12 C.F.R. § 229.12(b)(1) (emphasis added). This same second-day rule also applies to various specialized items that almost, but not quite, meet the next-day availability rule. 12 C.F.R. § 229.12(b)(2), (3), (4). Similarly, the depositary bank must make funds from the deposit of a *nonlocal check* available to the depositor "not later than the *fifth* business day following the banking day on which funds are deposited." 12 C.F.R. § 229.12(c)(1)(i) (emphasis added). This same fifth-day rule also applies to some specialized items, 12 C.F.R. § 229.(c)(1)(ii), and a longer time is permitted for certain other specialized items prescribed by the Federal Reserve Board of Governors, 12 C.F.R. § 229.12(c)(2).

b. Adjustments for Risk Factors

Once you have determined the general availability rule that applies to a particular check, you're off to a good start but not yet done. You must adjust the availability time that you determined under the general rule to reflect additional risk factors in Reg. CC.

The exceptions in sections 229.10 and 229.12, and some of the exceptions in section 229.13, specify the revised time by which funds must be made available. If the exception itself does not provide a specific revision to the availability schedule, you go to section 229.13(h) for further guidance as to what the revised time period should be. The depositary bank is also required to give the depositor notice of the exception. 12 C.F.R. § 229.13(g).

Deposits not in person. For most low-risk items that generally get next-day availability, a depositary bank is permitted to postpone availability to the second business day if the item is not deposited "in person to an employee of the depositary bank." 12 C.F.R. § 229.10(a)(2), (c)(2). Therefore, even if deposited in an ATM or night depository, banks still must give next-day availability for U.S. Treasury checks deposited in the payee's account, § 229.10(c)(1)(i), "on-us" checks (i.e., checks drawn on the depositary bank), § 229.10(c)(1)(vi), and the first $100.00 of any deposit, § 229.10(c)(1)(vii).

Withdrawals in cash. The general second-day and fifth-day availability rules are extended by one day if the depositor is withdrawing the funds in cash rather than by writing a check on the deposit account. 12 C.F.R. § 229.12(d). An exception to this exception requires the depositary bank to permit up to $400.00 to be withdrawn on the general two-day or five-day schedule. *Id.*

Deposits beyond the continental U.S. The second-day and fifth-day availability rules are also extended by one day for checks deposited in Alaska, Hawaii, Puerto Rico, and the U.S. Virgin Islands, if the check was not drawn on a bank in the same state or territory. 12 C.F.R. § 229.12(e).

Nonproprietary ATMs. A "nonproprietary ATM" is an automated teller machine that is not identified with the depositary bank. *See* 12 C.F.R. § 229.2(x), (aa), (c). Deposits of checks *or cash* in nonproprietary ATMs are subject to a fifth-day availability rule. 12 C.F.R. § 229.12(f). Notice that this rule not only trumps the two-day and five-day rules in section 229.12; it also trumps the next day availability rules in 229.10. *See* 12 CFR Part 229 Appendix E Commentary to Section 229.12(f).

New accounts. If an account has been open less than 30 days and one or more of the accountholders has not had another account with the depositary bank for at least 30 days, the depositary bank is permitted to use a ninth-day availability schedule for the portion of any check deposit in excess of $5,000.00. 12 C.F.R. § 229.13(a)(1)(ii), (a)(2). New accounts are also excluded from the general availability requirements for "on-us"checks and the first $100.00 of any deposit. 12 C.F.R. § 229.13(a)(1)(iii). However, cash deposits and electronic deposits are subject to the general availability rules even for new accounts. 12 C.F.R. § 229.13(a)(1)(i).

Large deposits. Check deposits are not subject to the general availability requirements to the extent that they total more than $5,000.00 for one customer in any one banking day. 12 C.F.R. § 229.13(b).

Redeposited checks. The general availability rules do not apply to most checks that have been redeposited after they were previously deposited and returned unpaid. 12 C.F.R. § 229.13(c). However, this exception does *not* apply to checks returned because of a missing indorsement or postdating, if the problem has been fixed by the time the check is redeposited. 12 C.F.R. § 229.13(c)(1), (2).

Repeated overdrafts, reasonable cause to doubt collectibility, and emergency conditions. Depositary banks are also permitted to extend the times specified by the general availability rules for check deposits in cases where the depositor's account has been repeatedly overdrawn, 12 C.F.R. § 229.13(d), or the bank has a reasonable and well-grounded basis to doubt the collectibility of the check, 12 C.F.R. § 229.13(e), or emergency conditions interfere with check collection such as communication or computer facilities interruptions, failure of another bank, war, or another emergency beyond the control of the depositary bank, 12 C.F.R. § 229.13(f).

3. Bank Liability for Noncompliance

A bank that violates the funds availability requirements of Reg. CC is liable to "any person" for actual damages, plus a statutory penalty set by the court, plus "a reasonable attorney's fee as determined by the court." Reg. CC § 229.21(a). The statutory penalty is permitted to range from $100.00 to $1,000.00 in an individual action. Reg. CC § 229.21(a)(2)(i). No minimum penalty is set for class actions, but the maximum is set at "the lesser of $500,000.00 or 1 percent of the net worth of the bank involved." Reg. CC § 229.21(a)(2)(ii).

A bank may avoid liability if "the violation was not intentional and resulted from a bona fide error, notwithstanding the maintenance of procedures reasonably adapted to avoid such error. Reg. CC § 229.21(b).

Checkpoints

- The EFAA and Reg. CC impose stricter deadlines than the UCC for when a depositary bank must make funds available to the depositor.

- The Reg. CC definition of "banking day" is significantly different than the UCC definition, requiring close attention to definitions when counting days.

- The starting point in Reg. CC is next-day availability for cash and certain low-risk items, second-day availability for local checks, and fifth-day availability for nonlocal checks.

- Reg. CC may adjust the availability deadline beyond the starting point for an item based on various measures of the risk of different types of deposits and customers.

Chapter 14

Dishonor, Return Mechanisms, Deadlines, and Bank Liability

Roadmap

- Dishonor
- Wrongful dishonor
- Provisional settlement
- Final payment
- Midnight deadline
- Reg. CC
  - Two-day/four-day test
  - Forward collection test
  - Two-day notice of nonpayment for $2,500.00+ checks
- Check 21
  - Truncation
  - Substitute check
  - Expedited recredit

As we saw in Chapter 12 above, when a check is deposited at a bank the normal and expected sequence is that the depositary bank will present the check to the payor bank, and the payor bank will pay the check. The vast majority of cases follow this process without incident. However, the law must also provide for the relatively few, but still significant, cases where things don't go according to the tidy plan. This Chapter explores the mechanism built into the check collection mechanism for dealing with problems.

The mechanisms described in this Chapter are usually the simplest and most certain way for a bank to avoid getting stuck with a bad check. However, in order to take advantage of these mechanisms, the banks involved must recognize the problem promptly and act swiftly, usually within a day or two at most. A depositary bank that has taken on a risk that it is not required to take—such as allowing the depositor to take away funds in exchange for the deposit earlier than required by the availability rules (Chapter 13 above)—may also find this avenue to be limited as a practical matter.

Because the direct dishonor-and-return path explored in this Chapter isn't always available, the law provides alternative mechanisms for dealing with problems involving checks. We will explore those alternative mechanisms in Chapters 15 and 16. Those alternatives tend to be more complex and less certain than simply dishonoring and returning the check, but they are important to have if the passage of time or some other problem has eliminated the dishonor-and-return option.

As discussed more extensively in Chapters 12 and 13, the rules of check collection and deposit availability involve a complex interaction of state law (mostly found in Articles 3 and 4 of the UCC) and federal law. The advice for dealing with that interaction is the same as in those two previous Chapters: The safest assumption for a bank to make is that it must comply separately with both the UCC and EFAA/Reg. CC rules, except in the few instances where a UCC rule is clearly preempted by the applicable federal rule. Similarly, the best strategy for a student or lawyer trying to understand these rules is to examine each system separately and consider how a particular fact pattern would be treated under each system individually, leaving analysis of the interaction between the UCC and federal systems for last.

A. UCC Rules

1. Dishonor

The concept of dishonor is deceptively simple: essentially, a check or other negotiable instrument is dishonored if it isn't paid when it was supposed to be.

However, the statutory definition of dishonor is complex. *See* UCC § 3-502. That quasi-definition is also hard to find if you don't know to look for it in section 3-502, because it isn't included in the UCC provisions that provide cross-references to most other definitions. *See* UCC §§ 3-103(b), (c), 4-104(b), (c). As if that much didn't already provide enough complexity, effective dishonor of a check by a bank is subject to rules in UCC Article 4, and it's sometimes hard to see the rules in the actual words of the Article 4 provisions. But fear not: we'll work through the rules here, and they are understandable once you work through them sufficiently.

It's important to remember that in the UCC Article 4 framework, *only the payor bank* can pay or dishonor a check. When a check is presented to the payor bank, the essential decision that bank must make is whether it will pay or dishonor the check. So far, this is the same process as for any negotiable instrument: whenever a draft is presented to the drawee, or a note presented to the maker, the drawee or maker must decide whether it will pay or dishonor the instrument. ("Accepting" a draft is also an option, but one that occurs only rarely, as explained in Section G of Chapter 4.)

We explored the ways that a payor bank can pay a check in Section E of Chapter 13. As we saw there, a payor bank may pay a check by an affirmative act, such as handing over cash or giving irrevocable credit. UCC § 4-215(a)(1), (2). Most often, however, the payor bank pays a check simply by retaining it without taking action to dishonor it. UCC § 4-215(a)(3). The other alternative is usually to dishonor the check. If the payor bank returns the check before the applicable deadline, the check is "dishonored." UCC § 3-502(b)(1).

(Dishonor is the other alternative "usually," rather than always, because of the provision for rare cases where a bank may be "accountable" for a check that it neither paid nor returned. *See* UCC §§ 4-302(a)(1), 4-302 Official Comments 1 and 2, 3-502(b)(1) (last clause), 3-502 Official Comment 4 (second and third paragraphs); Fred H. Miller & Alvin C. Harrell, The Law of Modern Payment Systems ¶ 8.02[3] (2003). However, this third alternative is for situations that occur infrequently, and are probably best left for later as you seek an initial understanding of the system.)

2. Wrongful Dishonor

As we saw in Section C of Chapter 3 above, the payor bank has no liability to the payee on the check itself, except in the rare instance where the bank signed the check as drawer or acceptor. The payor bank's incentive to pay a check comes from its potential liability to the drawer for *wrongful dishonor* if it dishonors a check that it was obligated to pay. *See* UCC §4-402.

A payor bank should be concerned about wrongful dishonor, because the potential liability is vast. The liability is limited to "actual damages proved," but those actual damages "may include damages for an arrest or prosecution of the customer or other consequential damages." UCC § 4-402(b).

3. UCC Return Mechanism

The UCC rules for returning checks do not impose strict deadlines by which collecting banks must *receive* returned checks. Instead, for many cases the UCC provides only a deadline by which the payor bank or another bank must act to *send* the check on its way. The possibilities of delay in the mail, or a check being returned through multiple banks, prevent a depositary bank from being certain as to how quickly it should receive a dishonored check.

If a clearinghouse is not involved, return is accomplished under the UCC when the check is either "sent or delivered" to the appropriate recipient. UCC § 4-301(d)(2). The definition of "send" indicates that something is "sent" when it is "deposited in the mail." UCC § 1-201(b)(36)(A). Consequently, for non-clearinghouse returns, a check may be effectively returned, and therefore dishonored, when the payor bank deposits the check (in a properly addressed envelope with adequate postage, of course) in the local mailbox. However, the depositary bank may not receive this check for several days, as you probably know from your own experience with the U.S. Mail.

For checks presented through a clearinghouse (a cooperative arrangement where banks get together, exchange the checks drawn on each of them, and settle up the net amounts that they owe each other), return of a check requires that it be "delivered" to the appropriate bank or the clearinghouse "or ... sent or delivered in accordance with clearinghouse rules." UCC § 4-301(d)(1); UCC § 1-201(b)(36). "Delivery" of a negotiable instrument is defined as "voluntary transfer of possession." UCC § 1-201(b)(15). The absence of "sending" here as an option for completing the return of a check suggests a greater focus on the time of receipt by the recipient. However, even here, the UCC rule does not precisely specify the time by which the recipient must *receive* the check. One could argue that delivery is complete when the courier (as agent for the recipient) gets the check, even though the recipient may not actually see the check until later. Even more troublesome, even a fully completed delivery to a clearinghouse or intermediary bank does not get the check to the depositary bank; at least one more step will be required before the depositary bank gets the check. For all these reasons, the Reg. CC rules discussed below have substantially clarified the time frames by which checks must be returned. Consequently, the Reg. CC rules substantially limit the time a depositary bank must wait before concluding that a check has been paid.

4. Payor Bank Return Deadlines and Liability

Generally, a check is dishonored by returning the check (or, if permitted, by sending notice of dishonor) by a deadline specified in UCC Article 4. *See*

UCC §§ 3-502(b)(1), 3-502 Official Comment 4 (first paragraph), 4-301, 4-302. In the normal case, that deadline is the "midnight deadline." UCC §§ 4-215(a)(3), 4-301(a). A bank's "midnight deadline" is "midnight on its next banking day following the banking day on which it receives the relevant item." UCC § 4-104(a)(10). Thus, if a bank wants to dishonor a check that it received on its Wednesday banking day, it must return the check by midnight on Thursday, assuming that the bank is open on both of those days. (To count days correctly for this rule, you also need to remember that a bank may treat a check received late in the day on Wednesday as being received on its *Thursday* banking day. *See* UCC § 4-108.)

In the usual case, the payor bank makes provisional settlement for a check when it is presented by a collecting bank; in that usual case, the check is "finally paid" when the payor bank's midnight deadline for that check passes. UCC §§ 4-215(a)(3), 4-301(a). In order to dishonor the check instead of paying it, the payor bank generally must return the check before the midnight deadline. UCC § 4-301(a)(1), (c).

5. Collecting Bank Return Deadlines and Liability

When a collecting bank (a depositary or intermediary bank, *see* UCC § 4-105) receives a dishonored check for which it has previously given credit, the collecting bank is permitted to get back the credit or money that it gave. UCC § 4-214(a). The collecting bank's responsibility is to return the dishonored check or send notice "by its midnight deadline or a longer reasonable time after it learns the facts." *Id.* Further delay in the return or notice does not take away the collecting bank's right to get back the credit or money that it gave, but the collecting bank "is liable for any loss resulting from the delay." *Id.*

The definition of "return" for collecting banks requires that the item be "sent or delivered." *See* UCC § 4-214(b). Sending or delivery by the midnight deadline meets the collecting bank's obligation to use "ordinary care." *See* UCC § 4-202.

So, as was the case for payor banks, the UCC rule focuses on when the collecting bank must start the dishonored check on the next leg of its journey; the UCC does not specify the time by which the recipient must *receive* the check. If the check were to pass through multiple intermediary banks on its way back to the depositary bank, perhaps retracing the path it took to reach the payor bank initially, the succession of midnight deadlines plus the time in transit could result in a long delay under the UCC system before the check actually arrives at the depositary bank. Consequently, a depositary bank was often anxious for a considerable length of time before gaining confidence that a particular check would not be returned. This potential delay and related uncertainty in the UCC system led to the EFAA and Reg. CC, to which we turn next.

B. EFAA/Reg. CC Rules

1. Overview of Subpart C Expedited Collection and Return Rules

As we saw in Chapter 13, the EFAA and Reg. CC require depositary banks to make funds from deposits available to the depositor much more quickly than the UCC rules do. If the EFAA and Reg. CC simply imposed faster availability times, but left the existing UCC check collection mechanisms and time frames intact, depositary banks might be at risk to suffer losses from uncollectible checks that aren't returned until after the depositor has taken the funds and disappeared. To alleviate this problem, Reg. CC imposes stricter return deadlines and faster procedures than are required by the UCC rules. 12 C.F.R. §§ 229.30–229.43. *See also* 12 U.S.C. § 4008 (b), (c) (authorization for the regulations).

As discussed more fully in Section B of Chapter 13, the Reg. CC terms and definitions have many similarities to those in the UCC, but differ in various ways. Reg. CC contains an extensive set of definitions. *See* 12 C.F.R. § 229.2. Reg. CC also incorporates the UCC definitions for terms that do not have a specific Reg. CC definition. 12 CFR § 229.2 (first sentence). For this discussion, you should particularly note that a "returning bank" in Reg. CC has a special and potentially counterintuitive definition. Neither the paying bank nor the depositary bank is a returning bank. *See* 12 C.F.R. § 229.2(cc). A returning bank corresponds to an "intermediary bank" under Article 4, though "returning bank" is used only for banks handling dishonored checks in the return process. By contrast, an intermediary bank may participate in either the forward collection process or the return process. *See* UCC § 4-105(4).

In contrast to the UCC focus on the deadline for the bank *returning* a check, Reg. CC focuses on making sure the depositary bank promptly *receives* the returned check. It does so first by requiring the paying bank and returning banks to return checks in an "expeditious manner." In addition, Reg. CC imposes a notice requirement on the paying bank for any dishonored check of $2,500.00 or more.

2. Expeditious Return

Reg. CC requires both paying banks and returning banks to return checks "in an expeditious manner." 12 C.F.R. §§ 229.30(a), 229.31(a). A bank may meet this requirement by complying with either the "two-day/four-day test" or the "forward collection test."

a. Two-Day/Four-Day Test

The two-day/four-day test requires that the depositary bank receive the check by the applicable time deadline. This rule and the UCC Article 4 midnight deadline rule (discussed in Section A of this Chapter) differ in important ways.

First, the UCC midnight deadline doesn't set a deadline for getting the check back to the *depositary* bank. See UCC §§ 4-301(d), 4-214(b). Because checks may be presented to the paying/payor bank via intermediary banks, the UCC rule leaves uncertainty as to when the check may actually arrive at the depositary bank. Except for checks presented via a clearinghouse, the UCC only requires that the check be "sent or delivered" by the deadline. UCC §§ 4-301(d), 4-214(b). By contrast, Reg. CC focuses clearly on the depositary bank's *receipt* of the check. 12 C.F.R. §§ 229.30(a)(1), 229.31(a)(1).

Turning our focus back to the Reg. CC rule itself: Reg. CC requires paying and returning banks to "send[] the returned check in a manner such that the check would normally be received by the depositary bank not later than 4:00 p.m." on the two-day or four-day deadline. 12 C.F.R. §§ 229.30(a)(1), 229.31(a)(1). The two-day deadline applies if both banks are in the same Federal Reserve "check processing region." See 12 C.F.R. §§ 229.30(a)(1)(i), 229.31(a)(1)(i). The four-day deadline applies if the banks are in different check processing regions. See 12 C.F.R. §§ 229.30(a)(1)(ii), 229.31(a)(1)(ii). This is the same distinction as the deposit availability rules make between "local checks" and "nonlocal checks," discussed in Subsection B 1 of Chapter 13 above.

For *both* paying banks and returning banks, the two-day deadline runs on "[t]he second business day following the banking day on which the check was presented to the *paying* bank." 12 C.F.R. §§ 229.30(a)(1)(i), 229.31(a)(1)(i) (emphasis added). Similarly, the four-day deadline runs on "[t]he fourth business day following the banking day on which the check was presented to the *paying* bank." 12 C.F.R. §§ 229.30(a)(1)(ii), 229.31(a)(1)(ii) (emphasis added). Counting days accurately for these rules require that you understand the Reg. CC definitions of "business day" and "banking day," which are discussed in Subsection B 1 of Chapter 13 above.

b. Forward Collection Test

Instead of complying with the two-day/four-day test, banks have the option of sending the returned check in the same way that a similar bank would handle a similar check in the forward collection process. 12 C.F.R. §§ 229.30(a)(2), 229.31(a)(2). The theory behind this option is that banks sending checks for forward collection have an economic incentive to act promptly, because the sooner a depositary bank presents a check to the paying bank, the sooner the depositary bank will get usable funds in exchange for that check. As a result of this incentive, banks have developed highly sophisticated methods for collecting checks, and these methods take into account the size of the check; a check for $25.00 doesn't merit heroic measures to collect it in the least possible time, but a bank wants to collect a check for $25,000,000.00 as quickly as it possibly can, because even one day's interest on $25,000,000.00 is a significant amount of money. (A deposit of $25,000,000.00 invested for one day at 5% annual interest would earn $3,424.66 in interest.) The forward collection test relies on this economic incentive to expedite the forward return process. If the bank uses the same method for returning a check as a similar bank would use to present a similar check for forward collection, Reg. CC recognizes that this method reflects a careful analysis of how much effort is warranted to move the check through the system, taking into account the amount of the check.

3. Notice of Nonpayment of $2,500.00+ Checks

In addition to returning the check itself, Reg. CC requires a paying bank dishonoring a large check ($2,500.00 or more) to give "notice of nonpayment such that the notice is received by the depositary bank by 4:00 p.m. (local time) on the second business day following the banking day on which the check was presented to the paying bank." 12 C.F.R. § 229.33(a). Unlike the two-day/four-day test discussed above for returning the check itself, this is *always a two-day rule,* whether the check is local or nonlocal. The purpose of this rule is to make sure that even if the depositary bank and paying bank are a great distance from each other, the depositary bank will get a relatively quick alert if there's a problem with a large check. The faster the depositary bank gets such information, the less likely it is to allow the depositor to get away with the funds from the check that the depositary bank won't be able to get from the payor bank.

4. Special Rule Extending the UCC Deadlines

Reg. CC contains a provision as to deadlines that explicitly overrules the UCC midnight deadline rule. If a paying bank uses an extra-prompt delivery method, *see* 12 C.F.R. § 229.30(c)(1) and (2), the UCC return deadline "is extended to the time of dispatch." 12 C.F.R. § 229.30(c). This gives a payor bank—if it moves quickly enough the morning after it misses the midnight deadline—an opportunity to make an effective return of a check despite having held it beyond the midnight deadline.

5. Reg. CC Liability

Reg. CC sets out a detailed set of rules for imposing liability on banks that fail to comply with its requirements. *See* 12 C.F.R. § 229.38. Similar to the UCC, Reg. CC requires banks to "exercise ordinary care and act in good faith in complying with the requirements [for collecting and returning checks]." 12 C.F.R. § 229.38(a). Ordinary care is not separately defined in Reg. CC, so the UCC definition applies in Reg. CC as well. *See* 12 C.F.R. § 229.2 (first sentence); UCC § 3-103(a)(9). Reg. CC adopts the newer UCC definition of good faith: "...honesty in fact and the observance of reasonable commercial standards of fair dealing." 12 C.F.R. § 229.2(nn). (The evolution of the UCC definition of good faith is discussed in Section D of Chapter 7.)

A bank that fails to exercise ordinary care may be liable for "the amount of the loss incurred, up to the amount of the check, reduced by the amount of the loss that party would have incurred even if the bank had exercised ordinary care." 12 C.F.R. § 229.38(a). Lack of good faith exposes the misbehaving bank to liability "for other damages, if any suffered by the [injured] party as a proximate consequence." *Id.* These liabilities only apply in bank-to-bank situations; liability of banks to their customers is left to "the U.C.C. or other law." *Id.* (last sentence). Reg. CC limits multiple recoveries for a problem with a single check in some circumstances. 12 C.F.R. § 229.38(b). Reg. CC also adopts a comparative negligence regime. 12 C.F.R. § 229.38(c).

A bank that fails to meet the return or notification requirements is also subject to warranty liability. A bank that returns a check warrants that (1) it met the applicable UCC or federal return deadlines; "(2) It is authorized to return the check; (3) The check has not been materially altered; and (4) In the case of a notice in lieu of return, the original check has not been and will not be returned." 12 C.F.R. § 229.34(a). Similarly, a bank that gives the notice of nonpayment required by Reg. CC section 229.33 warrants that (1) it has met or will meet the applicable U.C.C. or federal return deadlines, "(2) It is authorized to send the notice; and (3) The check has not been materially altered." 12 C.F.R. § 229.34(b). Accuracy of settlement amounts and check encoding are also subject to warranties. 12 C.F.R. § 229.34(c). Reg. CC also contains a warranty for "remotely created checks" that corresponds to the UCC transfer and presentment warranty for remotely created consumer items discussed in Section B of Chapter 15. *See* 12 C.F.R. § 229.34(d); UCC §§ 3-416(a)(6), 3-417(a)(4), 4-207(a)(6), 4-208(a)(4).

Warranty-based damages are limited to "the consideration received by the bank that presents or transfers a check or returned check, plus interest compensation and expenses related to the check or returned check, if any." 12 C.F.R. § 229.34(e). A warranty claimant must give notice of the claim within 30 days of learning the pertinent facts, or the claim may be discharged. 12 C.F.R. § 229.34(g).

C. Check 21

1. Overview

In 2003 Congress passed the "Check Clearing for the 21st Century Act," often referred to as "Check 21," codified at 12 U.S.C.A. §§ 5001–5018. Check 21 is designed to facilitate "check truncation," and reduce the check processing system's reliance on physical transfer of the paper checks themselves.

Traditionally, check processing has involved physically moving the actual paper check to each location where processing takes place. The advent of reliable and secure mechanisms for transmitting data electronically has raised awareness of the effort, energy, and expense devoted to shipping paper checks from place to place.

Check truncation allows the information captured from the check to be transmitted electronically from bank to bank in the check collection process, to the paper check doesn't have to travel. This allows check collection to move faster, at lower cost. The original paper check is typically retained by the bank that converted it into an electronic image, then destroyed when it is no longer needed.

You have probably experienced at least a limited form of check truncation with your own checking account. Until just a few years ago, most of us expected our bank to send our actual paper cancelled checks to us with our account statement each month. Even without the Check 21 Act, banks have increasingly sent electronic images of cancelled checks with depositors' monthly statements, in place of the actual cancelled checks. The payor bank can do this simply by agreement with its customer, the drawer of the checks on the account. That does save the postage and other costs of delivering the checks from the payor bank to the drawer/account holder. However, it realizes only a portion of the potential benefits from check truncation, because the paper check still has to make its way from the depositary bank to the payor bank, often via one or more intermediary banks. Additional savings and efficiencies are possible from stopping the paper check's travels earlier when it reaches the *depositary* bank. That requires a much more elaborate set of arrangements than just the agreement between the payor bank and that bank's customer. That's where Check 21 comes in. Even after Check 21, check truncation is optional, not mandatory. However, for banks that want to send checks electronically instead of by snail-mail, Check 21 provides a useful mechanism.

Check 21 authorizes the Federal Reserve Board of Governors to issue implementing regulations. 12 U.S.C.A. § 5014. Those regulations have been added to Reg. CC, mostly in a new Subpart D. *See* 12 C.F.R. §§ 229.51–229.60.

2. Definitions

Many of the terms used in Check 21 will be familiar to you from study of the UCC and Reg. CC, though it's always a good idea to look at the definition of even familiar terms, to make sure the definition is as familiar as you expect. *See* 12 C.F.R. § 5002. Check 21 also defines some new terms, like "indemnifying bank," "reconverting bank," "substitute check," and "truncate." *See* 12 U.S.C.A. § 5002(11), (15), (16), (18). You'll probably find it easiest to understand these terms as you consider the concepts to which they relate, discussed below (and above, for "truncate"). As with the already-familiar terms, you'll want to refer back to the definitions as you go along.

3. Substitute Checks

Perhaps the central event in the Check 21 Act framework is the creation of a substitute check. That term means:

a paper reproduction of the original check that—
(A) contains an image of the front and back of the original check;
(B) bears a MICR line containing all the information appearing on the MICR line of the original check, except as provided under generally applicable industry standards for substitute checks to facilitate the processing of substitute checks;

(C) conforms, in paper stock, dimension, and otherwise, with generally applicable industry standards for substitute checks; and

(D) is suitable for automated processing in the same manner as the original check.

12 U.S.C.A. § 5002(16).

More importantly, Check 21 declares that "A substitute check shall be the legal equivalent of the original check for all purposes ... and for all persons if the substitute check ... accurately represents all of the information on the front and back of the original check as of the time the original check was truncated;" and bears a specified legend. 12 U.S.C.A. § 5003(b). The bank that creates a substitute check is called the "reconverting bank." 12 U.S.C.A. § 5002(15).

4. Warranties and Indemnity

Whenever a bank "transfers, presents, or returns a substitute check and receives consideration for the check," that bank gives various automatic warranties to essentially anyone and everyone involved with the check. 12 U.S.C.A. § 5004. The warranties are given to anyone likely to be concerned about the use of a substitute check in place of the original check. *Id.* The substitute check is warranted to meet all its requirements under Check 21. 12 U.S.C.A. § 5004(1). The recipients of the warranties also get assurance that they won't have to pay twice (or more) if the original check or a duplicate substitute check shows up after a substitute check has been paid. 12 U.S.C.A. § 5004(2).

All the numerous recipients of the warranties also get an indemnity from all the warrantors and from the reconverting bank. 12 U.S.C.A. § 5005(a). Each of those banks giving the indemnity is an "indemnifying bank." 12 U.S.C.A. § 5002(11). This indemnity protects against "any loss incurred by any recipient of a substitute check if the loss occurred due to the receipt of a substitute check instead of the original check." 12 U.S.C.A. § 5005(a). If there was *no* breach of warranty, the indemnity is limited to the amount of the substitute check plus "interest and expenses (including costs and reasonable attorney's fees and other expenses of representation)." 12 U.S.C.A. § 5005(b)(2)(A) and (B). If there *was* a breach of warranty, the indemnity covers "the amount of ... loss (including costs and reasonable attorney's fees and other expenses of representation) proximately caused by [the] breach...." 12 U.S.C.A. § 5005(b)(1).

If someone suffers a loss from a breach of warranty in connection with a substitute check, but does not qualify for the indemnity provided in section 5005, a more limited alternative remedy is available for the breach of warranty. The amount of this alternative remedy is similar to the amount of the indemnity in the *absence* of a breach of warranty. *See* 12 U.S.C.A §§ 5009(a)(1), 5005(a)(2).

An indemnifying bank may be able to limit its liability in various ways. If the party claiming the indemnity was negligent, the indemnification may be limited using principles of comparative negligence. 12 U.S.C.A. § 5005(c). Producing the original check or a sufficient copy of the check can also cut off an indemnifying bank's liability. 12 U.S.C.A. § 5005(d). An indemnifying bank that has to make good on an indemnity is entitled to subrogation rights and the cooperation of the indemnified parties. 12 U.S.C.A. § 5005(e).

5. Expedited Recredit

a. Consumer Claims for Recredit

If a consumer claims a loss because a substitute check was not sufficient to determine the validity of a related charge to the consumer's account, the consumer "may make a claim for expedited recredit from the bank that holds the account of the consumer...." 12 U.S.C.A. § 5006(a)(1). The consumer generally may submit the claim for expedited recredit within 40 days from the later of the date the statement was mailed or "the date on which the substitute check [was] made available to the consumer." 12 U.S.C.A. § 5006(a)(2). This 40-day limit may be extended if the consumer shows extenuating circumstances. 12 U.S.C.A. § 5006(a)(3).

If the bank determines that the consumer's claim is valid, the bank must recredit the consumer's account by the next business day. 12 U.S.C.A. § 5006(c)(2)(A). If the 10 business days pass without a determination by the bank, the bank is obligated to recredit the first $2,500.00 of the amount of the substitute check (plus interest if the account earns interest). 12 U.S.C.A. § 5006(c)(2)(B)(i). If the bank still has not made its determination after 45 days, the bank must recredit the remaining amount of the substitute check, if any (plus interest if the account earns interest). 12 U.S.C.A. § 5006(c)(2)(B)(ii). The bank may delay the recredit if the account is new, or has had repeated overdrafts, or if the bank otherwise reasonably believes that the claim is fraudulent. 12 U.S.C.A. § 5006(d)(2). However, the bank is limited in its ability to charge overdraft fees on amounts for which recredit is delayed. 12 U.S.C.A. § 5006(d)(3).

The bank must give the consumer prompt notice of any action or determination. 12 U.S.C.A. § 5006(f).

b. Bank Claims for Recredit

A bank that receives a consumer's claim for expedited recredit gets a corresponding right to claim expedited recredit from an indemnifying bank. *See* 12

U.S.C.A. § 5007(a)(1). The bank making the claim has 120 days from the date of the relevant transaction to make the claim. 12 U.S.C.A. § 5007(a)(2). The indemnifying bank must take specified actions designed to resolve the matter (including a recredit, if appropriate) within ten business days after receiving the claim. 12 U.S.C.A. § 5007 (c) and (d).

Checkpoints

- Only the payor bank may pay or dishonor a check.

- The UCC rules do not specify the time by which a depositary bank must receive a dishonored check, which led to long periods of uncertainty before a depositary bank could be confident that a check had been paid.

- Reg. CC tightens the deadlines for availability of funds deposited, and mandates corresponding acceleration of the check return process.

- Check 21 facilitates check truncation by establishing a framework for creating and dealing with substitute checks.

- The UCC, Reg. CC, and Check 21 impose separate and distinct liability regimes.

Chapter 15

Fundamental Loss
Allocation under the UCC

Roadmap

- Liability on an instrument
  - Drawer
  - Indorser
- Transfer warranties
- Presentment warranties
- *Price v. Neal*
- Forgeries
  - Forged drawer's signature
  - Forged indorsement
- Alterations
- Remotely created consumer items

When there's a problem with a check, the simplest way for the banking system to deal with it is the dishonor and return mechanism discussed above in Chapter 14. As long as all the banks involved meet the applicable deadlines, returning the check and revoking the provisional settlements is simple and straightforward (at least by comparison with the other alternatives).

This Chapter describes mechanisms beyond dishonor and return. The mechanisms in this Chapter are often more cumbersome than dishonor and return. However, a bank that has missed the deadline for dishonor will be very interested in these alternatives. So will many other parties to check transactions who don't have the dishonor option.

As we saw in Chapters 12, 13, and 14, federal law now encroaches on some aspects of the UCC system, though the extent of that encroachment can be uncertain in particular cases. Here again, as discussed in Section B of Chap-

147

ter 12, the safe assumption by a bank or anyone else planning their transactions is that compliance with all the requirements will be required separately, with independent liability for failure to comply with any piece. For these reasons, it's useful to understand the UCC system first, and only then focus on the alternative mechanisms in federal law. Therefore, this chapter focuses on the UCC system. If you're litigating an already-complete set of facts, you'll need to do extensive and detailed research to determine the extent to which the UCC rules may be preempted, but you'll need to understand the UCC rules first.

A. Drawer and Indorser Liability

One liability mechanism you're already familiar with is the liability that arises when someone signs a check. As we saw in Chapter 8, someone who signs a negotiable instrument takes on liability depending on the nature of the signature.

If you sign a check as "drawer" (i.e., the person ordering your bank to make payment) and the draft is dishonored, you are obligated to pay the amount of the check to a holder, anyone else who qualifies as a person entitled to enforce the check, or to an indorser who had to pay because of indorser liability. UCC §§ 3-414(b), 3-301. An indorser's obligation is generally similar to a drawer's. *See* UCC § 3-415(a).

However, the ability to recover on drawer or indorser liability is subject to significant limitations. Probably the most significant limitation is that the drawer and indorsers are only liable if the check is dishonored. UCC §§ 3-414(b); 3-415(a). Therefore, if the payor bank paid the check and only found out about the problem later — usually after sending the drawer a monthly account statement showing that the check was paid — it will be too late for anyone to use drawer or indorser liability to shift the loss.

Another limitation of drawer and indorser liability is that only a person entitled to enforce the check (usually a holder, *see* UCC § 3-301(i)) can assert the liability. UCC §§ 3-414, 3-415. If the problem with the check is a missing or forged indorsement that's essential to make the check payable to the person currently in possession, that person cannot use drawer or indorser liability to shift the loss. An example of this scenario appears in Section C of this Chapter.

B. Transfer and Presentment Warranties

Presenting a check to the payor bank, and transferring a check (or any other negotiable instrument) in exchange for consideration, create implied warranties that can be a basis for shifting liability if there is a problem. The transfer warranties appear in UCC sections 3-416 and 4-207. The presentment warranties appear in UCC sections 3-417 and 4-208.

1. Comparing the Article 3 and Article 4 Versions of the Warranties

Other than terminology, the UCC Article 3 and Article 4 versions of the transfer warranties are essentially identical, except for minor differences between sections 3-416 and 4-207 as to whether an indorsement is required for the warranty to apply. *See* UCC §§ 3-416(a), 4-207(a); UCC § 4-207 Official Comment 1. Similarly, the Article 3 and 4 versions of the presentment warranties are essentially identical. *See* UCC §§ 3-417(a), 4-208(a); UCC § 4-208 Official Comment 1.

You might someday litigate a dispute for which the subtle differences between the Article 3 and Article 4 versions of the warranties might matter; in such a case, you will need to carefully compare each word in the Article 3 and 4 versions side-by-side and consider the possible impact of any difference in excruciating detail. However, for purposes of planning transactions, and for the purpose of understanding how these warranties work, it's best to treat the Article 3 and Article 4 versions of the warranties as saying the same thing. There's plenty here to occupy your mind without worrying about the very detailed (and usually unimportant) differences between the Article 3 and Article 4 versions

2. Differences between the Transfer Warranties and the Presentment Warranties

Subsection 3 below will discuss the warranties that are the same for both transfer and presentment. First, however, we focus on some differences between the transfer warranties and the presentment warranties that you need to understand, because you're undoubtedly eager to get into the ancient case of *Price v. Neal.* 3 Burr. 1354 (1762).

a. Who Gets Which Warranties

First, the easy difference between the transfer and presentment warranties: the drawee (payor bank) gets the presentment warranties. UCC §§ 3-417(a),

4-208(a). Transferees (collecting banks and their customers) get the transfer warranties. UCC §§ 3-416(a), 4-207(a). Therefore, in considering whether a warranty is available, you first need to analyze whether the party claiming the warranty is the drawee (or payor bank) of the draft, or a transferee (collecting bank or collecting bank's customer).

b. Effect of a Forged Drawer's Signature

Probably the key difference between the transfer warranties and the presentment warranties is the effect of a forged drawer's signature. A drawee or payor bank that pays a check with a forged drawer's signature has no claim for breach of the presentment warranty. By contrast, a *transferee* that suffers a loss as the result of a forged drawer's signature *can* claim a breach of the transfer warranty and thereby shift the loss elsewhere (assuming that a solvent defendant can be found). This rule is relatively easy to state, though a little harder to find in the statutory language and understand.

To see the distinction in the statute, you need to compare UCC section 3-416(a)(2) (or 4-207(a)(2)) with section 3-417(a)(3) (or 4-208(a)(3)). A transferee gets a warranty that "all signatures on the [instrument or item] are authentic and authorized." UCC §§ 3-416(a)(2), 4-207(a)(2). That warranty is not included in the presentment warranties; the corresponding presentment warranty is that "the warrantor has no knowledge that the signature of the [purported] drawer of the draft is unauthorized." UCC § 3-417(a)(3), 4-208(a)(3). In other words, a transferee gets a warranty that all the signatures, including the drawer's signature, are valid. The drawee or payor bank doesn't get that warranty, and can only recover for breach of the presentment warranty in the relatively rare case where the person giving the warranty actually knew about the forgery of the drawer's signature. (As we'll see in Subsection 3 below, the validity of indorsers' signatures is covered by a different warranty.)

The origin of the different warranties given to drawees (payor banks) and transferees with respect to the drawer's signature is the ancient case of *Price v. Neal*. 3 Burr. 1354 (1762). *See* UCC § 3-417 Official Comment 3. The current rule is based on the principle, distilled from *Price v. Neal*, that the drawee or payor bank is in a better position than transferees to know whether the drawer's signature is genuine or not. The drawee will typically have a relationship with the drawer of a draft, and therefore the opportunity to verify the drawer's signature. Transferees, on the other hand, may never deal directly with the drawer. This rationale does not entirely withstand detailed scrutiny around the edges. *See* James J. White & Robert S. Summers, Uniform Commercial Code § 17-2 at 614-15 (5th ed. 2000). However, students and lawyers often find it a useful way to understand and justify the more-limited warranty given to drawees.

c. No Defense, Claim in Recoupment, or Insolvency Proceeding

Two other warranties are given to transferees, but not to payor banks or drawees. The transfer warranties, but not the presentment warranties, include warranties that no applicable defense or claim in recoupment affects enforcement of the instrument or item. UCC §§ 3-416(a)(4), 4-207(a)(4). Similarly, only the transferor, and not the presenter, warrants that he, she, or it does not know of any "insolvency proceeding" (e.g., bankruptcy) affecting the liability of any obligor. UCC §§ 3-416(a)(5), 4-207(a)(5). The rationale for leaving these out of the presentment warranties is not clearly expressed. However, one might infer from the Official Comments that these warranties are designed to protect intermediate purchasers of instruments—perhaps notes, in particular—against problems that are peculiar to that type of transaction. *See* UCC § 3-416 Official Comments 3 and 4.

3. Warranties Given for Both Transfer and Presentment

There is no difference between the transfer and presentment warranties for three of the issues that are warranted. Both sets of warranties include assurances that:

- The transferor or presenter appropriately is or was a person entitled to enforce the instrument or item. UCC §§ 3-416(a)(1), 3-417(a)(1), 4-207(a)(1), 4-208(a)(1).
- No alteration affects enforcement of the instrument or item. UCC §§ 3-416(a)(3), 3-417(a)(2), 4-207(a)(3), 4-208(a)(2).
- If the item transferred was a "remotely-created consumer item" (e.g., a telephone check that isn't manually signed by the drawer because it was authorized over the telephone, *see* UCC § 3-103(a)(16)), it was appropriately authorized. UCC §§ 3-416(a)(6), 3-417(a)(4), 4-207(a)(6), 4-208(a)(4).

Each of these warranties is discussed in turn below.

a. Person Entitled to Enforce

Both the transfer and presentment warranties include a warranty that the warrantor is or appropriately was a person entitled to enforce the check. UCC

§§ 3-416(a)(1), 3-417(a)(1), 4-207(a)(1), 4-208(a)(1). As we saw in Chapter 6, the typical way to be a person entitled to enforce a check or other negotiable instrument is to be a holder.

In essence, this warranty is a warranty that all the indorsements are present and valid that were necessary to negotiate the check effectively. Forged or missing indorsements often occur in cases where a check has been stolen and the thief tries to negotiate it. As we saw in Chapters 6 and 7, if a check is payable to a particular person, only that person can be a holder until the check is indorsed. If a necessary indorsement is missing or forged, there was no effective negotiation past that point; the only person who can be a holder of the check is the person whose necessary indorsement is missing or forged. Moreover, as we saw in Chapter 12, a check is not properly payable if it lacks a necessary indorsement. Therefore, the payor bank will not be able to charge such a check against the drawer's account. This warranty provides a mechanism for shifting the loss back to the thief or other person who created the problem, if he or she can be found, or to the person who dealt most closely with the original wrongdoer.

The presentment warranty on this subject (UCC §§ 3-417(a)(1), 4-208(a)(1)) is stated in more complex terms than the corresponding transfer warranty (UCC §§ 3-416(a)(1), 4-207(a)(1)). This is because the presentment warranty only becomes a basis for liability when the check is actually presented to the drawee or payor bank, but the warranty is given at the time of transfer, which may occur long before presentment. By the time of presentment, one or more transferors may no longer be a person entitled to enforce the check, either because they no longer have possession of the check or because it has been specially indorsed and thereby made payable to someone else. However, as long as each transferor was a holder of the check at the time of that transfer, his, her, or its indorsement was effective to negotiate the instrument to the transferee (or unnecessary if the instrument was then a bearer instrument).

b. No Alteration

The transfer and presentment warranties also both include a warranty that the check has not been altered. UCC §§ 3-416(a)(3), 3-417(a)(2), 4-207(a)(3), 4-208(a)(2). When a check is altered, the drawee or payor bank is only permitted to charge the drawer's account for the original amount of the check (except in the unusual case where the drawer facilitated the alteration by leaving a space blank.) UCC § 3-407(b), (c). If a payor bank pays an altered check as altered, the difference resulting from the alteration is a potential loss to the payor bank. The presentment warranty of no alteration enables the payor bank to shift the loss from an alteration back to the person who presented the check. That person and other transferees can then use the corresponding transfer warranty to shift the loss back to the person who altered the check, if he or she can be found, or to the person who dealt most closely with the original wrongdoer.

An example involving a typical alteration scenario appears at the end of this Chapter, for comparison to the forgery scenarios. Further consideration of alterations appears in Section A of Chapter 16.

c. Special Warranty for Remotely Created Consumer Items

Until recent years, transactions in checks and other negotiable instruments were paper-only transactions. A check could only be issued if the drawer (or an authorized agent of the drawer) wrote on a piece of paper, and all checks were collected entirely by moving the actual paper check itself from one place to another. The vast majority of check transactions still occur by moving paper. However, electronic alternatives to payment by check are increasing in importance, as discussed in Part Three of this book, and electronic mechanisms are starting to move into the check-collection world, as discussed in Section C of Chapter 14.

Yet another innovation now permits a consumer to authorize someone—over the telephone or over the Internet—to issue a "remotely-created consumer item" which functions as a check drawn on the consumer's account. These quasi-checks are sometimes referred to as "telephonically generated checks" or simply "telephone checks."

The 2002 amendments to UCC Articles 3 and 4 added the definition of a remotely-created consumer item in section 3-103(a)(16), and added the related special transfer and presentment warranty provisions in sections 3-416(a)(6), 3-417(a)(4), 4-207(a)(6), and 4-208(a)(4). The effect of these warranties is to shift the loss for an unauthorized telephone check to the *depositary* bank, instead of leaving it with the payor bank as is typical for forged drawer's signatures on regular written checks. This rule represents a limited repudiation of the rule of *Price v. Neal*, discussed above. *See* UCC § 3-416 Official Comment 8. This departure from the ancient policy is justified because the purported drawer's signature is not put on by the drawer, so the payor bank has no advantage in determining whether the drawer's signature is valid or authorized. Because the depositary bank typically deals with the person who puts the drawer's signature on a telephone check, the depositary bank is probably in the best position to evaluate the reliability of the purported drawer's signature.

Of course, you could authorize someone over the telephone to sign your name to a check drawn on your account. That signature would be treated as your signature. UCC §§ 3-401(a)(ii), 3-402. Assuming that this check met all the requirements discussed in Chapters 3 and 5 of this book, it would be simply a check governed by the usual rules for checks in Articles 3 and 4, including *Price v. Neal*. This check manually signed by your telephonically-authorized agent would *not* be a remotely-created consumer item, because it would have "a handwritten signature purporting to be the signature of the drawer." *See* UCC § 3-103(a)(16).

The UCC definition of "remotely-created consumer item" indirectly acknowledges that these payment mechanisms may be valid and governed under UCC rules without the written signature usually required under Article 3. *See* UCC § 3-103(a)(16) (such an item "does not bear a handwritten signature purporting to be the signature of the drawer"). However, these are "items," not "instruments," so they aren't subject to the requirement that a negotiable instrument (i.e., a "promise or order") be "written." *See* UCC §§ 3-104(a), 3-103(a)(8), (10), 4-104(a)(9), 3-104(c). This creates dissonance in the UCC Article 3 versions of these rules, thereby perhaps making application of the rule uncertain.

A remotely-created consumer item cannot be a draft or other negotiable instrument. Therefore, it's not clear how the initial language of UCC subsections 3-416(a) and 3-417(a), which clearly apply the warranties to transfer of an "instrument" and presentment of a "draft," respectively, should apply in paragraphs 3-416(a)(6) and 3-417(a)(4) to items that are defined so that they are clearly not negotiable instruments. The same problem doesn't occur in the parallel Article 4 provisions, because subsection 4-207(a) refers to "items," and the broader Article 4 definition of a "draft" in section 4-104(a)(7) causes the subsection 4-208(a) reference to a "draft" to include an "item." If a case involving a remotely-created consumer item arises in which the Article 3 warranties apply, but not the Article 4 warranties, the court may have to decide whether to expand the Article 3 version of the warranties beyond their precise terms by analogy.

4. General Effects of a Breach of Warranty

When there's a problem with a check, the transfer and presentment warranties give the person who initially suffers the loss the opportunity to shift it to someone with greater culpability (at least in theory). Of course, there are other loss-shifting mechanisms that may be simpler to use in particularly circumstances. For example, if the payor bank recognizes a problem with a check quickly enough, the payor bank can dishonor the check and return it under the mechanisms discussed in Chapter 14, without having to use the transfer and presentment warranties. However, often a problem will not be apparent until after a check is paid and included on a bank statement sent to the drawer (or purported drawer) at the end of the month. In those cases, transfer and presentment warranties may be the best opportunity for shifting the loss, because the banks won't learn of the problem until long after the deadlines for returning the check have passed. (Also, neither drawer nor indorser liability will be an option for loss-shifting in these typical cases, because imposing liability on drawers and indorsers as such only works if the check was dishonored. *See* UCC §§ 3-414(b), 3-415(a).)

If a presentment warranty is breached, the payor bank can obtain damages for the loss from anyone who presented or transferred the check. UCC §§ 3-417(b), 4-208(b). This shifts the loss to one of the persons who participated in transferring and ultimately presenting the check to the payor bank or drawee. That person can then use a transfer warranty to shift the loss to his, her, or its transferor. UCC §§ 3-416(b), 4-207(c). Each person to whom the loss is thereby shifted can use those same transfer warranty provisions (or the additional warranties provided to transferors but not to payor banks or drawees) to shift the loss back to his, her, or its transferor, until the loss reaches someone who either cannot claim a breach of warranty or cannot find the person who transferred the check to them.

The analysis is similar in a case where a collecting bank or other transferee rather than the payor bank or drawee suffers the loss. The person that initially suffers the loss can use the breach of transfer warranty to shift the loss to a transferor; that person in turn can use the breach of transfer warranty to another transferor, and so forth.

A breach of a presentment warranty will also give rise to a breach of a transfer warranty. In addition, because the transfer warranties include things that aren't warranted under the presentment warranties (i.e., forged drawer's signature, defense or claim in recoupment, and knowledge of insolvency proceedings, as discussed above), transferees have the potential to claim breaches of warranty that aren't available to the payor bank. The most significant of these is forged drawer's signatures, as discussed above.

C. Examples

1. Forged Drawer's Signature

A forged drawer's signature breaches the *transfer* warranties. UCC §§ 3-416(a)(2), 4-207(a)(2). However, a forged drawer's signature only breaches the *presentment* warranty given by someone who actually knew of the forgery. UCC §§ 3-417(a)(3), 4-208(a)(3). Consequently, a forged drawer's signature does not give the payor bank the opportunity to shift the loss if it pays the check.

In the unusual case where the payor bank knows about the forgery and dishonors the check before making final payment (*see infra* Chapter 14), any collecting bank or other transferee of the check to which the loss is shifted can use the breach of the transfer warranty to shift the loss to their transferor. However, those cases are relatively rare.

Suppose Thomas steals one of Dorothy's checks, forges Dorothy's signature as drawer on that check, and makes the check payable to the order of himself. Suppose Thomas then indorses the check by signing his name on the back, and cashes it at a local retail store. The store then deposits the check in its account at Cooperative Bank, which presents the check to Paramount Bank, where Dorothy has her checking account.

Thomas' forgery of Dorothy's signature is not effective as Dorothy's signature. UCC § 3-403(a). However, Thomas' forgery *is* treated as Thomas' signature as drawer of the check. *Id.*

Transfer warranties are given (1) by Thomas to the retail store and Cooperative Bank, and (2) by the retail store to Cooperative Bank. UCC §§ 3-416(a), 4-207(a). Presentment warranties are given to Paramount Bank by Thomas, the retail store, and Cooperative Bank. UCC §§ 3-417(a), 4-208(a).

Thomas' forgery of Dorothy's signature as drawer breaches the *transfer* warranties given by each of the transferors (Thomas and Cooperative Bank). UCC §§ 3-416(a)(2), 4-207(a)(2). However, assuming the usual case that no one else knew that the drawer's signature was forged, *only Thomas* breaches the *presentment* warranty. UCC §§ 3-417(a)(3), 4-208(a)(3).

If Paramount Bank doesn't recognize the forgery and Dorothy doesn't alert Paramount Bank to the theft of her check, Paramount Bank will probably pay the check when it is presented. However, Paramount will not be able to charge the check against Dorothy's account, because the forged drawer's signature prevents the check from being properly payable, as discussed in Section F of Chapter 12. Typically, Paramount Bank will charge the check to Dorothy's account, then recredit her account for the amount of the check when Dorothy sees the charge on her statement and objects to it due to the forgery. In this scenario, Paramount will be able to shift the loss *to Thomas* using the presentment warranty, because Thomas knew about the forgery and therefore breached the presentment warranty he gave to Paramount when he transferred the check. UCC §§ 3-417(b), 4-208(b). However, Paramount will *not* be able to use a presentment or transfer warranty to shift the loss to anyone *except* Thomas. Paramount, as payor bank, does not get the transfer warranties. No one but Thomas breaches the presentment warranty in the usual case where only Thomas knew that the drawer's signature on the check was forged. Typically, Thomas will either be gone or judgment-proof.

Alternatively, if Paramount Bank recognizes the forgery before making final payment (perhaps because they check the signature, or perhaps because Dorothy alerted Paramount of the theft), Paramount could dishonor and return the check using the mechanisms discussed in Chapter 14 of this book. Cooperative Bank will then be able to shift the loss to the retail store by charging the check against the retail store's account. Cooperative Bank would be able to recover from the retail store (or from Thomas, if he and his assets can be found) using the transfer warranty. UCC §§ 3-416(b), 4-207(c). If the retail store has to make good on the loss, it can pursue Thomas on his breach of the transfer warranty (though again, it may be difficult to find Thomas or any available assets of his). One of the specialized loss-shifting mechanisms discussed in Chapter 16 might also be available to Paramount Bank, Cooperative Bank, or the retail store if the necessary additional facts are present.

If Paramount Bank pays the check, neither Cooperative Bank nor the retail store will be liable on their indorsement, nor will Thomas be liable as drawer, because indorser and drawer liability only arise if a check is dishonored. UCC §§ 3-414(b), 3-415(a). (Dorothy is not liable as drawer because she never signed the check. UCC § 3-401(a).) However, if Paramount Bank dishonors the check, indorser and drawer liability will be an alternative basis for shifting liability.

To summarize: the payor bank will be able to avoid the loss from a forged drawer's signature in the unusual case where the payor bank recognizes the forgery before making final payment, or where one of the specialized loss-shifting mechanisms discussed in Chapter 16 is available. However, the payor bank will bear the loss from a forged drawer's signature in the typical case where the payor bank pays the check without realizing that the drawer's signature was forged.

2. Forged Indorsement

A forged indorsement breaches the transfer warranty that all the signatures are valid. UCC §§ 3-416(a)(2), 4-207(a)(2). More importantly, though, forgery of an indorsement that was necessary for the effective negotiation of the check will breach the transfer and presentment warranty that the transferors and presenters appropriately are or were persons entitled to enforce the check. UCC §§ 3-416(a)(1), 3-417(a)(1), 4-207(a)(1), 4-208(a)(1). The forged indorsement is not effective to change the person to whom the check is payable; consequently, no one else can be a holder of that check and thereby a person entitled to enforce.

Suppose Tina steals a check, payable to the order of Peter, before Peter receives it. (If Tina steals the check *after* Peter receives it, Peter will be interested in the conversion remedy discussed in Section F of Chapter 16.) The check is drawn on Dan's account at Paramount Bank. Suppose Tina then forges Peter's signature as indorser on the back of the check, and cashes it at a local retail store. The retail store deposits the check into its account at Cooperative Bank.

Tina's forgery of Peter's signature is not effective as Peter's indorsement. UCC § 3-403(a). However, Tina's forgery *is* treated as Tina's indorsement of the check. *Id.*

Transfer warranties are given (1) by Tina to the retail store and Cooperative Bank, and (2) by the retail store to Cooperative Bank. UCC §§ 3-416(a), 4-207(a). Presentment warranties are given to Paramount Bank by Tina, the retail store, and Cooperative Bank. UCC §§ 3-417(a), 4-208(a).

In the typical case, Paramount Bank will pay the check, charge it against Dan's account, and include the check (or an electronic image of it) with Dan's bank statement at the end of the month; no one except Tina will realize that the indorsement is a forgery until much later, when Peter complains to Dan that Dan hasn't paid Peter. Dan will produce the cancelled check or electronic image, and Dan and Peter will together figure out that Peter's indorsement was forged. Because the check was not properly payable due to the forged indorsement (*see* Section F of Chapter 12), Dan can demand that Paramount Bank recredit his account for the amount of the check. By this time, it will be too late for any bank to use the dishonor and return mechanisms discussed in Chapter 14. Also, drawer and indorser liability will not be available, because they only arise when a check is dishonored. UCC §§ 3-414(b), 3-415(a).

Tina's forgery of Peter's indorsement causes breaches of both the transfer and presentment warranties. UCC §§ 3-416(a)(1) and (2), 3-417(a)(1), 4-207(a)(1) and (2), 4-208(a)(1). Peter remains the person to whom the check is payable. Therefore, only Peter can be a holder. UCC § 1-201(b)(21)(A). None of the other specialized facts is present that would make Peter a person entitled to enforce the check by any means other than being a holder. UCC § 3-301(ii) and (iii).

Paramount Bank can shift the loss to Cooperative Bank, the retail store, or Tina using the presentment warranty. Cooperative Bank, the retail store, and Tina all breached the presentment warranty, because none of them was a person entitled to enforce the check. UCC §§ 3-417(a)(1), 4-208(a)(1). If the loss is shifted to Cooperative Bank, it can shift the loss to the retail store or to Tina, using the corresponding transfer warranty, or the warranty that all signatures are valid. UCC §§ 3-416(a)(1), (2), 4-207(a)(1), (2). If the retail store has to make good on the loss to Cooperative Bank or Paramount Bank, the retail store can pursue Tina using the transfer warranty. *Id.* However, Tina will typically have disappeared or be judgment-proof.

If the check was paid, as in the typical case, neither the drawer nor any indorser will have drawer or indorser liability, because such liability only arises if a check is dishonored. UCC §§ 3-414(b), 3-415(a). Moreover, even in the unusual case where the check was dishonored, no one will be able to enforce either drawer or indorser liability, because neither Cooperative Bank, the retail store, nor Tina can be a person entitled to enforce the check without Peter's valid indorsement. *Id.* One of the specialized loss-shifting mechanisms discussed in Chapter 16 might also be available to Paramount Bank, Cooperative Bank, or the retail store if the necessary additional facts are present.

To summarize: the transfer and presentment warranties allow the loss from a forged indorsement to be shifted to the forger, or to the person who dealt most closely with the wrongdoer in cases where the actual wrongdoer cannot be found or is judgment-proof. (However, as we will see, the specialized loss shifting mechanisms discussed in Chapter 16 may change this result, by treating the indorsement as valid if the appropriate circumstances are present.)

3. Alteration

An example of a typical alteration scenario is included here to illustrate the similarities to the forgery analysis. Alterations are considered more fully in Section A of Chapter 16.

An alteration of a check breaches both the transfer and presentment warranties. UCC §§ 3-416(a)(3), 3-417(a)(2), 4-207(a)(3), 4-208(a)(2). The analysis is somewhat similar to that for a forged indorsement, except that the check remains properly payable as originally written. UCC § 3-407(b) and (c). Consequently, the payor bank will be permitted to charge the check against the drawer's account to the same extent as if it had not been altered, and recoveries for breach of the transfer and presentment warranties will be limited to the loss from the alteration.

Suppose David draws a check on his account at Paramount Bank, payable to the order of Pam. David fills in the amount of the check as $50.00, but Pam skillfully changes the amount to $500.00. Suppose Pam then signs her name on the back of the check as indorser, and cashes the check at a local retail store. The retail store then deposits the check into its account at Cooperative Bank, which presents the check to Paramount Bank.

Transfer warranties are given (1) by Pam to the retail store and Cooperative Bank, and (2) by the retail store to Cooperative Bank. UCC §§ 3-416(a), 4-207(a). Presentment warranties are given to Paramount Bank by Pam, the retail store, and Cooperative Bank. UCC §§ 3-417(a), 4-208(a).

In the typical case, Paramount Bank will pay the check as altered, charge it against David's account, and include the check (or an electronic image of it) with David's bank statement at the end of the month. No one except Pam will know of the alteration until David compares the amount shown for the check on his bank statement with the amount he wrote in his check register.

The check remains properly payable for the original $50.00, so Paramount Bank is permitted to deduct that amount from David's account. UCC § 3-407(b) and (c)(i). However, Paramount Bank was not authorized to charge David's account for the additional $450.00 resulting from the alteration, and Paramount will have to recredit David's account for that $450.00.

Pam's alteration causes breaches of both the transfer and presentment warranties. UCC §§ 3-416(a)(3), 3-417(a)(2), 4-207(a)(3), 4-208(a)(2). Liability on the check is assessed as if the alteration had not been made. UCC § 3-407(b) and (c)(i). One of the specialized loss-shifting mechanisms discussed in Chapter 16 might also be available to Paramount Bank, Cooperative Bank, or the retail store if the necessary additional facts are present.

Paramount Bank can shift the loss to Cooperative Bank, the retail store, or Pam using the presentment warranty. Cooperative Bank, the retail store, and Pam all breached the presentment warranty, because the check was altered. UCC §§ 3-417(a)(2), 4-208(a)(2). If the loss is shifted to Cooperative Bank, it can shift the loss to the retail store or to Pam, using the transfer warranty. UCC §§ 3-416(a)(3), 4-207(a)(3). If the retail store has to make good on the loss to Cooperative Bank or Paramount Bank, the retail store can pursue Pam using the transfer warranty. *Id.* However, Pam will typically have disappeared or be judgment-proof. The amount of the damages for breach of the warranty will be the $450.00 loss, plus expenses and loss of interest. UCC §§ 3-416(b), 3-417(b), 4-207(c), 4-208(b).

To summarize: The transfer and presentment warranties allow the loss from an alteration to be shifted to the forger, or to the person who dealt most closely with the wrongdoer in cases where the actual wrongdoer cannot be found or is judgment-proof. The specialized loss shifting mechanisms discussed in Chapter 16 may change this result, by denying the opportunity to assert the alteration if the appropriate circumstances are present.

Checkpoints

- Drawer and indorser liability provide the potential to shift a loss from a negotiable instrument problem from one party to another.

- However, drawer and indorser liability are subject to significant limitations.

- Transfer and presentment warranties may offer more opportunities to shift losses.

- The presentment warranty is more limited than the transfer warranty, reflecting the doctrine of *Price v. Neal.*

- The loss from a forged drawer's signature will often fall on the payor bank or drawee under the fundamental rules of this Chapter.

- The loss from a forged indorsement or alteration will often fall on the depositary bank, under the fundamental rules of this Chapter.

- The specialized rules in Chapter 16 offer a further opportunity to shift losses.

Chapter 16

Specialized UCC Loss Allocation Rules for Negotiable Instruments

---

Roadmap

- Alterations
  - Completed instruments
  - Incomplete instruments
- 3-406 general negligence
- 4-406 failure to examine bank statements
- 3-405 fraudulent indorsements by employees
- 3-404 imposters and fictitious payees
- Conversion

This Chapter focuses on some specialized liability rules that apply where the general liability rules are not thought to impose liability for a loss on the most appropriate party. Four of these rules are found in UCC Article 3; the fifth, considered in subsection B below, is found in UCC Article 4. Although the focus of this Part of this book is on UCC Article 4, we examine these provisions in this Chapter because they apply primarily to check transactions. These rules come into play after you complete the analysis using the basic rules outlined in the next two paragraphs, which are discussed more fully in Chapters 8, 14, and 15.

Transactions in negotiable instruments, particularly in those instruments that also qualify as "checks," are governed by a complex matrix of liability rules found in UCC Article 3, UCC Article 4, and federal law. Chapter 8 above lays out the basic liability framework applicable to all negotiable instruments under UCC Article 3. Chapters 13 and 14 explain the basic mechanism for collecting checks and dealing with dishonor and return in the check collection system. Chapter 15 explains the fundamental rules (outside the basic check collection system) that assigns liability when there's a problem with a check.

The UCC's general liability rules discussed in Chapters 8 (UCC Article 3, for all negotiable instruments) and Chapter 15 (UCC Article 4, for check collection) assign liability to each party who deals with a negotiable instrument based on the party's role in the transaction. Those rules work reasonably well to establish a first approximation for assigning liability when something goes wrong in a negotiable instrument transaction. However, some further adjustment may be appropriate in particular circumstances, to take into account the individualized behavior and characteristics of certain parties.

As you work through these rules, one of the characteristics you should keep in mind is the scope of each rule. A full understanding requires you to distinguish between *alterations, forged drawer's signatures* (also often called *"forged checks"*), and *forged indorsements*. An "alteration" occurs when someone changes or adds to the writing on an instrument and thereby modifies a party's liability. UCC § 3-407(a). "Forged drawer's signatures" and "forged indorsements" are subcategories of "forged signatures." These phrases are not defined as such in Article 3 or Article 4, but as the words suggest, the subcategories focus on the different capacities in which the forger placed the signature on the instrument. Chapter 8 above explains the significance of the different ways in which someone may sign a negotiable instrument.

The UCC provisions covered in this Chapter vary in their coverage of alterations, forged drawer's signatures, and forged indorsements. We start our consideration with section 3-407, which deals specifically with alterations. As you work through the other provisions, you should notice that the UCC sections discussed in this Chapter address alterations, forged drawer's signatures, and forged indorsements in varying combinations.

You should also notice that sections 3-406 and 4-406 operate by declaring someone to be "precluded from asserting" a forgery or alteration on the instrument. UCC §§ 3-406(a), 4-406(c). Sections 3-405 and 3-404 operate by making an indorsement effective that would otherwise be ineffective. UCC §§ 3-405(b), 3-404(b)(2). The significance of validating forged signatures is not obvious from these UCC provisions themselves; you have to examine their effect in light of the signatures' functions in creating liability, which is governed by the rules discussed in Chapters 8 and 15. The short version of those general rules, and the impact of the special rules in this Chapter, is this: a valid signature is usually required to impose liability in connection with a negotiable instrument; however, if you are prohibited from challenging the validity of a particular signature, you may lose the opportunity to avoid the related liability.

Finally, after you have mastered the mechanics of each rule discussed below, you should consider the ways in which they may interact with each other, and with the other liability rules for negotiable instruments that are considered in this book. The range of possible scenarios is vast. The examples at the end of Chapter 15 suggest possible starting points for such exercises. Often a particular fact situation may invoke more than one of these rules. In some cases, liability may be shifted under multiple rules as alternatives to each other. In other cases, it will be necessary to put different rules together to figure out who ultimately bears the loss. And in every case, the effect of the rules considered in this chapter has the potential to shift the liability away from the person who normally would be liable under the rules discussed above in Chapters 8 and 15.

A. Section 3-407: Alterations

We start with UCC section 3-407 because it defines the term "alteration" and applies solely to alterations, not to forged signatures. Alterations are also addressed to varying degrees in the other four UCC provisions we consider in this Chapter.

An "alteration" is "(i) an unauthorized change in an instrument that purports to modify in any respect the obligation of a party, or (ii) an unauthorized addition of words or numbers or other change to an incomplete instrument relating to the obligation of a party." UCC § 3-407(a). One classic example of an alteration would be the payee changing the amount of the check from $10.00 to $10,000.00. Another example would be Jim Jones finding a check on the sidewalk payable to Sam Smith, and changing the name of the payee to "Jim Jones."

An alteration may have a different effect depending on whether or not the instrument was an "incomplete instrument," which is an instrument that was signed but not completed with other significant information such as the name of the payee or the amount payable. See UCC § 3-115(a). Issuing an incomplete instrument subjects the issuer to liability for the terms *as completed,* even if the person who filled in the blanks did so in a way that was not authorized. UCC §§ 3-407(c)(ii), 3-115(b), (c). Adding further to the risk of issuing an incomplete instrument, the person complaining of the alteration (typically the issuer) has the burden of proof. UCC § 3-115(d). On the other hand, if a *completed* instrument is altered, the bank is only permitted to enforce the instrument as it was originally completed. UCC § 3-407(c)(i).

For example, if Mother signs a check payable to School to pay for lunch, and gives the check to Son with an agreement that he should fill in the amount for a maximum of $10.00, Mother has issued an incomplete instrument. Mother bears the risk that Son may buy lunch for his friends and fill in the amount as

$70.00. If Mother's bank pays the check for $70.00, Mother's bank can charge her account for the $70.00. Similarly, if Mother left the name of the payee blank, instructing Son to fill in the name of the school, but Son instead fills in the name of the local game arcade and uses the check there, Mother bears the risk of this completion as well. (Most of the remedies available to Mother when she finds out what Son has done are beyond the scope of this book. Whatever they are, they probably won't make Son happy.)

Suppose instead that Mother writes the check to School for $10.00, and Son skillfully changes the amount payable to $70.00. Mother's bank would only be permitted to charge Mother's account for the $10.00 specified in the check as originally completed. UCC § 3-407(c)(i).

Similarly, if Mother wrote the check payable to School but Son skillfully changed it to be payable to the game arcade, Mother's bank could only charge the check against Mother's account based on School being the payee. As explained more fully in Chapters 12 and 15, this probably means that Mother's bank will *not* be able to charge the check against Mother's account, because the check will lack the indorsement of School necessary to make the check "properly payable." *See* UCC § 4-401(a) and Official Comment 1.

A fraudulent alteration of an instrument "discharges a party whose obligation is affected by the alteration unless that party assents or is precluded from asserting the alteration." UCC § 3-407(b). That probably sounds like broader protection than it actually provides, because there are lots of ways that a party might be "precluded from asserting the alteration." *Id.* Someone who issues an incomplete instrument is so precluded, as discussed above. Other instances appear in sections 3-406 and 4-406, discussed below.

B. Section 3-406: General Negligence

The most general, and perhaps the simplest, of the specialized liability rules is found in UCC section 3-406. This section introduces general negligence concepts into the mix. It is designed to shift to the negligent party the loss from a forged signature (*either* a forged drawer's signature/forged check, or a forged indorsement, or perhaps even a forged maker's signature on a note). If more than one party is negligent, the loss is apportioned using comparative negligence.

Section 3-406 operates by denying a negligent party the normal right to complain of an alteration or forgery. A couple of examples make the significance of this clearer.

Normally if someone forges my name as drawer on one of my checks without my authorization, I have no liability for that forged drawer's signature (as discussed in Chapter 8 of this book), and my bank cannot charge that check against my account because it's not properly payable (as discussed in Chapter 12). However, if I negligently left my checkbook lying around in a public place, so as to make it easy for the forger, I may be "precluded from asserting ... the forgery." UCC § 3-406(a). As a result, I would have the drawer's liability on the check under UCC section 3-414(b), and the forged drawer's signature will no longer prevent the check from being properly payable under UCC section 4-401(a).

For another example, suppose I wrote a check on my account at North Carolina Bank to Barney, but negligently left it on the counter at the Post Office. Suppose further that Ernest found the check, skillfully forged Barney's name as indorser on the back, and cashed the check at a distant branch of North Carolina Bank, using a driver's license with Ernest's picture and Barney's name and address. Under the rules discussed in Chapter 12, this check would not be properly payable under UCC section 4-401 because it lacks a necessary (valid) indorsement; this would deny North Carolina Bank the right to charge the check against my account. However, the effect of adding UCC section 3-406 to the analysis is that my negligence may prevent me from complaining of the forgery, so that the check *can be* properly payable and North Carolina Bank may charge it against my account.

In both of the preceding examples, if someone (a bank or another party) is negligent in taking the check, or if my bank is negligent in paying the check, part of the liability for the loss will be apportioned to the other negligent party using principles of comparative negligence. UCC § 3-406(b). The person trying to shift liability to someone else for the latter's negligence bears the burden of proof. UCC § 3-406(c).

C. Section 4-406: Failure to Examine Bank Statements

UCC section 4-406 requires bank depositors to "exercise reasonable promptness in examining" their bank statements. UCC § 4-406(c). Depositors who fail to meet this requirement run the risk of being tagged with liability for alterations and unauthorized (i.e., forged) signatures. UCC § 4-406(d). (Revised Official Comment 5 indicates that section 4-406 is only concerned with unauthorized *drawer's* signatures, *not* with indorsements.) A depositor who ignores bank statements for a year risks the imposition of even broader liability for unauthorized signatures and alterations. UCC § 4-406(f). Threshold requirements are imposed on banks in the provision of the statements and related information to customers, UCC § 4-406(a) and (b), but these are not usually difficult for the banks to meet. Finally, if the depositor and the bank are both negligent, the loss is apportioned between them based on comparative negligence. UCC § 4-406(e).

Probably the hardest thing to understand about this set of rules is the two-step liability structure of section 4-406(d)(1) and (2). Most depositors who have liability shifted to them under section 4-406(d) are caught under subsection (2), not subsection (1). Understanding this requires close reading and some reflection.

Subsection (2) of section 4-406(d) applies when there are multiple, sequential unauthorized signatures or alterations by the same person. It applies when the depositor has received one statement showing unauthorized signatures or alterations, then more unauthorized signatures or alterations subsequently occur after the depositor should have noticed the problem and alerted the bank. Understanding that much requires you to work through the lengthy and detailed language of section 4-406(d)(2), but the meaning of the words in the statute leads directly to the conclusions stated in this paragraph.

Paragraph (1) of subsection 4-406(d) has the potential to shift losses to the depositor for any unauthorized signature or alteration, not just those that occur after the depositor has received statements showing that someone is forging or altering checks. However, paragraph (1) is subject to a qualification in its last clause that limits recovery by the bank to unusual cases. Paragraph (1) only applies "if the bank also proves that it suffered a loss by reason of the [depositor's] failure [to examine bank statements promptly and alert the bank to problems shown on a statement]." UCC § 4-406(d)(1) (referring to the depositor's duties in § 4-406(c), via the reference in the initial language of § 4-406(d)). This limitation is harder to understand than other parts of section 4-406, because it requires careful interpretation of when the bank "suffer[s] a loss by reason of the [depositor's] failure." *Id.* The third paragraph of Revised Official Comment 2 to section 4-406 hints at the meaning of this interpretation, but doesn't make it entirely clear.

In the usual situation involving alterations or forged signatures, the depositor is entirely unaware that anything is wrong until the problem is identified on a bank statement. Under the proximate-cause analysis typically applied to these situations, the cause of the bank's loss is *the alteration or forgery itself*, not the depositor's failure to see the problem. Only with respect to a subsequent alteration or forgery, that occurs after the depositor has the opportunity to review a bank statement showing prior forgeries, does the bank suffer a loss "by reason of the" depositor's failure to check the statement. *See* UCC § 4-406 Revised Official Comment 2 (third paragraph). Liability for those subsequent alterations and forgeries is shifted to the depositor via section 4-406(d)(2), *not* 4-406(d)(1).

If the bank was negligent or failed to act in good faith, the bank's customer has an opportunity to shift a portion of the loss back to the bank. UCC §4-406(e). However, if the customer fails to check bank statements for a year, the opportunity to complain of the bank's negligence disappears. UCC §4-406(f).

D. Section 3-405: Fraudulent Indorsements by Employees

UCC section 3-405 deals with a narrow but important class of situations. This provision imposes liability on employers for "fraudulent indorsements" by "employees" who are given "responsibility" in the employer's systems and processes for dealing with negotiable instruments. These three terms are defined in section 3-405(a).

Section 3-405 deals with two types of schemes. One involves instruments (usually checks) received by the employer. The other involves the employer's processes for issuing instruments (again, usually checks) to pay employees or suppliers. The common thread between both types of schemes is that a fraudulent indorsement is necessary to make the instrument appear legitimate so that it can be negotiated.

1. Checks Payable to the Employer

In the normal case, when you receive a check it is payable to you, and you indorse it before depositing it in your account at your bank or negotiating it to someone else. Unless and until it is indorsed, it remains payable only to you, the payee. (UCC section 4-205 provides a limited exception for checks deposited in the payee's account at the bank; note that section 4-205(1) generally only applies to cases where the bank's "customer"—defined in section 4-104(a)(5)—is legitimately a holder of the check.)

Most businesses receive so many checks that they have to use employees to process them. If the employees indorse the checks in the name of the employer and deposit them into the employer's bank account, everything is ok. In that normal scenario, the money ends up in the employer bank account. However, there is ample opportunity for creative employee dishonesty.

a. Cashing the Check

Suppose a dishonest employee wants to steal checks and get the money for himself or herself. Perhaps the simplest way to do this would be to indorse the check in the name of the employer and cash the check. If the dishonest employee is thereby successful in cashing the check, and if the bank or other person taking the check acts "in good faith" (a concept discussed in Subsection D 2 of Chapter 7) and "pays" the check or "takes it for value or collection" (concepts discussed in Section E of Chapter 7), section 3-405(b) treats the dishonest employee's indorsement as "effective" as the employer's indorsement. The net effect of this (working through the rules of Chapters 8 and 15) is that the employer will be stuck with the loss unless the employer can recover from the dishonest employee (a topic discussed in Chapter 15).

Because of the risks described in the preceding paragraph, banks and other businesses are typically reluctant to cash checks that are payable to a business or a person they don't know and who isn't present to verify the validity of their indorsement.

Of course, any dishonest employee could steal checks and indorse them in the name of the employer. However, this will be much easier for an employee who is involved in processing the checks and therefore already has access to the checks and the necessary tools for turning them into cash. Therefore, section 3-405 shifts the liability to the employer more quickly than the other special liability rules considered in this chapter, but the easy liability-shifting is only available if the problem is created by someone in the narrow class of employees who pose this special set of risks to the check processing system.

b. Depositing the Check in the Dishonest Employee's Account

A more complex, but often more effective, way for a dishonest employee to steal from his or her employer is to set up a bank account in the name of the employer, with withdrawal rights by the dishonest employee. Recognizing that a bank may be suspicious if an individual asks to cash a check payable to a business, a sophisticated dishonest employee may go to a bank other than the employer's usual bank and open an account in the name of the employer. Bank security procedures may require documentation from a corporation, limited liability company, etc. evidencing the business' intent to open the account and the employee's authority to act for the business. However, such documentation can be forged.

Once the fraudulent account is established, the dishonest employee can steal incoming checks from the employer, enter the employer's indorsement on the back of the checks, and deposit them in the employee's fraudulent account. The bank will collect the checks from the drawers, and the money will be readily available to the dishonest employee. Here again, if the bank or other person taking the check acts "in good faith" and "pays" the check or "takes it for value or collection," section 3-405(b) treats the dishonest employee's indorsement as "effective" as the employer's indorsement. The net effect of this (again working through the rules of Chapters 8 and 15 above) is that the employer will be stuck with the loss unless the employer can recover from the dishonest employee. The necessary showing of good faith may be harder, but not impossible, for the bank in this situation.

This type of scheme, like cashing stolen checks, is much easier for an employee who is involved in processing the checks and therefore already has access to the checks and the necessary tools for turning them into cash. Therefore, section 3-405 shifts the liability to the employer more quickly than the other special liability rules considered in this chapter, but the easy liability-shifting is only available if the problem is created by someone in the narrow class of employees who pose this special set of risks to the check processing system.

Examples in the UCC Official Comments illustrate these types of schemes. *See* UCC § 3-405 Official Comment 3 Case #3 and Case #4.

c. Comparative Negligence

As with the other provisions we have examined, the possibility exists that the employer may not be the only one liable. This is a highly fact-specific determination, and depends on the cleverness of the dishonest employee. If the dishonest employee is clumsy and unsophisticated, the person who takes the check from the dishonest employee may be found negligent because better procedures, or better adherence to the procedures already in place, might have caught the fraud. In such cases, the loss will be apportioned between the employer and the person who took the check using comparative negligence principles. UCC § 3-405(b) (last sentence).

2. Checks Issued by the Employer

Another possibility for a creative and dishonest employee is to steal money via checks issued *by* the employer. The employee might have the authority to issue the employer's checks or might be able to affect the preparation of the employer's checks that are prepared by another employee. In either case, the dishonest employee will have to forge the indorsement of the payee to get access to the funds (unless the check is made payable to the dishonest employee, which would be easy for the employer to spot).

Except for the source of the check and the name in which the forged indorsement must be made, these scenarios are quite similar to those for stolen checks payable *to* the employer. Again, examples in the UCC Official Comments illustrate these types of schemes. *See* UCC § 3-405 Official Comment 3 Case #5, Case #6, and Case #7.

E. Section 3-404: Impostors and Fictitious Payees

We have saved the least intuitive of the special liability rules for last. This gives you the opportunity to warm up your skills in simpler situations, getting accustomed to the idea that things may not always be as they appear on the face of a negotiable instrument. UCC section 3-404 deals with the possibility that the issuer of the negotiable instrument may be fooled into thinking that the instrument is issued to one person, but it is actually issued to someone else. As with any good mystery, it takes some reflection and study to work through the layers of deceit and identify the underlying reality.

UCC section 3-404 deals with both "impostors" and "fictitious payees." An *impostor* is someone who pretends to be another actual person. See UCC § 3-404(a). A *fictitious payee* is someone who does not exist at all. See UCC § 3-404(b)(ii). Section 3-404(a) deals with situations involving impostors. Section 3-404(b)(ii) deals with fictitious payees, and section 3-404(b)(i) deals with the in-between situation where the named payee actually exists, but the instrument is created with the intention for someone else to actually get the money.

The general effect of section 3-404 is to validate the forged indorsement made in the name of the fictitious payee or the person impersonated. In fact, checks drawn to impostors and fictitious payees are essentially converted to bearer instruments. See UCC §§ 3-404(b)(1), 1-201(b)(21)(A) (first clause).

Like we have seen for other provisions elsewhere in this Chapter, the loss from a check payable to an impostor or fictitious payee may be apportioned using comparative negligence principles. See UCC § 3-404(d).

Another reason for saving section 3-404 for last is that problems involving it also often involve other provisions discussed above in this chapter. Consequently, working through impostor or fictitious payee problems can be a good way to test your mastery of these other rules, too. The Official Comments to section 3-404, while complex, offer good hypotheticals for working through the issues, as well as helpful commentary explaining how to apply the various rules. See UCC § 3-404 Official Comments 2 and 3.

F. Conversion

Liability may also be imposed for conversion of a negotiable instrument. UCC Article 3 imports the general tort law of conversion, then adds specific rules applicable to negotiable instruments. See UCC § 3-420. "Conversion" in general is "[t]he wrongful possession or disposition of another's property as if it were one's own." Black's Law Dictionary 356 (8th ed. 2004).

Once you get past the first sentence, the rules in UCC section 3-420 are so laden with specific inclusions and exclusions that it can be hard to get a general sense of what this remedy is for. One scenario in which the conversion remedy is essential to appropriate loss-shifting is the case where a payee receives a check, but it is stolen before the payee indorses it or negotiates it. Once the payee has "taken" the check, the underlying obligation is suspended, as discussed in Chapter 11:

> If the person entitled to enforce the instrument taken for an obligation is a person other than the obligee, the obligee may not enforce the obligation to the extent the obligation is suspended. If the obligee is the person entitled to enforce the instrument but no longer has possession of it because it was lost, stolen, or destroyed, the obligation may not be enforced to the extent of the amount payable on the instrument, and to that extent the obligee's rights against the obligor are limited to enforcement of the instrument.

UCC § 3-310(b)(4). UCC Article 3 provides a mechanism for enforcing lost or stolen instruments. *See* UCC § 3-309. However, this mechanism requires "that the person required to pay the instrument [be] adequately protected against loss that might occur by reason of a claim by another person to enforce the instrument." UCC § 3-309(b). The cost of providing this protection may be so great as to make the right to enforce a stolen instrument essentially worthless in a particular case.

The availability of the conversion remedy in this scenario gives the payee a crucial alternative way to recover the value of the stolen instrument. Best of all, the remedy is not limited to enforcement against the thief who converted the instrument. As we have seen in many contexts, remedies against thieves are rarely valuable. The payee of the stolen instrument has the more-valuable opportunity to recover in conversion from the depositary bank, the payor bank, and any intermediary bank that still holds the proceeds from collecting the instrument. *See* UCC § 3-420(a) (second sentence), (c).

This UCC Article 3 conversion remedy will not be available if the instrument was payable to bearer, either originally or as the result of a valid indorsement in blank. In that case, the thief would be a holder and a person entitled to enforce the instrument, merely by having possession. *See* UCC § 3-420(a) (second sentence) (requiring transfer from or payment for, "a person *not* entitled to enforce the instrument") (emphasis added). However, the UCC

Article 4 conversion right can be quite valuable to many payees who suffered the theft of a check payable to them.

Checkpoints

- Specialized UCC liability provisions reallocate losses from negotiable instrument problems to achieve results thought to be appropriate for particular situations.

- The rules are generally designed to place responsibility for problems on the person best able to prevent them.

- Comparative negligence is often available to apportion liability when more than one party contributed to the problem.

Part Three

Other Payment Systems

Chapter 17

The Law of Credit Cards

Roadmap

- Consumer Credit Protection Act
- TILA
- Reg. Z
- Unsolicited credit card
- Accepted credit card
- Initial disclosures
- Periodic statement disclosures
- Other disclosures
- Unauthorized use
- Assertion of claims and defenses
- Billing errors

A. Overview

Credit card transactions are largely governed by federal law. The initial portion of the Consumer Credit Protection Act, codified at 15 U.S.C.A. §§ 1601–1666j and commonly referred to as the "Truth in Lending Act" (TILA), sets out a number of important rules governing credit card issuance and use. Although many of the rules appear in the statute, the statute authorizes the Federal Reserve System Board of Governors to issue regulations, which often provide a more detailed and helpful presentation. *See* 15 U.S.C.A. § 1604(a). These regulations appear at 12 C.F.R. Part 226, and are referred to as "Regulation Z" or "Reg. Z" for short, following the convention widely used for referring to Federal Reserve Board regulations. The lettering system reflects the fact that A is the first letter of the alphabet, so the regulations in 12 CFR Part 201 are "Regulation A." Z is the 26th letter, so the regulations in Part 226 are "Regulation Z." We will focus primarily on the rules in Reg. Z.

TILA applies to many different kinds of consumer credit arrangements besides credit cards. Consequently, we will not explore all the many rules and issues addressed in TILA, and we will instead focus here only on the provisions relevant to transactions using credit cards.

TILA and Reg. Z primarily create disclosure requirements. The theory behind them is that consumers should be able to agree to any credit terms they wish, as long as they have sufficient information to evaluate the credit they are offered. If you suspect that disclosure is not the answer to solving problems with credit (or other types of contracts), you have company. *See, e.g.,* Robert A. Hillman, Boilerplate in Consumer Contract: Online Boilerplate: Would Mandatory Website Disclosure of E-Standard Terms BackFire? 104 Mich. L. Rev. 837, 850 n.72 (2006). However, that debate is best left for another day. More important for our purposes here, TILA and Reg. Z contain both disclosure requirements and substantive requirements governing credit cards. Some of the TILA and Reg. Z provisions are specific to credit cards; others also apply to other types of credit arrangements. For this Chapter, the term "consumer" and "cardholder" are used interchangeably, because the consumers we're interested in are the ones holding credit cards. The terms "creditor" and "card issuer" are also used interchangeably in this Chapter, for similar reasons.

A card issuer that violates the Consumer Credit Protection Act requirements for credit cards is potentially liable for actual damages, plus a statutory penalty, plus costs and attorney's fees if the cardholder brings a successful action. 15 U.S.C.A. § 1640(a). The statutory penalty for an individual action is twice the finance charge, with a minimum of $100.00 and a maximum of $1,000.00 (with higher limits if collateral for the credit includes real property or a dwelling, though that would be unusual for credit cards). 15 U.S.C.A. § 1640(a)(2)(A)(i). For a class action, the statutory penalty is within the court's discretion, subject to a maximum of "the lesser of $500,000.00 or 1 per centum of the net worth of the creditor." 15 U.S.C.A. § 1640(a)(2)(B). However, a number of specific limitations apply to liability for disclosures (section 1637 of the statute). *See* 15 U.S.C.A. § 1640(a) *following* paragraph (a)(4).

B. Issuance Restrictions

In the early days of credit cards, issuers sent unsolicited cards to consumers. This created a number of problems, particularly when a card went to someone other than the intended recipient. Sadly, some people seem all-too-willing to use a credit card issued in someone else's name. The limitations on liability for unauthorized use, discussed in Section D of this Chapter, address a number of these problems, but TILA and Reg. Z also include a specific prohibition against issuing an unsolicited credit card. 15 U.S.C.A. § 1642; 12 C.F.R. § 226.12(a).

You may have noticed that once you have a credit card, you routinely and automatically get renewal cards. Card issuers are permitted to issue cards "[a]s a renewal of, or substitute for, an accepted credit card." 12 C.F.R. § 226.12(a)(2). The definition of "accepted credit card" is surprisingly broad, and even harder to find (in a footnote in Reg. Z):

> "accepted credit card" means any credit card that a cardholder has requested or applied for and received, or has signed, used, or authorized another person to use to obtain credit. Any credit card issued as a renewal or substitute in accordance with this paragraph becomes an accepted credit card when received by the cardholder.

12 C.F.R. § 226.12(a)(2) n.21a. Notice that once you authorize the issuance of a credit card to yourself *or anyone else*, the card issuer is allowed to keep sending renewal cards, and the renewal cards will be accepted credit cards.

Learning about these restrictions may cause you to wonder about a card sent to you after a card issuer called you up and asked if you wanted a credit card. Notice that an "oral request" is enough to authorize the issuance of a credit card. 12 C.F.R. § 226.12(a)(1). If you told the telephone solicitor that yes, you would like to have their credit card, you made an oral request for the card, thereby authorizing the card issuer to send it to you: "The request or application may be oral [in response to a telephone solicitation by a card issuer, for example] or written." *See* 12 C.F.R. Part 226 Supplement I, Official Staff Interpretation to Section 226.12.

C. Disclosure of Credit Card Terms

TILA and Reg. Z are primarily disclosure statutes, and they require three sets of extensive disclosures in connection with credit card transactions. The first group of disclosures is required up-front, as part of the initial solicitation and issuance process. The second group of disclosures is required with the periodic (usually monthly) statements sent for the account. The third—and usually least important, for most cardholders—group of disclosures is a set of miscellaneous requirements. We will consider each of these three groups in turn, below.

All of the disclosures are subject to overarching general disclosure requirements. *See* Reg. Z § 226.5.

1. Initial Disclosure Requirements

A prospective cardholder needs a lot of information at the front end of the relationship with a card issuer. Ideally the prospective cardholder will be comparison shopping at this stage, looking for the credit card that best suits his or her needs. Reg. Z requires extensive and detailed disclosure of numerous essential terms that govern the credit card relationship. Although subject to criticism, as noted above, TILA and Reg. Z do mandate disclosure of much information that is potentially useful for comparing one credit card offer to another. Moreover, even for a cardholder who says "I really need to borrow some money right now, so I'm going to grab this credit offer that came in today's mail," the disclosures do give the *opportunity* to understand much detail about the obligations he or she is agreeing to. A particular consumer, in particular circumstances, might legitimately complain that they needed different information, or in a different format, in order fully to understand the obligations. However, it's usually best to leave those more-difficult questions until after you have mastered the basics.

Reg. Z mandates the format of the disclosures. 12 C.F.R. §226.5a(a)(2). Reg. Z also provides model disclosure forms for credit card issuers to follow. *See* 12 C.F.R. Part 226 Appendix G. These model disclosures offer a safe harbor to creditors who follow them to meet their disclosure obligations. 15 U.S.C.A. §1604(b).

The actual disclosure requirements are extremely detailed. *See* 12 C.F.R. §§226.5, 226.5a, 226.6. They also vary depending on the context of the application or solicitation. *See* 12 C.F.R. §226.5a(c), (d), (e), and (f). Unfortunately, there is no substitute for working through the regulatory language, though the model disclosures in 12 C.F.R. Part 226 Appendix G can help.

In general, the disclosures are designed to focus on important terms of the credit arrangement that typically vary from one credit card issuer to another: the "annual percentage rate," 12 C.F.R. §226.5a(b)(1); fees and other charges, 12 C.F.R. §§229.5a(b)(2), (3), (4), (8), (9), (10), and (11), 226.6(b); the "grace period" allowed before finance charges begin to accrue (or if charges begin to accrue a finance charge from the day of the charge, the lack of a grace period must be disclosed), 12 C.F.R. §226.5a(b)(5).

The initial disclosures also must include the ways that finance charges are imposed and calculated. *See* 12 C.F.R. §§226.5a(b)(6), (g), 226.6(a). This is probably the most complex information in the disclosures. Here, again, the unfortunate reality is that fully understanding the byzantine details requires extensive and careful study of the regulatory language. As you study that language, it's appropriate to wonder how helpful these disclosures are to the average consumer. Another unfortunate reality, though, is that the disclosures are complex because the terms of the transactions are complex.

The initial disclosures also must tell the prospective cardholder if a card issuer will take a security interest to secure the credit extended. 12 C.F.R. §226.6(c). The initial disclosures also must include a statement as to particular rights and responsibilities imposed by TILA and Reg. Z, which are discussed below in Section D of this Chapter. *See* 12 C.F.R. §226.6(d).

2. Periodic Statement Disclosures

The "periodic" (usually monthly) statement is where the cardholder gets to see what he or she owes the card issuer and how much the credit is actually going to cost. Reg. Z imposes detailed requirements for what must be disclosed. *See* 12 C.F.R §§226.7, 226.8. Model disclosure forms are available for these requirements. *See* 12 C.F.R. Part 226 Appendix G. These model disclosures offer a safe harbor to creditors who follow them to meet their disclosure requirements. *See* 15 U.S.C.A. §1604(b).

As with the initial disclosures, full understanding requires you to work through the details of the regulatory language (with the help of the model disclosure forms). In general, the card issuer must disclose the beginning balance, 12 C.F.R. §226.7(a), the ending balance, 12 C.F.R. §226.7(i), the transactions during the period covered by the statement, 12 C.F.R. §§226.7(b) and (c), 226.8, and the finance charge and other charges for extending credit, 12 C.F.R. §226.7(d), (e), (f), (g), and (h). The periodic statement must also indicate the deadline for paying the bill without incurring a finance charge. 12 C.F.R. §226.7(j).

3. Other Disclosure Requirements

Reg. Z imposes various other disclosure requirements. Cardholders must be reminded at least annually of their rights for dealing with certain types of problems with their account. *See* 12 C.F.R. §§226.9(a), 226.6(d). Card issuers must also provide specified disclosures in connection with changes in the terms of the credit arrangement, 12 C.F.R. §226.9(b), (c), and (f), and at renewal, 12 C.F.R. §226.9(e).

D. Cardholder Rights for Addressing Problems with Transactions

TILA and Reg. Z go beyond simply requiring disclosure, and impose substantive requirements on the structure of credit card rights and responsibilities. These are particularly important when problems occur with the credit account. Cardholders have limited liability for unauthorized use of their credit cards. If a cardholder has a claim or defense that is good against a merchant, that claim or defense may be asserted against the card issuer. TILA and Reg. Z also prescribe elaborate procedures for dealing with "billing errors." Each of these protections is discussed in turn below.

1. Unauthorized Use

TILA and Reg. Z limit a cardholder's liability for unauthorized use of his or her credit card. 15 U.S.C.A. § 1643; 12 C.F.R. § 226.12(b). "Unauthorized use" is defined as "the use of a credit card by a person, other than the cardholder, who does not have actual, implied, or apparent authority for such use, and from which the cardholder receives no benefit." 12 C.F.R. § 226.12(b)(1) n.22.

The maximum liability for unauthorized use is set at $50.00. 12 C.F.R. § 226.12(b)(1). If the cardholder notifies the card issuer of the loss or theft of the card, the cardholder's liability for unauthorized use will be the *lesser* of $50.00 or the amount of unauthorized charges. 12 C.F.R. § 226.12(b)(1), (3). Notification of loss or theft can be made orally or in writing. 12 C.F.R. § 226.12(b)(3). Of course, the advantage of giving written notification is having a copy of the written notice to prove that notice was given.

A cardholder is only liable for unauthorized use of an "accepted credit card," so a cardholder who has not accepted a credit card from the issuer is not even liable for the first $50.00 of unauthorized use. *See* 12 C.F.R. § 226.12(b)(2)(a). As discussed above in Section B of this Chapter, the definition of "accepted credit card" is both broad and somewhat difficult to find.

An employer with ten or more employees is permitted to contract around these limitations on liability for unauthorized use and accept that liability (presumably in exchange for the card issuer's charging lower fees or interest). *See* 15 U.S.C.A. § 1645; 12 C.F.R. § 226.12(b)(5). However, the employer must retain the obligation, and the liability may not be shifted to employees. *Id.*

At least one reported case has denied a cardholder the defense for unauthorized use where the cardholder's dishonest employee obtained a credit card for herself on the cardholder's account and ran up a series of charges over a period of more than a year. *See Minskoff v. Am. Express Travel Related Serv. Co.*, 98 F.3d 703 (2d Cir. 1996). Although the decision reaches an appealing result on the equities, it seems wrong on the law. Applying New York law, the Second Circuit held that the cardholder's negligence in failing to examine statements for more than a year could result in the dishonest employee getting apparent authority to use the card she fraudulently obtained. *Id.* at 709. The most troubling part of the opinion is the application of a policy the court found in UCC section 4-406 that a cardholder should be liable for subsequent unauthorized use after he has received statements showing prior unauthorized use. *Id.* This seems a peculiar form of reverse preemption, since the court is using a state statute (UCC section 4-406) to insert a new rule into the federal statutory scheme. Congress chose to put a rule similar to UCC section 4-406 into the Electronic Funds Transfer Act. See 15 U.S.C.A. § 1693g(a); 12 C.F.R. § 205.6(b)(3). The lack of a similar rule in the statute for credit cards suggests that it should not be read in by a court.

2. Assertion of Claims and Defenses

When you buy something, you generally have various contractual rights to refuse to pay if you don't get what you bargained for. If your payment obligation is owed to the seller, refusing to pay can be a simple and effective way to get the seller's attention and motivate a favorable resolution of your complaint.

However, you could lose a lot of that leverage if you borrowed the purchase price from someone other than the seller. If the seller has already been paid, and you're obligated to pay your creditor who financed your purchase, the seller may not be as motivated to resolve your complaint.

In the negotiable instrument context, this problem is addressed for consumer transactions by the FTC Holder in Due Course regulation, discussed in Subsection C 4 of Chapter 7. TILA and Reg. Z offer similar protections to credit card holders. *See* 15 U.S.C.A. § 1666i; 12 C.F.R. § 226.12(c).

If you have a dispute with a merchant over a purchase made with a credit card, you may be able to enlist the help of the card issuer by withholding payment for the charge related to the dispute. 12 C.F.R. § 226.12(c)(1). The card issuer is forbidden to report the amount you withheld as delinquent if you comply with the Reg. Z requirements for asserting this right. 12 C.F.R. § 226.12(c)(2).

The right to withhold payment is subject to several important restrictions. First, the cardholder must make "a good faith attempt to resolve the dispute with the person honoring the credit card." 12 C.F.R. § 226.12(c)(3)(i). Second, the credit extension must exceed $50.00. 12 C.F.R. § 226.12(c)(3)(ii). Third, the transaction must have occurred in the same state as the cardholder's address, or within 100 miles of that address. *Id.* Last, and hardest to find, the cardholder must not have paid the charge for the disputed transaction. 12 C.F.R. § 226.12(c)(1) (last sentence). A footnote to Reg. Z specifies that partial payments on an account balance are applied first to late charges, then to finance charges, and then to other charges on a first-in-first-out basis. *See* 12 C.F.R. § 226.12(c)(1) n.25.

The restrictions described in the preceding paragraph generally make sense, except for the requirement that transactions occur in the same state or within 100 miles of the cardholder's address. This probably made sense in the early days of credit cards, when card issuers only covered a limited geographic area. Today, however, credit card networks are national and international in scope, so geographic restrictions on dispute resolution are outdated.

3. Billing Errors

TILA and Reg. Z provide an elaborate mechanism for dealing with "billing errors." *See* 15 U.S.C.A. §§ 1666–1666j; 12 C.F.R. § 226.13. The term "billing error" is defined broadly to encompass a variety of problems that might occur with a credit card account. *See* 12 C.F.R. § 226.13(a).

In order to invoke the billing error procedures, a consumer (not just a cardholder, because this provision applies to other types of credit besides credit cards) must first file a "billing error notice," which must be in writing and sufficiently identify the consumer, the account, and the problem complained of. *See* 12 C.F.R. § 226.13(b). The creditor must receive the billing error notice within "60 days after the creditor transmitted the first periodic statement that reflects the alleged billing error." 12 C.F.R. § 226.13(b)(1).

The receipt of a timely billing error notice imposes a number of obligations on a creditor. First, the creditor must acknowledge receipt of the billing error notice within 30 days (unless the problem is resolved within the 30-day period). 12 C.F.R. § 226.13(c)(1). The maximum time period for completely resolving the matter runs from the date the billing error notice is received until the earlier of two billing cycles or 90 days. 12 C.F.R. § 226.13(c)(2). The consumer is permitted to withhold payment for the disputed amount until the matter is resolved. 12 C.F.R. § 226.13(d)(1). Collection efforts and adverse credit reports are also forbidden while the matter is pending. 12 C.F.R. § 226.13(d)(1), (2).

The creditor is obligated to conduct a "reasonable investigation." 12 C.F.R. § 226.13(f) and n.31. If the creditor discovers that the consumer was right about the billing error, the creditor is obligated to make the correction, credit the account, and notify the consumer. 12 C.F.R., § 226.13(e). If the creditor determines that the consumer owes all or part of the disputed amount, the creditor must so notify the consumer, with documentation. 12 C.F.R. § 226.13(f), (g)(1), (g)(2). The creditor is then permitted to collect the disputed amount and report the account as delinquent if it remains unpaid past any applicable grace period. 12 C.F.R. § 226.13(g)(3). If the consumer disagrees with the creditor's resolution, the creditor is required to acknowledge that fact in its reports on the delinquency and send the consumer the name and address of report recipients. 12 C.F.R. § 226.13(g)(4). A creditor is only required to go through this process once for each alleged billing error. 12 C.F.R. § 226.13(h).

E. Other Cardholder Protections

TILA and Reg. Z impose various other protections for credit cardholders. Payments must be credited promptly. 15 U.S.C.A. § 1666c; 12 CFR § 226.10. Credit balances must be refunded within seven days of the consumer's request and within six months in any case (if the consumer can reasonably be located). 15 U.S.C.A. § 1666d; 12 C.F.R. § 226.11. A card issuer may not offset a balance in a cardholder's deposit account to repay amounts owed on a credit card account without the cardholder's consent or the use of judicial process. 15 U.S.C.A. § 1666h; 12 C.F.R. § 226.12(d). A card issuer must credit refunds promptly. 12 U.S.C.A. § 1666e; 12 C.F.R. § 226.12(e). Card issuers may not prohibit merchants who honor the issuer's cards from offering discounts for payment in cash. 15 U.S.C.A. § 1666f; 12 C.F.R. § 226.12(f)(1). TILA and Reg. Z impose extensive requirements for credit advertising. 15 U.S.C.A. §§ 1661–1665b; 12 C.F.R. § 226.16.

Checkpoints

- TILA (a part of he Consumer Credit Protection Act) and Reg. Z impose both disclosure and substantive requirements for credit cards.

- Issuance of unsolicited credit cards is prohibited.

- Specific and extensive disclosures are required at the beginning of the relationship between issuer and cardholder, and periodically (usually monthly) while a credit card account is open; certain other disclosures are required at least annually.

- TILA and Reg. Z limit cardholder liability for unauthorized use of a credit card, enable the cardholder to assert claims against the card issuer that would be available against the merchant who took the card, require creditors to follow an elaborate mechanism for addressing billing errors, and impose various other requirements.

Chapter 18

The Law of Debit Cards

Roadmap

- Consumer Credit Protection Act
- Reg. E
- Electronic fund transfer
- Consumer
- Access device
- Issuance limitations for unsolicited cards
- Disclosure requirements
- Limits on liability for unauthorized use
- Error resolution mechanism

A. Overview

Debit cards, like credit cards, are largely governed by federal law. The Consumer Credit Protection Act (CCPA), which we examined in Chapter 17 for credit cards, also contains rules for debit cards. This time the applicable rules are in Subchapter VI of the CCPA, sometimes referred to as the Electronic Fund Transfer Act (EFTA). *See* 15 U.S.C.A. §§ 1693–1693r. Also like the Truth in Lending Act (TILA) rules we examined in Chapter 17, the statute enacted by Congress authorizes the Federal Reserve System Board of Governors to issue regulations to accomplish the purposes of the statute. 15 U.S.C.A. § 1693b. These regulations appear at 12 C.F.R. §§ 205.1–205.18, and are often better-organized and more detailed than the original statute. These regulations are commonly referred to as "Regulation E," or "Reg. E" for short, reflecting the convention of assigning letters to Federal Reserve Board regulations: the regulations in 12 C.F.R. Part 201 are referred to as "Reg. A," Part 202 is "Reg. B," Part 226 is "Reg. Z," Part 227 is "Part AA," etc. We will focus primarily on the statements of the rules in Reg. E, which usually are better organized, clearer, and more detailed than the corresponding versions in the statute. Similar to the credit card regulations, Reg. E provides model disclosure clauses and forms, as well as interpretations of the regulation by the Federal Reserve Board of Governors Staff. *See* 12 C.F.R. Part 205 Appendix A, Appendix C, and Supplement I.

Definitions of terms appear in section 1693a of the statute and sections 205.2 and 205.3 of the regulation. The typical transaction covered by the EFTA involves a "consumer" using an "access device" (Reg. E's term for a debit card) to initiate an "electronic fund transfer" to move money into or out of the consumer's "account" at a "financial institution." *See* 12 C.F.R. §§ 205.2(a), (b), (e), (i), 205.3(b). This indicates that the EFTA and Reg. E cover transactions beyond those initiated with a debit card.

You should note that the EFTA and Reg. E only apply to *consumer* electronic fund transfers. The scope provision and definition of "electronic fund transfer" in Reg. E are clear and explicit that the coverage only extends to transactions that "debit or credit a consumer's account." *See* 12 C.F.R. § 205.3. This limitation is a bit harder to find in the statute, but it's there: an "electronic fund transfer" must involve an "account," which is limited to those "established primarily for personal, family, or household purposes." *See* 15 U.S.C.A. § 1693a(6), (2). That phrase is customarily applied to set apart consumer transactions from other transactions. *See* 15 U.S.C.A. § 1602(h) (definition of the adjective "consumer" in TILA). Congress' intent to limit the EFTA and Reg. E to *consumers'* electronic fund transfers is also clear in the preamble of the statute. *See* 15 U.S.C.A. § 1693.

You may be aware that a system also exists for making "wire transfers" of money, primarily for large business transactions. (Those transactions are sometimes referred to as "wholesale wire transfers," reflecting the fact that they often involve enormous amounts of money.) The wire transfer system is governed by Article 4A of the Uniform Commercial Code (UCC), which we explore in Chapter 19. Although the wire transfer and debit card systems have some similarities, the nature of the two systems is sufficiently different for the dual legal regimes to work well. UCC Article 4A explicitly steps aside and excludes funds transfers covered by the EFTA. UCC § 4A-108. Similarly, Reg. E steps aside and excludes the types of wire transfers covered by UCC Article 4A. *See* 12 C.F.R. § 205.3(c)(3).

In general, you will find that the rules for debit cards are simpler than the rules for credit cards. This reflects the fact that the range of possible debit card transactions is not as broad as the range of possible credit card transactions. A electronic fund transfer governed by the EFTA and Reg. E is generally limited to an immediate movement of money on deposit from one party to another. When you swipe your debit card through the card reader at the grocery store to pay for your groceries, you move money from your account at your bank to the grocery store. Once that money moves, the transaction is complete. By contrast, if you use a *credit* card to pay for your groceries, not only are you initiating an immediate (or nearly-immediate) movement of money (from your card issuer to the grocery store), the system also must deal with the mechanism by which you will repay your card issuer for the money it advanced to the grocery store on your behalf.

A financial institution that inappropriately fails to make an electronic funds transfer is potentially liable to the consumer for "all damages proximately caused." *See* 12 U.S.C.A. § 1693. To avoid liability, the financial institution must show a justification recognized in the statute. *See id.*

B. Issuance

The EFTA and Reg. E generally prohibit the issuance of unsolicited debit cards, similar to the TILA and Reg. Z prohibition of issuing unsolicited credit cards discussed in Chapter 17. *See* 15 U.S.C.A. § 1693i(a); 12 C.F.R. § 205.5(a). Unlike the credit card rules, however, the EFTA and Reg. E permit the issuance of unsolicited debit cards in certain circumstances. *See* 15 U.S.C.A. § 1693i(b), (c); 12 C.F.R. § 205.5(b). Any unsolicited debit card must be "not validated" when sent, meaning that it cannot be used unless the consumer requests the issuing financial institution to activate it, and the financial institution is required to verify the customer's identity before doing so. *See id.* The financial institution that sends an unsolicited debit card must also include instructions on how to validate the card, as well as an explanation of the customer's liability for use of the card if validated. *Id.*

C. Disclosure

As we saw with the rules for credit cards, there is no substitute for working through the statutory and regulatory language that mandates the required disclosures. That language is the authoritative statement of the rules. Fortunately, the disclosure rules (and most of the other rules) for debit cards are simpler than those for credit cards, reflecting the relative simplicity of debit card transactions.

All of the disclosures are subject to general requirements that they be "clear and readily understandable, in writing, and in a form the consumer may keep."

12 C.F.R. § 205.4(a)(1). The regulation includes various detailed requirements that all financial institutions' disclosures must meet. *See* 12 C.F.R. § 205.4. Special rules govern disclosures provided electronically. 12 C.F.R. §§ 205.4(c), 205.17.

1. Initial Disclosure

A consumer needs substantial information at the beginning of any commercial relationship, to reduce the chances of nasty surprises later. Reg. E specifies a number of things that must be disclosed "at the time a consumer contracts for an electronic fund transfer service or before the first electronic fund transfer is made involving the consumer's account." 12 C.F.R. § 205.7(a). Particularly important disclosures include the liability rules (discussed in Section D of this Chapter), 12 C.F.R. § 205.7(b)(1), the fees to be charged, 12 C.F.R. § 205.7(b)(5) and (11), and information on how to resolve problems with the account, 12 C.F.R. § 205.7(b)(2), (7), (8), and (10). Disclosure is also required if the addition of new services results in different terms and conditions. 12 C.F.R. § 205.7(c).

2. Post-Issuance Disclosure

Reg. E requires financial institutions to send monthly statements of electronic fund transfer activity, and a statement at least quarterly in the absence of activity. 12 C.F.R. § 205.9(b). The statement must disclose specified information about each transaction (amount, date, type, location of any electronic terminal used, and identity of any recipient of the funds other than the consumer), the account number, fees charged, account balances, and contact information for the financial institution. *Id.* Special rules apply to particular types of accounts, 12 C.F.R. § 205.9(c), and to preauthorized transfers, 12 C.F.R. § 205.10.

Financial institutions must give 21 days advance notice of any change in terms that would impose increased fees, increased liability, or additional limitations on the consumer's electronic fund transfers. 12 C.F.R. § 205.8(a). Financial institutions must also send, at least annually, a notice of the error resolution procedures discussed in Section E of this Chapter below. 12 C.F.R. § 205.8(b). Automated teller machines (ATMs) must provide specified disclosures at the ATM as to fees. 12 C.F.R. § 205.16.

D. Limits on Liability

Reg. E, like Reg. Z for credit cards, limits consumers' liability for unauthorized use of their debit cards (and other types of unauthorized electronic access of their accounts). However, the limits are more complex than the liability limits for credit cards, and failure to notify the financial institution of a lost or stolen debit card can subject a consumer to substantial liability. Of course, debit card withdrawals are limited by the consumer's account balance plus the amount of any overdraft protection that the financial institution allows the consumer (or the thief) to draw against. However, such amounts can still be substantial.

As long as the consumer notifies the financial institution of the loss or theft of a debit card or other access device within two business days after learning of the loss or theft, the consumer's liability for unauthorized use is capped at $50.00. 12 C.F.R. § 205.6(b)(1). So far, this is similar to the credit card regime.

However, if the consumer doesn't give notice to the financial institution within two business days after learning of the loss or theft, the consumer's maximum liability goes up to $500.00. 12 C.F.R. § 205.6(b)(2). Even worse for the consumer, if unauthorized electronic fund transfers show up on the consumer's statement and the consumer doesn't notify the financial institution within 60 days after the statement was sent, the consumer's liability for subsequent unauthorized transfers is potentially unlimited. 12 C.F.R. § 205.6(b)(3).

The consumer may give notice to the financial institution "in person, by telephone, or in writing." 12 C.F.R. § 205.7(b)(5)(ii). Of course, written notice has obvious evidentiary advantages for the consumer

E. Error Resolution

In case of errors in electronic fund transfer transactions, Reg. E provides an error resolution mechanism similar to the billing error resolution mechanism for credit cards. The types of errors to which this resolution mechanism applies is defined broadly to include typical specific problems that might be expected. See 12 C.F.R. § 205.11(a)(1). However, certain types of routine inquiries don't qualify as an "error." See 12 C.F.R. § 205.11(a)(2).

The process requires the consumer to give notice to the financial institution sufficiently identifying the account and the alleged error. 12 C.F.R. § 205.11(b)(1). The financial institution must receive the notice within 60 days after the first statement or passbook documentation was sent reflecting the alleged error. Id. The notice may be written or oral. Id. However, the financial institution may require written confirmation of an oral notice. 12 C.F.R. § 205.11(b)(2).

The financial institution has 10 business days from receipt of the notice to investigate and determine whether an error occurred, and the financial institution must report the results of the investigation to the consumer within 3 days of completing it. 12 C.F.R. § 205.11(c)(1). If the financial institution discovers that an error occurred, the financial institution must correct it within 1 business day of that discovery. *Id.*

If the financial institution cannot complete its investigation within the 10-day period, it may take up to 45 days if it provisionally recredits the consumer's account and notifies the consumer of the events as they unfold. 12 C.F.R. § 205.11(c)(2). The time limits for investigation are extended for new accounts in certain circumstances. 12 C.F.R. § 205.11(c)(3).

If the financial institution determines that the error described by the consumer did not occur, the financial institution must provide a written explanation to the consumer and make the documents relied upon available to the consumer. 12 C.F.R. § 205.11(d)(1). If a financial institution takes back funds that were previously provisionally credited to the consumer's account while an investigation was pending, the financial institution must give notice to the consumer, and for five days thereafter the financial institution may not dishonor checks or drafts that it would have paid if it had not taken back the provisionally credit funds. 12 C.F.R. § 205.11(d)(2).

Once a financial institution has complied with these requirements for an alleged error, the consumer may not invoke the error resolution procedure again by asserting that same error. 12 C.F.R. § 205.11(e).

Checkpoints

- Reg. E, authorized by the Electronic Funds Transfer Act in the Consumer Credit Protection Act, provides protections to consumers in connection with electronic fund transfers.

- These rules apply only to consumer transactions; non-consumer wire transfers are covered in Chapter 19.

- Issuance of unsolicited debit cards is sometimes permitted, but only in particular circumstances.

- Various disclosures are required by Reg. E at the initiation of the consumer's account, and periodically throughout the relationship.

- Reg. E imposes limits on a consumer's liability for unauthorized electronic fund transfers, but (unlike the credit card rules) the Reg. E liability can increase over time if the consumer fails to notify the financial institution of the loss or theft of a debit card or other access device, or of unauthorized electronic fund transfers that appear on the consumer's account.

- Reg. E includes an error resolution mechanism similar to the billing error resolution mechanism for credit cards.

Chapter 19

Funds Transfers
(UCC Article 4A)

Roadmap
- Funds transfers and wire transfers
  - Originator
  - Originator's bank
  - Beneficiary
  - Beneficiary's bank
- Payment orders
  - Sender
  - Receiving bank
  - Acceptance
  - Rejection
  - Payment
  - Payment date

A. Overview

1. United States Law

Consumer electronic fund transfers, considered in the previous Chapter, are a relatively recent phenomenon. Funds transfers of large amounts of money, typically in connection with business transactions, have a much longer history. Surprisingly, these transactions, often called "wire transfers" in common parlance, lacked a comprehensive governing body of law until Article 4A was added to the UCC by the National Conference of Commissioners on Uniform State Laws in 1989. In the relatively few years since that time, this addition to the UCC has enjoyed almost universal enactment by state legislatures in the U.S.

The commonly-used term "wire transfer" suggests that these transactions proceed electronically. However, that may or may not be the case. Often a funds transfer or wire transfer does involve some form of electronic communication, especially between the banks involved. However, UCC Article 4A applies independently of the means of communication, and the settling-up for the money takes place in accounts at the bank or banks involved. *See* UCC § 4A-104 Official Comments 2 and 6.

Assume you're in California, I'm in Alabama, and suppose (hypothetically, unfortunately) I have agreed to send you $1,000,000.00. Because of the amount of money involved, you're likely to be a bit impatient to actually get the funds. Your impatience would likely arise both because you want to be sure that I have paid you, and also because you miss significant interest or other investment opportunities every day that you don't actually have that money. (For example, at 5 percent interest per year, the interest *per day* on $1,000,000.00 would be $136.99.)

The inconvenience and delay of delivering $1,000,000.00 in cash across a great distance is obvious. Alternatively, I could send you a check. However, you would probably wait at least two or three days for the check to arrive in the mail, or one day even if I sent the check by express courier. Moreover, your bank probably wouldn't allow you to withdraw the funds until several days after you deposited the check, due to uncertainty about whether my check might be dishonored and returned. (More on those issues appears in Chapters 12, 13, and 14.)

A funds transfer is ideally suited to this problem of promptly sending large sums of money across great distances. Assuming everything goes smoothly, the funds transfer system would allow you to receive the money at your bank the same day I instruct my bank to send it.

This Chapter provides a summary of the key terms, parties, events, and legal rules applicable to funds transfers that go through the system as planned, plus a brief listing of the UCC Article 4A provisions that apply for sorting out liability in the case of problems. Additional information on funds transfers appears in 2B Frederick M. Hart & William F. Willier, Negotiable Instruments Under the Uniform Commercial Code §§ 17.01–17.19 (2006); Frederick H. Miller, The Lawyer's Guide to Modern Payment Methods: ACH, Credit, Debit, and More 17–58 (2007); Fred H. Miller & Alvin C. Harrell, The Law of Modern Payment Systems 468–507 & Supp. 157–62 (2003 & Supp. 2006); James J. White & Robert S. Summers, Uniform Commercial Code 688–96 (5th ed. 2000); and Ronald J. Mann, Payment Systems and Other Financial Transactions: Cases, Materials, and Problems 198–250. (3d ed. 2006). The UCC Official Comments also have helpful examples and explanations. *See* UCC § 4A-104 Official Comment 1.

2. International Law

The UCC, of course, applies only in the U.S. states that have adopted it. International law governing funds transfers remains somewhat unsettled, at least around the edges. The principles of UCC Article 4A appear to have influenced the development of the related international law, particularly in the development, at about the same time as Article 4A, of the United Nations Commission on International Trade Law (UNCITRAL) Model Law on International Credit Transfers. *See* 2B Frederick M. Hart & William F. Willier, Negotiable Instruments Under the Uniform Commercial Code § 17A.01 (2004). However, the U.S. approach has not been uniformly embraced. *See id* at 17A-2 fn 6 and accompanying text.

B. Terminology and Parties

A *funds transfer* proceeds by a series of *payment orders*, starting with the *originator*, and ultimately (if all goes according to plan) resulting in receipt of the funds by the *beneficiary*. Each of the payment orders is given to the *receiving bank* by the *sender*. Consequently, the identity of the originator and beneficiary remain constant throughout the entire funds transfer, but the identities of the sender and receiving bank typically change from one payment order to the next as the funds transfer progresses.

1. Funds Transfer

The term "funds transfer" denotes the overall transaction for the movement of money from the originator to the ultimate beneficiary: " 'Funds transfer' means the series of transactions, beginning with the originator's payment order, made for the purpose of making payment to the beneficiary of the order." UCC § 4A-104(a). A funds transfer progresses by a series of "payment orders."

The key event with respect to each payment order is *acceptance* of that payment order. As in UCC Article 3, the definition and implications of acceptance are highly technical and perhaps counterintuitive, but the Article 4A meaning of the term is completely different than in Article 3. Acceptance of payment orders is discussed further below.

2. Payment Order

Payment orders are the building blocks of a funds transfer:

"Payment order" means an instruction of a sender to a receiving bank, transmitted orally, electronically, or in writing, to pay, or to cause another bank to pay, a fixed or determinable amount of money to a beneficiary if:
  (i) the instruction does not state a condition to payment to the beneficiary other than time of payment,
  (ii) the receiving bank is to be reimbursed by debiting an account of, or otherwise receiving payment from, the sender, and
  (iii) the instruction is transmitted by the sender directly to the receiving bank or to an agent, funds-transfer system, or communication system for transmittal to the receiving bank.

UCC § 4A-103(a)(1).

3. Beneficiary and Beneficiary's Bank

The beneficiary is the ultimate recipient of the funds transfer, although the definition of the term doesn't clearly say that: " 'Beneficiary' means the person to be paid by the beneficiary's bank." UCC § 4A-103(a)(2). Unsurprisingly, the beneficiary's bank is the bank that will finally make the money available to the beneficiary: " 'Beneficiary's bank' means the bank identified in a payment order in which an account of the beneficiary is to be credited pursuant to the order or which otherwise is to make payment to the beneficiary if the order does not provide for payment to an account." UCC § 4A-103(a)(3). The Official Comments are helpful in understanding the roles of the parties. See UCC § 4A-104 Official Comments 1 and 2.

4. Originator and Originator's Bank

The originator is the person who starts the funds transfer process: " 'Originator' means the sender of the first payment order in a funds transfer." UCC § 4A-104(c). The originator's bank is the first bank in the process: " 'Originator's bank' means (i) the receiving bank to which the payment order of the originator is issued if the originator is not a bank, or (ii) the originator if the originator is a bank." UCC § 4A-104(d).

5. Sender and Receiving Bank

Often a funds transfer is accomplished by a sequence of two or more payment orders. Each of those payment orders has a different sender and receiving bank; typically the receiving bank of one payment order becomes the sender of the next payment order in the sequence. "'Sender' means the person giving the instruction to the receiving bank." UCC § 4A-103(a)(5). "'Receiving bank' means the bank to which the sender's instruction is addressed." UCC § 4A-103(a)(4).

6. Intermediary Bank

If a funds transfer involves more than one bank, the banks involved must either have a relationship with each other for settling up the money owed, or use an intermediary bank. If the originator's bank and the beneficiary's bank do not have a direct relationship, they may turn to one or more intermediary banks as a go-between. The intermediary bank or banks can facilitate the funds transfer by receiving and then sending along payment orders in the middle of the process: "'Intermediary bank' means a receiving bank other than the originator's bank or the beneficiary's bank." UCC § 4A-104(b). The Federal Reserve Banks offer a popular intermediary for funds transfers in the U.S., through their "Fedwire" system. Funds transfers through Fedwire are subject to special rules found in Federal Reserve Board of Governors' Regulation J. *See* 12 C.F.R. §§ 210.25–210.32.

7. Payment Date and Payment

The "payment date" for a funds transfer is the date of receipt by the beneficiary's bank, unless the originator specified a later payment date. *See* UCC § 4A-401. The "payment" of a funds transfer is subject to additional detailed rules found in Part Four of UCC Article 4A. *See* UCC §§ 4A-401–4A-406.

C. Acceptance or Rejection of Payment Orders

1. Acceptance

"Acceptance" is the key event in a bank's taking responsibility for sending a payment order. Acceptance is significant for two fundamental reasons. First, acceptance of a payment order triggers the sender's obligation to pay the amount of the order to the receiving bank. *See* UCC § 4A-402(b), (c). The time at which that obligation to pay arises depends on whether the receiving bank is the beneficiary's bank or not. *See id.* Second, acceptance by the receiving bank cuts off the receiving bank's option to reject the payment and avoid liability for it. UCC § 4A-210(d). Prior to acceptance, the receiving bank has broad discretion to reject a payment order. *See* UCC § 4A-210(a).

The originator of a payment order has the opportunity to establish the earliest date on which the payment order may be accepted. *See* UCC § 4A-209(d). However, if the originator does not impose that limitation, the time of acceptance is the time when the receiving bank acts on the payment order. *See* UCC § 4A-209(a) and (b). That action is called "execution," and is subject to detailed rules found in Part Three of UCC Article 4A. *See* UCC §§ 4A-301–4A-305.

The type of action that constitutes acceptance of a payment order depends on whether the receiving bank is the beneficiary's bank or not. If the receiving bank is the beneficiary's bank, acceptance occurs at the earliest of three times: (1) when the beneficiary's bank makes the transferred money available to the beneficiary, *see* UCC § 4A-209(b)(1); (2) when the beneficiary's bank receives the entire amount of transferred money, *see* UCC § 4A-209(b)(2); or (3) at "the opening of the next funds-transfer business day following the payment date of the order," *unless* (i) the money is not fully available to the beneficiary's bank at that time, or (ii) the payment order has been effectively rejected by a time specified in the statute, *see* UCC § 4A-209(a)(3).

2. Rejection

A bank that effectively rejects a payment order has no liability with respect to that payment order, except in limited circumstances. *See* UCC §§ 4A-212, 4A-210(b).

3. Other Liability Rules

Additional rules affecting the liability for payment orders in particular circumstances appear in Parts Two and Five of UCC Article 4A. *See* UCC §§ 4A-202–4A-208, 4A-211, 4A-501–4A-507. These rules are generally not implicated in the normal case where the funds transfer goes through as planned.

However, they become important for assigning liability if a payment order was accepted, but turns out to have been erroneous or fraudulent.

Checkpoints

- Funds transfers are well suited to sending large amounts of money across great distances in a shorter time than other payment mechanisms.

- UCC Article 4A is the current source of the law governing funds transfers.

- Article 4A uses the term "funds transfer," but a transaction governed by Article 4A is also commonly called a "wire transfer."

- A funds transfer goes from an originator to a beneficiary.

- A funds transfer is accomplished by a series of payment orders, each of which is sent by a sender to a receiving bank.

- In the normal case, the funds transfer moves money effectively from the originator to the beneficiary.

- In cases of error or fraud, UCC Article 4A provides detailed rules of apportioning the related loss.

Epilogue

The law of payment systems continues to evolve, as do the institutions that facilitate payment transactions. Human society has spent centuries developing our current mechanisms for making payment. Our paper-based mechanisms may now seem antiquated compared to digital electronic systems, but we should not forget that even purely paper-based negotiable instruments were and are an enormous advance over the predecessor systems that required carrying and transferring gold, silver, or other items that were often heavy and bulky in addition to being valuable. The ability to transfer value symbolically — using pieces of paper that have no intrinsic value in themselves — still represents a remarkable technological achievement. Even in today's electronic age, this paper-based technology retains immense importance for our economic system and its efficient functioning.

Increasingly, electronic records are taking the place of paper, and transactions that once required moving pieces of paper now proceed over wires, or fiber-optic cable, or radio waves. This creates an inherent tension between the existing law of negotiable instruments and the desires of innovators. A "negotiable instrument" must still be written on a piece of paper, as discussed in Chapters 3 and 5. However, as electronic communication methods proliferate, as the pace of commerce continues to increase, and as more and more commerce crosses national borders, pressure grows to eliminate paper transactions and rely on electronic methods.

In one possible scenario, payment systems might adapt to the new electronic realities by allowing creation and transfer of negotiable instruments in electronic form. Legal innovations like the Check Clearing for the 21st Century Act, discussed in Chapter 14, represent a partial step in this direction. However, purely electronic negotiable instruments are still a long way away, and much work remains to be done before such a thing will be possible. Moreover, we must first decide whether our objectives are better served by creating purely electronic negotiable instruments, or by some new and different approach to the problem.

Other alternatives may (or may not) offer a better approach to electronic payments than the negotiable instrument model. As described in Part Three of this book, credit cards, debit cards, and funds transfers each provide a way of moving money without any particular piece of paper as a formal requisite. Each of those systems already has its own governing body of law.

Further developments will likely grow out of innovative combinations and extensions of the existing legal regimes described in this book. Many such innovations can proceed, at least at the experimental stage, based on private ordering arrangements within and across the existing legal frameworks. Many such experiments are already under way. *See* Frederick H. Miller, The Lawyer's Guide to Modern Payment Methods: ACH, Credit, Debit, and More 169–182 (2007); Fred H. Miller & Alvin C. Harrell, The Law of Modern Payment Systems ¶ 11.03 at 525–34 & Supp. ¶¶ 11.03–11.06 at 171–88 (2003 & Supp. 2006). Some of those experiments will reveal needs for additional revisions to the legal system. Adjustments to the existing legal system will probably suffice in the short run. A wholesale reworking of the law in this area might be appropriate at some point, though that point is probably years away.

In short: Our current payment systems work remarkably well, though improvements are always possible and many worthwhile experiments are under way. Payment systems and their governing law in the future will likely combine characteristics of the current regimes for negotiable instruments, credit cards, debit cards, and funds transfers. Increasing globalization is also likely to introduce new ideas and approaches into the mix. Only time will tell whether any one system will dominate the 21st-Century landscape in the way that negotiable instruments did in the 20th Century. In any event, the concepts and rules of the current systems are unlikely to disappear any time soon.

Master Checklist

❑ Payment systems in the United States are governed by a complex mixture of state law, federal law and regulation, judicial decisions, and private ordering arrangements. As international transactions become more frequent, the importance of other countries' law also increases.

❑ Credit cards, debit cards, funds transfers, and other types payment systems are growing in importance, but negotiable instruments remain the predominant mechanism.

❑ UCC Articles 3 and 4 provide the primary law governing negotiable instruments.

❑ Drafts and notes are the most common types of negotiable instruments.

❑ A check is a particular type of draft.

❑ The UCC also recognizes several categories of specialized negotiable instruments, including cashier's checks, teller's checks, certified checks, traveler's checks, certificates of deposit, and Article 9 instruments.

❑ A draft is only rarely "accepted" within in the narrow, technical, and counterintuitive meaning of that term in the UCC.

❑ The specialized rules of UCC Article 3 (including in particular the opportunity to become a holder in due course) only apply to a writing that qualifies as a "negotiable instrument" (except for unusual cases where a court might choose to apply the rules of Article 3 by analogy).

❑ To qualify as a negotiable instrument, a writing must be an unconditional promise or order for a fixed amount of money, payable to bearer or to order on demand or at a definite time, must not contain any non-monetary undertaking or instruction, and must not indicate the intent of the parties to opt out of treatment as a negotiable instrument.

❑ A negotiable instrument is initially "issued," then subsequently "transferred" from one party to another.

❑ A transfer is a "negotiation" if it results in the recipient becoming a "holder" of the instrument.

❑ Being a holder is the typical way to become a person entitled to enforce a negotiable instrument.

❑ Holder status with respect to a negotiable instrument requires physical possession.

❑ Holder status also requires either that the instrument be payable to bearer, or that it be payable to the person in possession.

❑ An indorsement is always either blank or special. In addition, it may be restrictive or anomalous.

❑ An indorsement can change the person to whom a negotiable instrument is payable.

❑ An indorsement also creates liability for the indorser on the instrument.

❑ Being a holder is required to become a holder in due course.

❑ A holder in due course must take the instrument for value, in good faith, and without notice of problems with the instrument.

❑ A holder in due course of a negotiable instrument gets immunity from claims and certain defenses to enforcement of that instrument.

❑ The "real defenses" are good against even a holder in due course, but they only arise in very exceptional circumstances.

❑ The shelter rule may allow someone, who doesn't qualify on their own, to exercise someone else's rights as a holder in due course.

❑ Only someone who signs a negotiable instrument can be liable on the instrument, though a signature may be made by an agent.

❑ Secondary obligors (often called guarantors, sureties or accommodation parties) may take liability by a signature on the instrument, or by a separate guaranty agreement.

❑ Someone who qualifies as a secondary obligor may have certain suretyship defenses that are not available to principal obligors.

❑ A letter of credit may be used for purposes similar to those involving secondary obligors.

❑ If more than one party signs a negotiable instrument in the same capacity, those parties have joint and several liability.

❑ Contribution or reimbursement may be used to settle up obligations among liable parties.

❑ A signer of a negotiable instrument will be liable as issuer (maker or drawer), indorser, or (rarely) acceptor.

❑ If an instrument is altered, each signer's liability varies depending on whether the instrument was incomplete at the time of the signature.

❑ Payment of an instrument is the most common way to discharge the related liability, though other discharge mechanisms are recognized.

❑ Usually, when someone takes a negotiable instrument for an underlying obligation, the underlying obligation is suspended until the instrument is paid or dishonored.

❏ Payment of the instrument discharges the underlying obligation; dishonor of the instrument revives the underlying obligation.

❏ In the unusual case when someone takes a certified check, cashier's check, or teller's check, the underlying obligation is discharged, not just suspended.

❏ Banks have developed an elaborate mechanism for collecting checks promptly and efficiently.

❏ The primary governing law for the check collection system is found in UCC Article 4, the EFAA, Reg. CC, and the Check 21 Act; Reg. J also applies to the Federal Reserve Banks' participation in the check collection process.

❏ Preemption of statutes and regulations is not always clear, so the best approach is to understand the requirements of each system separately.

❏ A depositary bank wants to be sure it does not give its depositor money for a deposited check that will subsequently be returned unpaid by the payor bank.

❏ Only the payor bank "pays" a check.

❏ The payor bank wants to make sure it does not pay a check if it cannot obtain the money from the drawer of the check.

❏ A payor bank is only permitted to charge "properly payable"checks against a customer's account.

❏ An overdraft in the drawer's account does not prevent a check from being properly payable, but it may make a payor bank reluctant to pay the check.

❏ Stop payment orders and postdated checks are subject to specialized rules.

❏ A forgery will prevent a check from being properly payable, though forgeries are often difficult for the payor bank to discover in time to dishonor the check.

❏ The UCC system requires a bank that wants to dishonor a check to return it by the bank's midnight deadline.

❏ The EFAA and Reg. CC focus on the time a returned check gets back to the depositary bank, and generally impose tighter deadlines (the two-day/four-day test or the forward collection test) than the UCC rules.

❏ The EFAA and Reg. CC also require a bank returning a large check ($2,500.00 or more) to send notice to the depositary bank.

❏ The EFAA and Reg. CC tighten the deadlines in the check collection process because they also impose stricter deadlines than the UCC on when a depositary bank must make funds available to the depositor.

❏ Check processing historically has required movement of each paper check physically through the system, but the Check 21 Act provides greater opportunities to send electronic images in place of paper checks, thus facilitating check truncation.

❏ Drawer and indorser liability, and the transfer and presentment warranties, provide mechanisms in addition to dishonor and return for allocating losses from problem checks.

❏ The law of conversion and rules found in UCC sections 3-407, 3-406, 4-406, 3-405, and 3-404 provide additional mechanisms for allocating loss in special situations.

❏ Credit cards, debit cards, funds transfers, and other experiments in electronic payments offer alternatives to paying by check.

❏ Credit cards, debit cards, and other consumer electronic transactions are primarily governed by federal law; the rules for each share similarities, but differ in important respects.

Index